Terry A.

MAKE DISCIPLES

Reaching the Postmodern World for Christ

COLLEGE PRESS PUBLISHING
JOPLIN, MO

Cover Design: Brett Lyerla

Library of Congress Cataloging-in-Publication Data

Bowland, Terry A. (Terry Allen), 1954–
    Make disciples!: reaching the postmodern world for
  Christ/Terry A. Bowland.
      p. cm.
    Includes bibliographical references
    ISBN 0-89900-856-9 (pbk.)
    1. Evangelistic work.   2. Great Commission (Bible).
  3. Postmodernism—Religious aspects—Christianity.   I. Title.
  BV3793.B63 1999
  269'.2—dc21   99-049164
                                                           CIP

Acknowledgements

The Preacher of Ecclesiastes knew of what he spoke when he said, "Of making many books there is no end, and much study wearies the body" (Eccl 12:12). This is my first adventure into the publishing world, so I hope the reader will give this book that consideration. All authors bear resemblance to the story of the midget and the giant. Left to himself, the horizons of the midget's vision are limited. However, when he is hoisted up to stand on the giant's shoulders, he can see as far as the giant.

There are many "giants" to whom this "midget" is indebted. I owe a deep debt of gratitude to my colleagues on the faculty of Ozark Christian College. Through numerous conversations, they have helped to refine my thinking on a great many issues, especially Dr. Gary Zustiak, an expert on Generation X. To a man, our faculty is concerned about and active in carrying out the Great Commission.

I also owe much thanks to the students who have sat in my Personal Evangelism classes. Through our dialogue, they have helped verify many of my insights, as well as dispel a few. A special word of appreciation to my student, now graduated and preaching, Ken Morris. Many of the insights from his study on the evangelistic mission of Jesus have found their way into Chapter 4. To him and many others, I say, "Thank you." My thinking on evangelism would be shallow indeed were it not for their wisdom. Of course, any shortcomings contained in this work are solely my responsibility.

I dedicate this book to the two individuals who have displayed to me the meaning of "incarnational evangelism." The first is my mother. She was the one who lived out the life of Christ before my eyes every day and introduced me to Jesus. "Thanks, Mom." The second is my wonderful wife, Carol. I have always said that if at the end of my ministry I had produced only two disciples — my own two lovely daughters — then my ministry would be a success. Carol has lived out Jesus so sweetly and completely that our daughters could not help but fall in love with Him. I have provided the head knowledge, but she has shown them the "heart of God." "Thank you, Carol."

May God use this humble project to glorify His name and aid His church in carrying out the Great Commission.

— Terry A. Bowland —

TABLE OF CONTENTS

Introduction
THE JOY OF SEEING PEOPLE COME TO CHRIST

> You must picture me alone in that room in Magdalen, night after night, feeling, whenever my mind lifted even for a second from my work, the steady, unrelenting approach of Him whom I so earnestly desired not to meet. That which I greatly feared had at last come upon me. In the Trinity Term of 1929 I gave in, and admitted that God was God, and knelt and prayed . . . . The hardness of God is kinder than the softness of men, and His compulsion is our liberation.[1]
> C.S. Lewis, *Surprised by Joy*

In 1904 William Booth, founder of the Salvation Army, was invited to Buckingham Palace to visit King Edward VII. The King asked Booth to write in his autograph album. Booth wrote these words:

> Your Majesty,
> Some men's ambition is art.
> Some men's ambition is fame.
> Some men's ambition is gold.
> My ambition is the souls of men.

A cynic once asked, "What in the world are you Christians doing?" I can think of no more relevant question for the church here at the beginning of the twenty-first century. When an individual comes to Christ, he/she enters into the greatest task in the world. Jesus said, "Go and make disciples of all nations, baptizing them in the name of the Father and of the Son and of the Holy Spirit, and teaching them to obey everything that I have commanded you. And surely I am with you always, to the very end of the age."

This is the mission of the church. This is the task of every Christian — not simply to become involved in, but to become immersed in, the spread of the good news of Our Lord Jesus Christ.

"Go and make disciples of all nations," Jesus said. These are our marching orders. This is our priority. This is our goal. This is our work. This is our labor. This is our joy.

No book on personal evangelism can be approached strictly from an academic viewpoint or even from a "how-to-do-it" approach. There is always a sense of the presence of the supernatural when God allows us to be actively present when the Holy Spirit does His mighty work in the heart of someone who is responding to Christ. C.S. Lewis was correct — when an individual comes to Christ, the only and best description is JOY!

I personally have experienced some amazing events in life. I was present at the seventh game of the World Series in 1982 when my St. Louis Cardinals won it all. We went crazy. I was in the delivery room (along with my wife) and experienced the birth of both of our beautiful daughters. We were humbled and awed. I have had the opportunity to climb several mountains in southwest Colorado. I was overwhelmed with the majesty of God's creation. But all of these pale into insignificance when compared with allowing the Holy Spirit to use us in the process of leading men and women to discover new and abundant life through Jesus Christ.

As we prepare to begin a study of carrying out the Great Commission, we must do it in the awareness that God is at work in the world when people are sharing their faith. If we can catch a glimpse of the divine in our labors, then we will be able to see the vast significance of speaking the name of Jesus to those who need to hear.

Long ago, King David wrote,

> Restore to me the joy of your salvation and grant me a willing spirit, to sustain me. Then I will teach transgressors your ways, and sinners will turn back to you (Ps. 51:12-13).

It seemed apparent that David believed "joy" to be a necessary element in sharing the good news of the Lord's reign in people's lives. It is impossible to carry out the Great Commission in a spirit of oppressive obligation. Consistent holy joy is one of the key elements for attracting the lost people of our present postmodern generation to the God who alone can forgive and renew them. When people come to Christ, there is JOY!

This is the story of every individual who comes to Christ. Here are a few examples of several famous individuals who were "surprised by joy" when they gave themselves to Christ:

Charles Haddon Spurgeon

Spurgeon lived from 1834 to 1892 and was the greatest preacher of his day in the English speaking world. Twice a week he would preach to overflowing crowds in the 6000 seat Metropolitan Tabernacle, and this was before the age of electronic amplification! Reporters from the London Times were present taking down Spurgeon's sermons verbatim to be published in the Monday edition. Talk about influence! It was a truly amazing set of circumstances which led young Spurgeon to be surprised by the joy of Christ. The great preacher tells the story of his own conversion in his autobiography.

> I sometimes think I might have been in darkness and despair until now had it not been for the goodness of God in sending a snowstorm one Sunday morning while I was going to a certain place of worship. When I could go no further, I turned down a side street and came to a little Primitive Methodist Chapel. In that chapel there may have been a dozen or fifteen people. I had heard of the Primitive Methodists, how they sang so loudly that they made people's heads ache; but that did not matter to me. I wanted to know how I might be saved, and if they could tell me that, I did not care how much they made my head ache. The minister did not come that morning; he was snowed up, I suppose. At last, a very thin-looking man, a shoemaker, or tailor, or something of that sort, went up into the pulpit to preach. Now, it is well that preachers should be instructed, but this man was really stupid. He was obliged to stick to his text, for the simple reason that he had little else to say. The text was- "LOOK UNTO ME, AND BE YE SAVED ALL THE ENDS OF THE EARTH."
>
> He did not even pronounce the words rightly, but that did not matter. There was, I thought, a glimpse of hope for me in that text. The preacher began thus: "My dear friends, this is a very simple text indeed. It says, 'Look.' Now lookin' don't take a deal of pain. It ain't liftin' your foot or your finger; it is just, 'Look.' Well, a man needn't go to College to learn to look. You may be the biggest fool, and yet you can look. A man needn't be worth a thousand a year to be able to look. Anyone can look; even a child can look. But then the text says, 'Look unto Me.'" "Ay!" said he, in broad Essex, "many on ye are lookin' to yourselves, but it's no use lookin' there. You'll never find any comfort in yourselves. Some look to God the Father. No, look to Him by-and-by. Jesus Christ says, 'Look unto Me.' Some on ye say, 'We must wait for the Spirit's workin'.' You have no business with that just now. Look to Christ. The text says, 'Look unto Me.'"
>
> Then the good man followed up his text in this way: "'Look unto Me; I'm sweatin' great drops of blood. Look unto Me; I'm hangin' on the cross. Look unto Me; I am dead and buried. Look unto Me; I rise again. Look unto Me; I ascend to Heaven. Look

unto Me; I am sittin' at the Father's right hand. O poor sinner, look unto Me! look unto Me!'"

When he had gone to about that length, and managed to spin out ten minutes or so, he was at the end of his tether. Then he looked at me under the gallery, and I daresay, with so few present, he knew me to be a stranger. Just fixing his eyes on me, as if he knew all my heart, he said, "Young man, you look very miserable." Well, I did, but I had not been accustomed to have remarks made from the pulpit on my personal appearance before. However, it was a good blow, struck right home. He continued, "and you always will be miserable — miserable in life, and miserable in death — if you don't obey my text; but if you obey now, this moment, you will be saved." Then, lifting up his hands, he shouted, as only a Primitive Methodist could do, "Young man, look to Jesus Christ. Look! Look! Look! You have nothin' to do but to look and live." I saw at once the way of salvation. I know not what else he said — I did not take much notice of it — I was so possessed with that one thought. Like as when the brazen serpent was lifted up, the people only looked and were healed, so it was with me. I had been waiting to do fifty things, but when I heard that word, "Look!" what a charming word it seemed to me. Oh, I looked until I could almost have looked my eyes away. There and then the cloud was gone, the darkness had rolled away, and that moment I saw the sun; and I could have risen that instant, and sung with the most enthusiastic of them, of the precious blood of Christ, and the simple faith which looks alone to Him. Oh, that somebody had told me this before, "Trust Christ, and you shall be saved."[2]

John Wesley (1703-1791)

Wesley was one of the leaders of the great revival that swept over Great Britain near the end of the eighteenth century. Many historians credit the social changes produced by that revival as saving England from the upheaval of the Terror of the French Revolution. Wesley had been trained for the ministry at Oxford and had even traveled to Colonial America to do mission work among the Indian tribes in Georgia. However, he had never personally given his life to Christ. In his journal he wrote, "I went to America to save the Indians, but who, oh who will save me?" Upon his return to England, he met a group of Moravians, followers of Count Zinzendorf. Wesley was tremendously affected by their simple and joyous faith. After his return to London, he was invited to a meeting of these Moravians. His conversion that evening, on May 24, 1738, marked the beginning of an itinerant ministry that lasted 50 years in which he traveled over 250,000 miles and preached nearly 50,000 sermons.

In his journal, Wesley tells the simple story of being surprised by joy:

> In the evening I went very unwillingly to a society in Aldersgate Street, where one was reading Luther's preface to the Epistle to the Romans. About a quarter before nine, while he was describing the change which God works in the heart through faith in Christ, I felt my heart strangely warmed. I felt I did trust in Christ, Christ alone for salvation: And an assurance was given me, that he had taken away my sins, even mine, and saved me from the law of sin and death.[3]

I have no way of being sure, but I suspect that the very section of Luther's Roman preface which so affected Wesley was the following:

> Faith, however, is a divine work in us. It changes us and makes us to be born anew of God (John 1); it kills the old Adam and makes altogether different men, in heart and spirit and mind and powers, and it brings with it the Holy Ghost. Oh, it is a living, busy, active, mighty thing, this faith; and so it is impossible for it not to do good works incessantly. It does not ask whether there are good works to do, but before the question rises, it has already done them, and is always at the doing of them. He who does not these works is a faithless man. He gropes and looks about after faith and good works, and knows neither what faith is nor what good works are, though he talks and talks, with many words, about faith and good works.
>
> Faith is a living, daring confidence in God's grace, so sure and certain that a man would stake his life on it a thousand times. This confidence in God's grace and knowledge of it makes men glad and bold and happy in dealing with God and all His creatures; and this is the work of the Holy Ghost in faith. Hence a man is ready and glad, without compulsion to do good to everyone, to serve everyone, to suffer everything, in love and praise to God, who has shown him this grace.[4]

Blaise Pascal (1623-1662)

Pascal was one of the true geniuses of his day. He achieved fame in mathematics, physics, philosophy, theology and literature although he died when only 39. When he was 21 years of age, Pascal underwent a tremendous conversion experience. So dramatic was his encounter with the living Christ, that Pascal wrote it down and sewed it into the lining of his jacket as a constant reminder of what Christ had done. It was not recovered until ten years after his death. A member of his family was preparing to finally give away all of Pascal's old clothes when she heard the sound of crinkling paper as she handled his coat. When she realized that the sound came from inside the lining, she tore open the threads and discovered Pascal's own account of the night when he was surprised by joy.

THE MEMORIAL

In the year of Grace, 1654

On Monday, 23rd of November, Feast of St. Clement, Pope and Martyr, and others in the Martyrology,

Vigil of Saint Chrysogonus, Martyr, and others,

From about half past ten in the evening until about half past twelve,

FIRE

God of Abraham, God of Isaac, God of Jacob, not of the philosophers and scholars (Ex. 3:6; Matt. 22:32).

Certitude. Certitude. Feeling. Joy. Peace.

God of Jesus Christ.

Deum mum e' Deum vestrum ("My God and your God," John 20:17).

Forgetfulness of the world and of everything except God.

He is to be found only by the ways taught in the Gospel. Greatness of the human soul.

"Righteous Father, the world hath not known Thee, but I have known Thee" John 17:25).

Joy, joy, joy, tears of joy.

I have separated myself from Him.

Derelinquerunt me fontem aquae vivae ("They have forsaken me, the fountain of living waters," Jer. 2:13).

"My God, wilt Thou leave me?" (Matt. 27:46)

Let me not be separated from Him eternally.

"This is the eternal life, that they might know Thee, the only true God and the one whom Thou has sent, Jesus Christ" (John 17:3).

Jesus Christ.

Jesus Christ.

I have separated myself from Him: I have fled from Him, denied Him, crucified Him.

Let me never be separated from Him.

We keep hold of Him only by the ways taught in the Gospel.

Renunciation, total and sweet.

Total submission to Jesus Christ and to my director.

Eternally in joy for a day's training on earth.

Non oblivisicar sermones tuos ("I will not forget Thy words" Psalm 118:16). Amen.[5]

Getting Involved in Joy

Let us make no mistake about it. Evangelism is not simply learning Bible facts. Evangelism is not simply understanding sociological information. Evangelism is taking part in God's great work of redeeming the world through Christ. It is to reach out and allow God's power and presence to extend into the lives of people through our daily lives. When we increasingly become aware of God working within us, the result will be joy — joy in our daily tasks and joy in the lives we touch. Wherever God's will is done, the ultimate result for us will be joy. Then those famous words from Jesus' parable will become the reality of our lives:

> Well done, good and trustworthy slave; you have been trustworthy in a few things, I will put you in charge of many things; enter into the joy of your master (Matt. 25:21, NRSV).

It's time to get involved in the joy!

---

1. C.S. Lewis, *Surprised by Joy*, in *The Inspirational Writings of C.S. Lewis* (New York: Inspirational Press, 1987), p. 125.

2. C.H. Spurgeon, *Autobiography, Vol 1: The Early Years* (Edinburgh: Banner of Truth, 1985), pp. 87-88.

3. John Wesley, *The Works of John Wesley*, Vol 1 (Peabody, MA: Hendrickson Publishers, 1986), p. 103.

4. Martin Luther, *Romans* (Grand Rapids: Kregel Publishing, 1979), p. xvii.

5. Blaise Pascal, *Great Shorter Works*, trans. Emile Cailliet and John C Blankenagel (Philadelphia: Westminster Press, 1948), p. 117, as found in Hugh Kerr & John Mulder, eds., *Conversions: The Christian Experience* (Grand Rapids: Eerdmans, 1985), pp. 36-38.

Chapter 1
THE GREAT COMMISSION:
ONE COMMAND – THREE TASKS

> It was the best of times, it was the worst of times, it was the age of wisdom, it was the age of foolishness, it was the epoch of belief, it was the epoch of incredulity; it was the season of Light, it was the season of Darkness; it was the spring of hope, it was the winter of despair.
>
> Dickens, *A Tale of Two Cities*

When we examine the church of Jesus Christ at the dawn of the twenty-first century, much the same can be said. According to some, it is the best of times; according to others, it is the worst of times. The optimists, for example, proclaim, "Is this not, as Dickens would say, 'the best of times?'" America seems to be caught up in the throes of religious revival. After all, Promise Keepers are filling stadiums around the country with literally hundreds of thousands of men, with over one million men having attended the great rally in Washington, D.C. in 1997.

Many would also point out that the church around the world is experiencing tremendous growth. Take South Korea for example. Six of the world's largest churches are there (five of them in the capital, Seoul): the two largest Presbyterian churches in the world, the two largest Methodist churches in the world, the largest Baptist church in Asia — all there; not to mention Paul Yonggi Cho's church — Yoido Full Gospel Church (the largest congregation in Christian history) founded in 1958 with 5 members. Today over 700,000 members honor the name of Christ!! The Yoido church has gone years where they *averaged 10,000 new members a month*!!!

Such amazing growth is not only happening in Korea. In formerly communist Russia, the Moscow Baptist Church meets each Sunday with over 5,000 in attendance. In Shanghai, China, one of the more religiously suppressed countries on earth, 6,000 will meet this Lord's Day in the Mo'en Church. Across our globe there are well over 40 congregations which average over 10,000 each Sunday.

Across our globe there are well over 40 congregations which average over 10,000 each Sunday.

In America hundreds of congregations are exploding with growth. The Willow Creek Community Church in Chicago over the past 20 years has gone from a small group meeting in a theater to over 17,000 in attendance. There are well over 450 congregations in the United States which run over 2,000 in morning worship attendance, with a new one passing that barrier every 2 weeks. Surely this is the best of times!

Yet, others are not quite so optimistic. In spite of all the growing churches nationwide, between 1960 and 1990 the United States population grew at a rate of 39%; and yet the number of Christians only grew by 28%; and the number of total churches only grew by 7%.

Americans are, as a rule, mostly illiterate when it comes to the truth of Christianity. A recent survey showed that of those who never attend worship services, 52% say they have made some sort of commitment to Jesus Christ, and yet they have no idea what this means. Forty-six percent of the unchurched could not even answer the question: "Why do we celebrate Easter?" Not only are they ignorant of what the church believes — they do not even know what they believe. Fifty-one percent of all Americans had absolutely no consistent philosophy of life![1]

Between 1960 and 1990 US population grew by 39%, yet the number of Christians only by 28%.

And what has become of the moral climate of our nation? George Gallup has said, "In America, religion may be up, but morality is down." Sixty-nine percent of all Americans declare that there are no moral absolutes. Peterson and Kim have done what they describe as the most complete morality survey in the nation's history and they have published their findings in *The Day America Told the Truth*.[2] These results are startling.

74% I will steal from those who won't miss it.

64% I will lie when it suits me if it doesn't cause any real damage.

53% I will cheat on my spouse; after all, given the chance, they would do the same.

50% At work I will do nothing about one full day in five. It's standard operating procedure.

41% I will use recreational drugs.

How should we in the church, view all this? Is it the best of times or the worst of times?

John Naisbitt has insightfully commented on these two contrasting views in his book *Mega Trends 2000.* He wrote that two of the most powerful trends in America for the decade of the 1990s would be: (1) a religious revival reaching into the 3rd Millennium in which baby boomers and busters will begin to seek spirituality in organized religion; and (2) something Naisbitt calls "the triumph of the individual," where each person will place him/herself at the center of the universe and strive for that which will empower and enlighten them.[3] While Naisbitt does not use the term "postmodern," his observations display an awareness of definite postmodern trends within our culture. We will discuss this in more detail in chapters 6 and 7.

For anyone even vaguely familiar with biblical Christianity, the above two trends are mutually exclusive. Individuals cannot seek spirituality and at the same time exalt themselves. The Lord Jesus is quite clear: "If anyone would come after me, he must deny himself and take up his cross daily and follow me. For whoever wants to save his life will lose it, but whoever loses his life for me will save it" (Luke 9:23-24).

With the above mutually exclusive trends playing themselves out in our present cultural environment, let's return to our original question: In view of carrying out the Great Commission, is it the best of times or the worst of times? Perhaps it is both. Never has there been a time of greater opportunity for the church of Jesus Christ, and yet never has there been a time of such peril. For while men and women today are indeed seeking spirituality, they are seeking it on their own terms according to their own rules instead of on Christ's terms and upon Christ's rules. Christianity may indeed be growing, but it runs the risk of growing into the image of contemporary self-seeking narcissism instead of into the image of the self-sacrificial Christ.[4]

Is this the best or the worst of times in relationship to the Great Commission? Perhaps both.

And so what is the solution? What is it to which we must attend in order to take advantage of the best of times and avoid the worst of times? What is it that must be the church's chief priority? What are our marching orders? What is it that Christ is calling us to do at the dawn of the twenty-first century?

Then Jesus came to them and said, "All authority in heaven and on earth has been given to me. Therefore go and make disciples of all nations, baptizing them in the name of the Father and of the Son and of the Holy Spirit, and teaching them to obey everything I have commanded you. And surely I am with you always, to the very end of the age" (Matt. 28:18-20).

As well worn as this text is, I believe that it is the only hope for our churches facing the best of times and the worst of times. Let's take a look once again at these familiar words as they challenge us anew with our marching orders.

Christ Calls Us to Make Disciples

The Great Commission has four main elements: (1) Go, (2) Make Disciples, (3) Baptize, and (4) Teach. In the Greek only one of these elements is an imperative verb (i.e., a verb of command).[5] The other three elements are what grammarians call participles. They tell us how to carry out the force of the command. For instance, I might say to my daughter, "Clean your room, vacuuming, dusting and making the bed." In my appeal the command is "clean your room." "Vacuuming, dusting, and making the bed" instruct my daughter on exactly how to go about carrying out the command to "clean."

In my class on evangelism at Ozark Christian College, I enjoy asking students to guess which of the four is indeed the command. Usually the first guess (unless there is a Greek scholar among the students) is "GO." Surely all those missionary sermons we have heard on the Great Commission were correct in placing the emphasis on "going!" But "Go" is not the command. Others think the main emphasis rests upon baptizing, since that has been a major emphasis in the Christian Churches/Churches of Christ. But again, the command is not primarily to "baptize." Being a teacher, I would truly enjoy knowing the command was to "teach." Yet this is not the verb of command in Jesus' words.

The *command* of the Great Commission is to make disciples.

The command of the Great Commission is: MAKE DISCIPLES. We would define a disciple as "a learner-follower of Jesus Christ."[6] We make disciples by going and baptizing and teaching. In making a disciple of Jesus Christ, first, we must GO to where individuals need the gospel. Next the commission assumes that we will share the good news of Jesus and call people to obedient faith in Him. In the New Testament the culmination of faith in Christ always displays itself in Christian BAPTISM. Finally, we must TEACH the new convert everything Jesus has commanded us. Many in the church seem to believe that the task of evangelism is over when an individual is "toweling off" after their baptism. Nothing could be further from the truth. Our job of "making a disciple" is just beginning when a person comes to Christ. The task of God's people is to bring to maturity those who give their lives to Christ. While I was sharing this in a class, one student raised his hand and complained, "But, Professor, a new Christian will spend the rest of their life learning EVERYTHING that Jesus taught, and still not be able to master it all!!" I responded, "That's right!" We will never be finished with carrying out the Great Commission. It is a lifelong task. Just as others are at work in the ongoing task of helping us to become mature disciples of Christ, so must we ever be at work in the lives of those we help lead to the Lord.

The Apostle Paul saw the purpose of "disciple making" when he wrote to the Ephesians about the function of leaders within the church. The goal of such disciple-making leadership is:

> . . . so that the body of Christ may be built up until we all reach unity in the faith and in the knowledge of the Son of God and become mature, attaining to the whole measure of the fullness of Christ. Then we will no longer be infants, tossed back and forth by the waves, and blown here and there by every wind of teaching and by the cunning and craftiness of men in their deceitful scheming. Instead, speaking the truth in love, we will in all things grow up into him who is the Head, that is, Christ (Eph. 4:12b-15).

Putting into practice Paul's vision of the church will solve the shallowness of nominal Christianity. Jesus never asked us to go into the world and make church members. He asked us to make *disciples*. A disciple is a learner and a follower whose greatest goal is to be like his master in everything he says and does.

I know many frustrated preachers who wonder where they should spend their time and energy. In my first full-time ministry, my wife and I served in a small farming community in Illinois. On Sunday evenings we would get together with a preacher and his family from another tiny community only two miles away. Usually, we would pile into one of our vehicles and travel 20 miles to the nearest Dairy Queen (These churches were really out in the sticks!). Then, over a banana split, we would discuss the joys and frustrations of ministry. I can remember my friend one time asking an interesting question. He pondered, "I don't know where I should spend the bulk of my time — with the unsaved outside the church or the unsaved inside the church." He was only half joking. At the time I remember saying, "I know where my heart lies. It is with the lost who have never heard. **I have always found it easier to give birth than to raise the dead!**"

However, upon reflection, the heart of our discussion revolved around the theological error that separates *evangelism* from *discipleship*. In the Great Commission there is no such separation. To evangelize is to make disciples of Jesus. In this book we have divided the chapters into the three sections which deal with the three aspects of disciple making in the Great Commission. But before we launch into our study, there are two other aspects of Jesus' command with which we must come to grips.

In Christ's Authority

One facet of the Great Commission that we often miss is the concept of Christ's authority. It is not in our own skill or expertise that we share the good news of Christ. It is in His authority! All authority in heaven and on earth is Christ's, and He gives that authority to us as we carry out the Commission.

In their book *A Passion for Excellence*, Peters & Austin declare that the #1 task of all leadership is to choose a priority — and clearly, repeatedly, religiously, urgently, attentively, passionately focus all your discussion and energy on that priority — right now!

Now I have to ask: What is it that we focus on — right now? Rick Warren has pointed out that churches can be driven by a wide range of factors.[7] Some churches are driven by tradition. Some are powered by the personality of the preacher. Other churches make every decision based upon the economic feasibility of any suggested activity. There are, in fact, an almost innumerable amount of issues which motivate the church and individual Christians to action. God's church needs to be driven by the Great Commission with the Lord at the wheel! It is under this unwavering authority that we must make disciples.

The church often places more emphasis on growth than on repentance.

Chuck Colson writes: "I don't want to generalize unjustly or be overly harsh, but it's fair to say that much of the church is caught up in the success mania of American society. Often more concerned with budgets and building programs than with the body of Christ, the church places more emphasis on growth than on repentance. Suffering, sacrifice and service have been preempted by success and self-fulfillment."[8]

The purpose of the church is not to make life easy. The church was never instructed to make non-Christians as comfortable as possible by entertaining them on Sunday morning and as self-fulfilled as possible by exercising them on Sunday afternoon. If the contemporary church has had little impact on society as a whole, it is because the church has failed to call its own members to repentance.

The words of the German martyr, Dietrich Bonhoeffer, need to once again ring in our ears: "When Jesus Christ calls a man, he bids him come and die . . . . In fact every command of Jesus is a call to die, with all our affections and lusts."[9] The basic message of the Christian faith has been, it is, and it always shall be that men and women must repent of their sins and turn their lives back to God through Christ. Jesus said in Luke 5:32, "I have not come to call the righteous, but sinners to repentance," and again in Luke 13:3, "I tell you, no! But unless you repent, you too will all perish."[10] The church must not obscure this truth by transforming a congregation into an audience, transforming proclamation into performance, or transforming worship into entertainment.

I like the way John MacArthur talks about his philosophy of ministry. While I don't agree with everything he writes, I truly appreciate his willingness to declare the hard demands of discipleship. MacArthur preaches at the Grace Community Church in Sun Valley, California. I heard him speak once about his church's growth techniques. His remarks conveyed the following philosophy:

> When people come to Grace Community Church, maybe it's because they have seen our advertising in the paper. It's first-rate. We want people to feel good when they see our ads. Maybe they come because of one of our community outreach programs to divorcees or unwed mothers or singles or what-have-you. We want people to feel good when they are reached by those programs. When they come to our services, I think they are impressed by our ample parking and by our beautiful building. And when they sit down in our worship services, we want them to feel great. Our singing and special music is second to none. Jesus blesses excellence. In fact, everything we do at Grace Community Church is geared to meet people's needs and make them feel comfortable until I get up to preach. Then I make it my job to preach the uncompromising gospel of salvation so clearly, that those people will become so uncomfortable that they will cry out like those at Pentecost, "men and brethren, what shall

we do?" and in repentance and obedience, they will give their lives to Christ.

The congregation should only be comfortable *until* the preacher gets up to preach.

May God grant us such wisdom and boldness in sharing the gospel in the authority of Christ.

Through the Power of the Holy Spirit

Sharing the gospel is a tremendous responsibility for each Christian. After all, it is the Great COMMISSION, not the Great SUGGESTION. In fact, many stress the personal responsibility of evangelism to such a great extent that many Christians believe that everything depends on them. This, however, ignores one of the most significant teachings of Matthew 28:18-20. Jesus wants us to realize that we are not alone. After the commission was given, Jesus presented a powerful promise : "I am with you always, even to the end of the age." Evangelism is to take place under God's authority through the power of the Holy Spirit.

Ken Hemphill has written:

> Church Growth is not produced by a program, plan or marketing strategy. Your church's greatest need is not a clearer understanding of it's demographics, but a clearer understanding of its God. Church Growth is not the result of any program or plan. Church growth is the by-product of a right relationship with the Lord of the church.[11]

The Lord Jesus said, "I will build my church" (Matt. 16:18). It is His power working within us which allows fruit in all our labors. Paul recognized this when he wrote to the Colossians, "To this end I labor, struggling with all his energy, which so powerfully works in me" (Col. 1:29). The Great Commission is preceded by "Great Authority" and it is followed by a "Great Promise." John Stott has written:

> But to those who go, who go into the world as Christ came into the world, who sacrifice their ease and comfort and independence, who hazard their lives in search of disciples — to them the presence of the living Christ is promised. In sending them out, he yet accompanies them.[12]

Seeing the Great Commission as Jesus Saw It

In this book we have divided the chapters into the three sections dealing with the aspects which describe disciple making in the Great Commission. In the first section (GO), we will outline a biblical understanding of evangelism and the difficulties and opportunities encountered as we take the gospel to our postmodern, post-Christian culture. In the second section (BAPTIZE), we will attempt to combine our understanding of the Bible and our society to determine what methodology will help us to maximize our efforts in carrying out the Commission. In doing this we will look at different models of evangelism, centering on the lifestyle approach as best suited to most contemporary Christians, as well as the needs of postmodern Americans. We will also examine the biblical model of accepting Christ as Savior and share numerous approaches for sharing the biblical teaching in practical presentations. The final section (TEACH) will emphasize the importance of a follow-up structure to be put in place by the local congregation to ensure that baby Christians receive nurture in their new walk with the Lord.

Our examination of evangelism will be admittedly limited. The goal of our study is to consider sharing Christ primarily within Western culture. Cross-cultural and Third World evangelism can obviously use many of the principles that will be outlined from Scripture. However, for the principles laid out in this study, the primary harvest field is contemporary, postmodern America.

The Commission is clear. We are to make disciples. The good news is: They are out there and they are ready. *"Lift up your eyes, the fields are ripe unto the harvest."*

---

1. Lee Strobel, *Inside the Mind of Unchurched Harry and Mary* (Grand Rapids: Zondervan, 1993), pp. 46, 51-52.

2. James Peterson and Peter Kim, *The Day America Told the Truth* (New York: Prentice Hall Press, 1991), pp. 25-26.

3. John Naisbitt and Patricia Aburdene, *Mega Trends 2000* (New York: William Morrow, 1990), pp. 270-309.

4. Compare Christopher Lasch's prophetic work *The Culture of Narcissism* (New York: W.W. Norton, 1978), as opposed to John MacArthur's fine study on true discipleship in *The Gospel According to Jesus* (Grand Rapids: Zondervan, 1988).

5. The imperative verb is μαθητεύσατε (πάντα τὰ ἔθνη) MAKE DISCIPLES (of all the nations). The other three elements, (1) πορευθέντες—going, (2) βαπτίζοντες—baptizing, and (3) διδάσκοντες—teaching, are participles. They tell us how to carry out the force of the imperative. It should be noted that when participles accompany an imperative verb they usually carry the force of the imperative (see Jesus' command earlier in Matt. 28:10). However, the main command in the commission is to "make disciples."

6. See the extensive article on discipleship by K.H. Regsdorf, "μαθητής," *Theological Dictionary of the New Testament* (Grand Rapids: Eerdmans, 1977). Also see C. Blendinger, "Disciple," *Dictionary of New Testament Theology* (Grand Rapids: Zondervan, 1981).

7. Rick Warren, *The Purpose-Driven Church* (Grand Rapids: Zondervan, 1995), pp. 75-84.

8. Charles Colson, *Against the Night* (Ann Arbor: Servant Publications, 1989), p. 103.

9. Dietrich Bonhoeffer, *The Cost of Discipleship*, trans., R.H. Fuller (New York: Macmillan, 1961), p. 99.

10. Luke 5:32; 13:3. John MacArthur is quite right when he observes: "Listen to the typical gospel presentation nowadays. You'll hear sinners entreated with words like, 'accept Jesus Christ as personal Savior'; 'ask Jesus into your heart'; 'invite Christ into your life'; or 'make a decision for Christ.' You may be so accustomed to hearing those phrases that it will surprise you to learn none of them is based on biblical terminology. They are products of a diluted gospel. It is not the gospel according to Jesus." MacArthur, *The Gospel According to Jesus*, p. 21.

11. Ken Hemphill, *The Antioch Effect* (Nashville: Broadman & Holman, 1994), p. 10.

12. John R.W. Stott, "The Great Commission" in *One Race, One Gospel, One Task*, vol. 1 (Berlin: World Congress on Evangelism, 1966) ed., Carl F.H. Henry & W. Stanley Mooneyham (Minneapolis: World Wide Publications, 1967), p. 49.

Section 1
"Go"

"Taking the Gospel to the world
requires two things:
knowing the gospel and
knowing the world to which
you would take the gospel."

Chapter 2
WHAT IS EVANGELISM?

> "A new command I give you: Love one another. As I have loved you, so you must love one another. By this all men will know that you are my disciples, if you love one another."
>
> John 13:34-35
>
> Hearing that Jesus had silenced the Sadducees, the Pharisees got together. One of them, an expert in the law, tested him with this question: "Teacher, which is the greatest commandment in the Law?" Jesus replied: "'Love the Lord your God with all your heart and with all your soul and with all your mind.' This is the first and greatest commandment. And the second is like it: 'Love your neighbor as yourself.' All the Law and the Prophets hang on these two commandments."
>
> Matt. 22:34-40

Love is an interesting command. And make no mistake about it, love is a command. This seems so strange to our modern American ears because in our culture "love" is usually thought of as an *emotion* and not what it biblically is: a commitment of the will.

The Two Greatest Commandments

When the canon lawyer came to Jesus in Matthew 22:34-40, he wished to know which of the hundreds of Old Testament laws was the most important. Jesus' famous reply boiled the summation of the Jewish Torah down into two simple commands — love God and love your neighbor.

In the New Testament there are several words in the Greek which are translated by our English word "love." One is φιλέω (*phileo*), which means "to have an appreciation or high regard for someone."[1] Another word used in our texts is the Greek term ἀγαπάω (*agapao*).[2] This word also means to have a deep appreciation or high regard for someone and these two words are very similar. There are, however, important distinctions. "*Phileo*-love" is usually based upon interpersonal relationships. "*Agapao*-love" is based upon higher principles — those of commitment, covenant and promise. In the New Testament people are never commanded to love one another with *phileo*-love! Every commandment in the New Testament for Christians to love, is a commandment to practice *agapao*-love.[3]

How will God know that we love Him? As Jesus has already instructed us, the New Testament teaches that God will recognize our love for Him in at least two of our activities.

First, we show God our love by obeying his commandments. "If you love me, you will obey what I command" (John 14:15). The context of this passage displays Jesus doing the work of the Father. The great work of Christ on earth was to bring people lost in sin back to a right relationship with God the Father. Jesus declared in Luke 19:10: "For the Son of Man came to seek and to save what was lost." Jesus' primary work on earth, was not as a miracle worker or a moral example or an ethical teacher. He came to be the Savior of all mankind through His sacrificial death on the cross and His glorious resurrection. The task of proclaiming His great work was given to the twelve disciples and to all those who would be His disciples in the centuries to follow. One of the greatest ways we can display our love for Christ is to take part in His great command to share our faith with others.

We also show our love to God by loving other people in His name.

> If anyone says, "I love God," yet hates his brother, he is a liar. For anyone who does not love his brother, whom he has seen, cannot love God, whom he has not seen. And he has given us this command: Whoever loves God must also love his brother (1 John 4:20-21).

A large amount of the instruction in New Testament Epistles centers on teaching us how to treat one another with love. We must contend that there is no greater way of showing love to our neighbors than by sharing with them the gospel of our Lord Jesus.

If we were awakened one night by the sound of crackling wood and the faint smell of smoke and looked out the bedroom window to see our neighbor's house on fire, what is the best way to show them love? We could show them love by sending them a note of appreciation, or by baking them some cookies, or by inviting them over for dinner. But with the crisis of the present moment, the only best way to show them love would be to run over and warn them of the fire or, if need be, pull them from the burning building. In fact, if their lives were in peril, no other action would show love unless it involved saving them from the fire. So it is with the Great Commission and the state of the lost. In a world enslaved by sin and doomed to destruction, the only best way to carry out Jesus' command to "love our neighbor" is to make our every action geared to helping lead lost people to Jesus.

It doesn't really matter which of the two great commandments we consider as Christians. Neither one of them can be accomplished unless we actively take part in our Master's work of saving the lost.

Neither one of the two great commandments can be accomplished unless we actively take part in our Master's work of saving the lost.

Five Versions — One Commission

We usually think of the Great Commission as it is found in Matthew's Gospel, but the command to share the good news of Jesus was so important that we find variations of this command in each of the Gospels and the Book of Acts. We've already examined Matthew 28:16-20 in chapter 1. Let's briefly look at the remaining versions of Christ's great mandate.

The Great Commission according to Mark

He said to them, "Go into all the world and preach the good news to all creation. Whoever believes and is baptized will be saved, but whoever does not believe will be condemned" (Mark 16:15-16).[4]

Mark's record of the Great Commission is brief and to the point. The command is twofold. First, the disciples are instructed to "go into all world." In the New Testament, the concept of the "world" is used several different ways, but in reference to the gospel, it is always a word designating those in need of the salvation found in Christ.[5] The lost cannot be expected to come to us. We must go to them.

Secondly, once we have placed ourselves in the presence of the lost, we must proclaim to them the good news of what Christ has done. Those who have faith in Christ will be saved. Acceptance of Christ, in Mark's rendition of the Commission has both an inward and outward aspect. Inwardly people believe the message of the apostolic preaching of Christ. Outwardly, they display their public allegiance to Christ in Christian baptism. Both are seen as indispensable displays of faith in Jesus. Those who do not respond to our evangelistic efforts of going and preaching will receive the condemnation for their sins. This places tremendous gravity on Christ's injunction that we must share our faith. The eternal destiny of those within our sphere of influence may hang in the balance of whether or not we take Jesus' command seriously.

The Great Commission according to Luke in His Gospel

> He said to them, "This is what I told you while I was still with you: Everything must be fulfilled that is written about me in the Law of Moses, the Prophets and the Psalms. Then he opened their minds so they could understand the Scriptures. He told them, "This is what is written: The Christ will suffer and rise from the dead on the third day, and repentance and forgiveness of sins will be preached in his name to all nations, beginning at Jerusalem. You are witnesses of these things. I am going to send you what my Father has promised; but stay in the city until you have been clothed with power from on high" (Luke 24:44-49).

Several aspects of the will of the Master come plainly into view here. First, we see that the plan of God to save the world is not a creation of the imagination of the New Testament authors. The Hebrew Bible was seen to exist in three divisions: law (*torah*), prophets (*nebhiim*) and writings (*kethubhim*). Hence, Jesus declared to His disciples that the whole of the Old Testament was a witness to both His mission and commission.

The Old Testament prophecy is threefold. Scripture prophesied concerning Christ's great work on the cross. It also prophesied about the call to repentance and the promise of forgiveness. These aspects of repentance and forgiveness speak of Christ's role as both Lord and Savior. Finally, Jesus declared that the whole of the Hebrew Scriptures predicted that this good news would be proclaimed to all the nations. The Judaism of the first century was quite exclusive. It was generally believed that salvation was the sole possession of the Jewish nation. Here, however, Jesus points out the universal aspect of the gospel (to all the nations — ἔθνη, *ethne* — ethnic groups) and that such an emphasis was part of the message of the entire Old Testament.

Secondly, the disciples are told that "you are witnesses of these things." A witness bears testimony. Not only did Jesus give these men a world-class lesson in Old Testament hermeneutics, He informed them that they were the ones who would enter into God's great work in the world. Notice that Jesus did not ask them to become witnesses. Jesus stated, "You are witnesses." To follow Jesus is to take part in spreading the good news.

Jesus told His disciples, "You *are* witnesses."

The Great Commission according to John

> On the evening of that first day of the week, when the disciples were together, with the doors locked for fear of the Jews, Jesus came and stood among them and said, "Peace be with you!" After he said this, he showed them his hands and side. The disciples were overjoyed when they saw the Lord.
>
> Again Jesus said, "Peace be with you! As the Father has sent me, I am sending you." And with that he breathed on them and said, "Receive the Holy Spirit. If you forgive anyone his sins, they are forgiven; if you do not forgive them, they are not forgiven" (John 20:19-23).

Several aspects of John's version of Jesus' commission stand out to us from the text. First, there is the double blessing of "Peace be with you" (19,21). Jesus had already promised them this peace in John 14:27.[6] Here in our text, sandwiched in between the blessings of peace, Jesus showed His disciples evidence of the reality of His resurrection by displaying His hands and feet. When the eleven realized that this was no ghost or imitator, but that their crucified master had indeed risen, they committed themselves to Him by addressing Him as Lord and experiencing extreme joy. Hence when anyone comes in faith to the risen Christ, the Lord grants peace that is a mixture of submission to His Lordship coupled with overwhelming joy.

Next, we see Christ sending out those who had received his peace. "As the Father has sent me, I am sending you."[7] It seems that Jesus intended the disciples to understand that they would be taking part in the same mission which Jesus Himself had received from the Father.

This mission would be accomplished through the power of the Holy Spirit. Jesus had already instructed the apostles that apart from Him, they could do nothing (John 15:5). What we see in this setting is a preview of Pentecost when the full blessing of the Spirit would come. And while there are certain aspects of the Spirit's power that were unique to the apostles, every believer is promised the presence of the Spirit within their life. The Spirit would grant the power for life and witness.[8]

Finally, Jesus promised results which would follow carrying out His commands. Those who responded in faith to the message would reap the benefits of the forgiveness of sins. Some have misunderstood these words of Christ to teach that the apostles themselves had the authority to forgive sins. To understand exactly what Jesus means here, we need to turn our attention to Peter on the Day of Pentecost as recorded in Acts 2. There we see the fulfillment of Jesus' commission given in John. The Holy Spirit came in power upon the apostles and through Peter offered the forgiveness of sins to all who repented and were baptized. Those who responded in faith to Christ were forgiven and those who did not respond to the gospel, as preached by Peter, were to retain their sins. Hence, we can say that, in a way, the power of forgiving sins is indeed placed within the hands of God's servants. The way we make forgiveness available to people is by proclaiming who Jesus is and what He has done for them on the cross. We, who have received peace with God, now have the opportunity to offer peace to a world in need. We do this with overwhelming joy in the power of His Spirit, assured by the reality of His resurrection.

The power of forgiving sins is indeed placed within the hands of God's servants.

The Great Commission according to Luke in Acts

> In my former book, Theophilus, I wrote about all that Jesus began to do and to teach until the day he was taken up to heaven . . . .
> So when they met together, they asked him, "Lord, are you at this time going to restore the kingdom to Israel?"
> He said to them: "It is not for you to know the times or dates the Father has set by his own authority. But you will receive power when the Holy Spirit comes on you; and you will be my witnesses in Jerusalem, and in all Judea and Samaria, and to the ends of the earth" (Acts 1:1-2a,6-8).

In the opening words of his second volume on the origins of the Christian faith, Dr. Luke addressed Theophilus with his intention to continue describing the ministry of Jesus: "I wrote about all that Jesus **BEGAN** to do and to teach" (emphasis mine). This implies that Jesus' ministry was not over, but just beginning at the time of His ascension! Now this ministry would be carried on through the work of the Holy Spirit in the lives of the apostles and the soon-to-be-established "church."

Jesus' instructions to the disciples during His forty days of postresurrection appearances centered upon two topics: 1) the kingdom of God;

and, 2) the coming of the Holy Spirit (Acts 1:3-4). Apparently, near the end of this teaching period the disciples asked a more pointed question: "Lord, are you at this time going to restore the kingdom to Israel?" It is not a silly question because Jesus had been discussing the kingdom. However, the disciples' question revealed a fundamental lack of understanding concerning the truth of Jesus' basic teaching on the kingdom. From the disciples' question, and their use of the word "restore," it appears that they were expecting a territorial/political kingdom. When they inquired about "Israel" being restored, they showed that they were expecting the kingdom to be nationalistic. And when they asked if the kingdom was going to be restored "at this time," they showed that they expected the establishment of the kingdom to be a sudden and immediate event.

Jesus' response to their question showed the inadequacy of the disciples' understanding. Jesus outlined three truths concerning the nature of the coming of the kingdom of God.[9]

First, **the kingdom of God is spiritual in its character.** Notice that the disciples asked a question about the kingdom. Jesus' reply was about the Holy Spirit (1:7-8a). The kingdom of God is not political. It is the rule of God in the lives of people through the work of the Holy Spirit. John Stott has written: "[The kingdom of God] is spread by witnesses, not by soldiers; through a gospel of peace, not a declaration of war, and by the work of the Spirit, not by force of arms, political intrigue or revolutionary violence."[10]

The kingdom of God is international in its membership.

Second, **the kingdom of God is international in its membership.** The apostles still cherished a narrow, nationalistic aspiration concerning the kingdom. They believed it was only for nationalistic Israel. In His reply, Jesus instructed the disciples to broaden their vision as to the extent of God's kingdom: ". . . and you will be my witnesses in Jerusalem, and in all Judea and Samaria and to the ends of the earth" (1:8). In the Old Testament several of the prophets had predicted the word of God going forth from Jerusalem and proceeding to the ends of the earth (Isa. 2:3; Micah 4:2). This reply by Jesus forms the basic structure of "how" the apostles carried out the Great Commission. The Book of Acts records that they began where they were (in Jerusalem) and ultimately spread the gospel throughout the civilized world, to both Jew and Gentile, ending in Rome.

The kingdom of God is gradual in its expansion. The disciples seemed to assume that the coming of the kingdom would be immediate and complete in its nature. Jesus' reply to such an assumption is twofold. First, he told the disciples that it was not necessary for them to know God's timetable for the flow of human history.[11] Then, Jesus told them that, although they would not see the whole of God's timetable, they would receive what was necessary for the kingdom's coming — power through the gift of the Holy Spirit. This would enable them to carry on the only task necessary for the spread of the kingdom — being witnesses of Jesus. The kingdom, through the church, would begin with the coming of the Spirit and it would consummate at the return of Christ at the *parousia*. The growth of the kingdom was to be gradual and steady.[12]

The job of a disciple is not to be a clock-watcher or Second-Coming predictor. God will take care of these things. A disciple's only concern is to carry out the Great Commission in the power of the Holy Spirit.

The job of a disciple is not to be a clock-watcher or Second-Coming predictor.

Jesus' teaching during His forty days on earth after the resurrection was basic and direct. When the Spirit came in power, the long promised reign of God, which Jesus had Himself inaugurated and proclaimed, would begin to spread. It would be spiritual in its character (transforming the lives and values of its citizens), international in its membership (including Gentiles as well as Jews) and gradual in its expansion (beginning at Jerusalem and spreading outward to the ends of the earth; beginning with Jesus and concluding with the Second Coming). This must also be our understanding, as disciples of Jesus, carrying out the commission into the 21st century.

What Evangelism Is Not

The goal of evangelism is not winning people to a particular point of view, although everyone evangelized will develop a point of view. Christ did not send us into the world to champion some great argument. The Great Commission is not, "Go into all the world and win every theological argument!" We are to win people.

Neither is the goal of evangelism to win individuals to a particular church family, although everyone evangelized should ultimately be united with a local congregation. I am reminded of a church where a friend went to minister. He followed a preacher who had been there for over 30 years. The congregation had over 1000 members listed on its membership roll.

Forty elders served as congregational leaders, although only half of them attended services regularly. The congregation obviously followed the precedent set by their leaders with fewer than 25% of the membership attending. I can remember my friend lamenting that the former minister had made many church members, but very few disciples of Jesus. Men won to an organization form a club, not a church.

The goal of evangelism is not to win people to a particular preacher or evangelist, God uses His people in the evangelism process. Many of the media evangelists of the 1980s and 1990s sold their souls to the perverted gospel of health and wealth. When the shallow nature of this false Christianity was revealed and many of these leaders fell into sin, they left in their wake an ocean of disillusioned followers. This cult of following the super-preacher-creature is not solely a 20th-century phenomenon. Paul had to deal with this very issue in 1 Corinthians 1:11-13.

Christ did not send us into the world to champion some great argument.

What Evangelism Is

In the 20th century there have been scores of definitions for evangelism.[13] There are very lengthy and precise definitions, such as one by the 1974 International Congress on World Evangelism in Lausanne, Switzerland:

> To evangelize is to spread the good news that Jesus Christ died for our sins and was raised from the dead according to the Scriptures, and that as the reigning Lord he now offers the forgiveness of sins and the liberating gift of the Spirit to all who repent and believe. Our Christian presence in the world is indispensable to evangelism, and so is that kind of dialogue whose purpose is to listen sensitively in order to understand. But evangelism itself is the proclamation of the historical, biblical Christ as Savior and Lord, with a view to persuading people to come to him personally and so be reconciled to God. In issuing the gospel invitation we have no liberty to conceal the cost of discipleship. Jesus still calls all who would follow him to deny themselves with his new community. The results of evangelism include obedience to Christ, incorporation into his church and responsible service in the world.[14]

There are also much briefer descriptions, such as the one made famous by D.T. Niles: "Evangelism is just one beggar telling another beggar where to get food."[15]

J.I. Packer has written:

> Evangelism means exhorting sinners to accept Christ Jesus as their Savior, recognizing that in the most final and far-reaching sense, they are lost without Him. Nor is this all. Evangelism also means summoning men to receive Christ Jesus as all that He is — Lord, as well as Savior — and therefore to serve Him as their King in the fellowship of His Church, the company of those who worship him, witness to Him and work for Him here on earth. In other words, evangelism is the issuing of a call to turn, as well as to trust; it is the delivering, not merely of a divine invitation to receive a Savior, but of a divine command to repent of sin. And there is not evangelism where this specific application is not made.[16]

It is not our purpose here to evaluate the numerous definitions put forward by concerned New Testament scholars. At times it is possible to overdefine a simple subject. The great English preacher Charles Haddon Spurgeon once said:

> We would bring men to Christ, and not to our own peculiar views of Christianity. Our first care must be that the sheep should be gathered to the great Shepherd; there will be time enough afterwards to secure them for our various folds. To make proselytes, is a suitable labor for Pharisees; to beget men unto God, is the honorable aim of ministers of Christ.[17]

The great goal of evangelism is to bring men and women into a saving relationship with Jesus Christ, the Lord of Glory.

New Testament Words Which Describe Evangelism

There are numerous words used in the New Testament which describe different aspects of evangelism.[18] Alan Watson has made several keen observations about the two New Testament words which are at the root of our English words "evangelize" and "evangelism."[19]

Evangelize — Sharing Good News

The first of these words is εὐαγγελίζω (*euangelizo*) which is the verb "to evangelize." This word is used 52 times in the New Testament (25 times by Luke and 21, by Paul). It means quite simply, "To announce, proclaim or bring good news." In the Greek Old Testament (LXX) it is some-times used of a runner coming with the news of victory. In the Psalms it occurs twice (40:10; 96:2) in the sense of proclaiming God's faithfulness and salvation. In the New Testament the word is used in a fuller context.

The Gospel of Luke records the dramatic announcement of Jesus' public ministry in the synagogue at Nazareth. Jesus was asked to take part in the service of the day. The Scripture records that he took the scroll of the prophet Isaiah and read the following:

> "The Spirit of the Lord is on me, because he has anointed me to preach good news to the poor. He has sent me to proclaim free-dom for the prisoners and recovery of sight for the blind, to release the oppressed, to proclaim the year of the Lord's favor" (Luke 4:18-19).

Here proclamation of the good news (*euangelizo*) is linked with demonstra-tion of the good news. Part of the proclamation of good news is the demonstration of the implications of that news.

When John the Baptist was languishing in Herod's dungeon and he sent his disciples to ask Jesus, "Are you the one who was to come, or should we expect someone else?" How did Jesus answer? Did He simply preach another sermon? No, He said, "Go back and report to John what you have seen and heard: The blind receive sight, the lame walk, those who have lep-rosy are cured, the deaf hear, the dead are raised, and the good news is preached to the poor" (Luke 7:22). Without the *demonstration* of the good news, the *proclamation* will fall on deaf ears. This is why, in many third-world countries, the most effective mission activity must include the distrib-ution of food and clothing and the giving of medical attention.

Watson points out how this was worked out in Jesus' ministry.[20] In Luke 8:1 we read: "After this, Jesus traveled about from one town and vil-lage to another, proclaiming the good news (*euangelizo*) of the Kingdom of God." What follows in the rest of Luke 8? We see Jesus give the Parable of the Sower. We see Christ calm the storm on Galilee (8:22-25). He cast out the demon Legion (8:26-29). Then He healed the woman with the hemor-rhage (8:40-48) and finally raised Jairus's daughter from the dead (8:49-56). What a way to bring the good news to the cities and villages of Galilee! In Jesus' ministry, the proclamation of good news was always combined with the demonstration of that good news. If the kingdom of God had come, then the good news would have real implications for daily life. It was not simply a doctrine of God to believe, but rather a life empowered by God to experience. And this dual aspect of proclamation and demonstration is not unique to Jesus in the New Testament. It shows up everywhere else as well.

When Paul wrote to the Roman Christians about the extent of his ministry, he declared:

> Therefore, I glory in Christ Jesus in my service to God. I will not venture to speak of anything except what Christ has accomplished through me in leading the Gentiles to obey God by what I have said and done — by the power of signs and miracles, through the power of the Spirit. So from Jerusalem all the way around to Illyricum, I have fully proclaimed the gospel [ευαγγε-λιον] of Christ (Rom. 15:17-19).

Notice that for Paul, part of fully proclaiming the gospel of Christ included "what I have said and done." Hence, for Paul, "evangelizing" included both words and deeds — proclamation and demonstration!

Watson continues to point out that such a display of words and actions are quite evident in the evangelism of the church displayed in the Book of Acts.[21] In Acts 8 when the church was scattered (8:4), the Christians went everywhere *preaching* the word (*euangelizo* — evangelizing). Philip went to Samaria and performed many wonderful works such as driving out demons and healing cripples. We note Acts 8:12 states: "But when they believed Philip as he preached the good news [*euangelizo*] of the kingdom of God and the name of Jesus Christ, they were baptized, both men and women." Here again, in "preaching the good news [*euangelizo*]," demonstration and proclamation cannot be separated.

In "preaching the good news," demonstration and proclamation cannot be separated.

The Gospel — Good News

The second main word in the New Testament relating to evangelism is the noun εὐαγγέλιον (*euangelion*). This is the word usually translated "gospel" in our English versions. It literally means "good news."[22] It is used 72 times in the New Testament, 54 of which occur in Pauline literature. Watson has observed that from these passages we can learn several truths about the gospel we are to proclaim.[23]

The "good news" is called the "gospel of the kingdom" in Matthew 4:23; 9:35; and 24:14. The first two examples in Matthew are in the context of Jesus' manifesting his authority over the powers of evil. We have already noted earlier that the "kingdom" is not a physical place or a social/political entity. It is the realm in which God is recognized as King and His will is done.[24] And so the gospel of the kingdom emphasizes Christ's authority over those who would respond to the message.

The "good news" is called the "gospel of God" in Mark 1:14 and 1 Thessalonians 2:2,8,9. This is true in two ways. First, it is good news *about* God. The Bible records His love for all men in Christ (John 3:16), His work for all men in Christ (Rom. 5:6-8), and His desire for all men to be saved in Christ (1 Tim. 2:3-4; 2 Pet. 3:9). Secondly, it is good news *from* God. The gospel is not the creation of the mind of man, but the revelation of the mind and heart of God for His lost people. Paul went to great lengths in affirming that the gospel he preached was not of human invention (Gal. 1:11-12). The gospel is not from man but from God Himself.

The "good news" is called the "gospel of Jesus Christ" (Mark 1:1; 2 Cor. 4:4; 9:13; 10:14). This is also true in two senses. Jesus brought the good news into the world. Matthew, Mark, and Luke all record that Jesus traveled about preaching the "good news" (Matt. 4:23; 9:35; Mark 1:14; Luke 8:1). Mark even begins his story of Jesus' life as a declaration of this "good news." Some have pointed out that the word "gospel" does not appear in John, but the concept of Jesus coming to bring the gospel of light and life to men is everywhere present (e.g., John 1:10-13; 3:16-21; 4:21-26). Without Jesus, there would be no good news. Also, in the New Testament, Jesus does more than simply bring "good news." He is "good news." Jesus is the embodiment of the message that He preached (John 1:17-18; 5:39-40). We will spend more time elaborating this point in the next chapter.

This gospel is for all men (Mark 13:10; 16:15; Acts 15:7). God's great work through Christ is for all people regardless of race, gender or social standing (Gal. 3:26-29). This makes spreading the good news such an urgent matter. One time Spurgeon was asked if the heathen who had never heard the gospel would be saved. Spurgeon answered, "It is more a question with me whether we who hear the gospel, and fail to give it to those who have not, can be saved."

This gospel must be personally appropriated. There must be a whole-hearted, personal response to the gospel, so that we not only believe it but also hold it fast. To do less is to have "believed in vain" (1 Cor. 15:1-2). Paul would sometimes speak of "our gospel" or even "my gospel" (2 Cor. 4:3; 1 Thess. 1:5; 2 Thess. 2:14). Our response must be a total one. We must be "unashamed of the gospel" (Rom. 1:16), do all "for the sake of the gospel" (1 Cor. 9:23), and even be willing to leave house and family for the gospel (Mark 10:29). The gospel can be missed (Rom. 2:16), neglected (Rom. 10:16), disobeyed (2 Thess. 1:7-8), and refused (1 Pet. 4:17). It must be our goal to present this "good news" of Jesus so that men and women can accept it and be saved.

The Apostle Paul's Summary of Evangelism

As we conclude our thoughts on defining evangelism, perhaps we should examine the Apostle Paul's great injunction to the church at Corinth. In 1 Corinthians 15:1-5, Paul reminds these early Christians of what it means to have been evangelized.

> Now, brothers, I want to remind you of the gospel I preached to you, which you received and on which you have taken your stand. By this gospel you are saved, if you hold firmly to the word I preached to you. Otherwise, you have believed in vain.
>
> For what I received I passed on to you as of first importance: that Christ died for our sins according to the Scriptures, that he was buried, that he was raised on the third day according to the Scriptures, and that he appeared to Peter, and then to the Twelve.

As we read this passage in our English version, we need to remember that the word "gospel" is the noun form of the "evangel" — good news (εὐαγγέλιον) and that the word translated "preached" is the verb form of "evangelize" — sharing the good news (εὐαγγελίζω). Hence, we could very easily translate the first two verses of 1 Corinthians 15 as:

> Now, brothers, I want to remind you of the *evangel* with which I *evangelized* you, which you received and on which you have taken your stand. By this *evangel* you are saved, if you hold firmly to the word with which I *evangelized* you.

In considering Paul's thinking on this vastly important subject, ten issues concerning the gospel become quite clear.

First, **the gospel is unifying and corrective**. Paul had just finished addressing the Corinthians who were flaunting their spiritual gifts (1 Cor. 12–14). He concluded 1 Corinthians 14 with an appeal to his own apostolic authority. Everyone in the church must recognize Paul's authority as an apostle of Christ and that Paul's own writings to them were indeed the Lord's command (1 Cor. 14:37). If the Corinthians "ignored" this basic truth, they were to be "ignored" (1 Cor. 14:38). What was the important truth which they had to "know" or be "reminded of"? It was the truth of the gospel. With all the doctrinal and internal conflicts of the church at Corinth, Paul saw the solution in an emphasis on the *evangel*, the good news of what Christ had done.

Second, **the gospel is "apostolic."** It is not a gospel received through the special revelations which some of the Corinthian Christians believed they were receiving (1 Cor. 12:7-11; 13:8-10; esp. 14:36-38). This was the gospel which Paul delivered with his own apostolic authority. In Ephesians, Paul wrote that the church was built upon the Lord Jesus Christ as proclaimed in the apostolic and prophetic witness (Eph. 2:20). This gospel was not available to everyone directly (through inspiration) but rather had been revealed to God's holy apostles and prophets in the Spirit (Eph. 3:2-5). Paul's conclusion to the Ephesians is the same as here with the Corinthians. By reading what he, as an apostle, had written, they would be able to understand the revelation of the good news of God (Eph. 3:4).

Third, **the gospel is personal**. Although it did not originate within the Corinthians through direct revelation, they were indeed to internalize it as they received the apostolic message. Paul recognized that they had "received" (15:1) it, for not to internalize the gospel is to remain outside of God's grace.

Fourth, **the gospel is foundational**. Not only are we to internalize the good news, but we are to clear all the other boulders of life out of the way and to take our stand solely on the message of what Christ has done. Paul has already reminded the Corinthians of this foundation earlier in his epistle.

> By the grace God has given me, I laid a foundation as an expert builder, and someone else is building on it. But each one should be careful how he builds. For no one can lay any foundation other than the one already laid, which is Jesus Christ (1 Cor. 3:10-11).

Outside of Christ, there is no place to stand.

Fifth, **the gospel brings salvation**. In the coming chapters we will deal at length with the concept of salvation. Here, Paul wished his readers to understand that without receiving this good news — without being "evangelized" — they were lost, in the greatest and most complete sense of that word. Paul described the state of those who had not received the gospel as ". . . separate from Christ, excluded from citizenship in Israel and foreigners to the covenants of the promise, without hope and without God in the world" (Eph. 2:12). Yet for those who received and stood upon that good news, to them Paul wrote ". . . now in Christ Jesus you who once were far away have been brought near through the blood of Christ" (Eph. 2:13).

Sixth, **the gospel must be firmly held**. The blessings of salvation come only to those who cling to the good news tenaciously. This was a favorite thought to the author of the Hebrew Epistle.[25] It was also the concept Jesus used in the parable of the soils in Luke 8:15.[26] While it is true that no power is great enough to separate a Christian from the loving embrace of the Heavenly Father (John 10:28; Rom. 8:35-39), the Scripture is equally clear that our relationship with Christ cannot be entered into without a great commitment on our part. Paul maintained that failure to hold firmly to faith in Christ is to have "believed in vain." Jesus will save those who cling to Him. But we must *"cling to Him!"*

The blessings of salvation come only to those who cling to the good news tenaciously.

Seventh, **the gospel is revelation from God**. While Paul had already emphasized his place in the delivery of the good news as an apostle, he was only the "one sent with the message." Paul also stresses the "one sending the message!" Even though the gospel had come to Paul directly through revelation, it was indeed — revelation. "I want you to know, brothers, that the gospel I preached is not something that man made up. I did not receive it from any man, nor was I taught it; rather, I received it by revelation from Jesus Christ" (Gal. 1:11-12).

Eighth, **the gospel is supreme**. "For what I received I passed on to you as of first importance" (1 Cor. 15:3). Of everything Paul preached, this one thing was to have primacy over all the others. "For I resolved to know nothing while I was with you except Jesus Christ and him crucified" (1 Cor. 2:2). The church has many members and touches many areas of life. One thing, however, must be the fulcrum around which everything else revolves — sharing the good news of what God has done through Christ. Evangelism is the supreme task of the church and every Christian.

Ninth, **the gospel is the culmination of history in the finished work of Christ on the cross**. That which was supreme for the Apostle Paul was the historical activity of God surrounding the death, burial, and resurrection of Christ. Paul emphasized that the cross was not simply an item of daily news. No, these things happened *"according to the Scriptures!"* In the gospel, the prophetic promises of the Old Testament concerning the coming Messiah collided with the actual events in the life of Jesus of Nazareth. The Passion of Christ was that to which the entire revelation of God looked forward in the Old Testament Scriptures (John 5:39-40; Luke 24:25-27; Heb. 1:1-4). Out of this understanding came the great confession of faith, "I believe that Jesus [the historic figure of the New Testament] is the Christ [the promised Savior of the Old Testament], the Son of the Living God" (Matt. 16:16).

And yet, Paul's understanding of the cross of Christ cannot remain simply an historical fact or even a prophetic reality. Someone might ask, "Fine. This is all very interesting. What does all this prophecy and history have to do with me?" Listen to Paul's understanding of the gospel ". . . Christ died for our sins according to the Scriptures, that he was buried and that he rose again according to the Scriptures."

Paul emphasized that the cross was not simply an item of daily news, but rather happened "according to the Scriptures!"

The key phrase in the entire paragraph of 1 Corinthians 15:1-5, as it relates to us, is — "for our sins." All of the story of Jesus would remain simply an historical peculiarity were it not for the fact that God revealed that it was all accomplished in order to deal with the problem of *my* sin. And so the events of the cross were predicted in Old Testament prophecy, they occurred historically in the life of Jesus of Nazareth, and they extend right up to the present day in that they are meant as the final solution to the problem of my own sin which separates me from God.

The hymn writer was correct when he wrote:

> My hope is in the Lord,
> Who gave himself for me
> And paid the price for all my sin on Calvary.
> For me He died;
> For me he lives,
> And everlasting light and life
> He freely gives.[27]

Tenth and finally, **the gospel is the message of a resurrection faith**. In the mind of the apostles, the resurrection of Jesus was that event through which God proved the reality of the work of Christ on the cross for our sins. It was at the heart of all the preaching recorded in the Acts of the Apostles.[28] Peter declared before the Sanhedrin, "It is by the name of Jesus Christ of Nazareth, whom you crucified but whom God raised from the dead, that this man stands before you healed" (Acts 4:10). Paul's message to the philosophers in Athens was the same: "He has given proof of this to all men by raising him from the dead" (Acts 17:31). The resurrection of Jesus was the ultimate testimony of God that the gospel is indeed real. Sins can be forgiven! New and abundant life is possible! God's kingdom can come and God's will can be done in the life of anyone who would accept this gospel! Because Jesus was raised from the dead, we can rise and walk in newness of life (Rom. 8:1-11). Because Jesus is raised, we can know that death will not defeat us (1 Cor. 15:51-58). God will raise us on the final day, just as He raised Christ (1 Thess. 4:13-18). This is the *evangel*, the good news. With it, we are to evangelize the nations. This is the great task of the church. This is the great commission of our lives.

The resurrection of Jesus was the ultimate testimony of God that the gospel is indeed real.

And so, what do we share when we tell the good news of Christ? We do not share simply Bible words and Bible doctrines. People are not saved by a book! We present Jesus Christ Himself, as presented in the Bible. "We do not preach ourselves, but Jesus Christ as Lord" (2 Cor. 4:5). There is no substitute for a life on fire that reflects Jesus Christ.

This is ultimately the task of the evangelist, and to this end we must not only be faithful to the message entrusted to us, but also dependent on the Holy Spirit who alone can glorify Christ and bring hearers in touch with the living God.

Long ago Richard Baxter wrote:

> I seldom come out of the pulpit but my own conscience strikes me that I have been no more serious and fervent. It accuses me not so much for want of ornaments and elegancy, nor for letting fall an unhandsome word; but it asks me, "How could you speak of life and death with such a heart? How could you preach of heaven and hell in such a careless, sleepy manner? Do you believe what you say? Are you in earnest or in jest? How can you tell people that sin is such a terrible thing, and that so much misery is upon them and before them, and be no more affected with it? Should you not weep over such a people, and should not your tears interrupt you words? Should you not cry aloud and show them their transgressions and entreat and beseech them as for life and death?
>
> Truly this is the peal that conscience does ring in my ears, and yet my drowsy soul will not be awakened. Oh, what a thing is an insensible, hardened heart! O Lord, save us from the plague of unfaithfulness and hardheartedness ourselves, or else how shall we be fit instruments of saving others from it? Oh, do that on our souls which you would use us to do on the souls of others![29]

1. The verb φιλέω is used 25 times in the New Testament.

2. In John 13:33-35 and Matt. 22:34-40, "love" is the translation of ἀγαπᾶτε/ἀγαπήσεις (ἀγαπάω).

3. For many years it was mistaken that φιλέω and ἀγαπάω were completely different in their meanings. Today, linguists inform us that the words are very similar and can at times be used synonymously (See John 21:15-17). However, ἀγαπάω is always the word chosen when the *command* of love is used. See Johannes Louw and Eugene Nida, "attitudes and emotions," *Greek-English Lexicon of the New Testament Based on Semantic Domains* (New York: United Bible Societies, 1988), sect: 25:43.

4. We recognize the questionable manuscript evidence for this passage. Nonetheless, it does display a remarkable consistency of content with the other "commission" passages.

5. In the New Testament, the word κόσμος is used 186 times. It can mean (1) the physical universe, Acts 17:24; (2) the sphere or place of human life, Matt 4:8; and (3) humanity, the world of men, especially those in need of salvation. The term never refers to the saved when used in this final way. See J. Guhrt, "earth," *Dictionary of New Testament Theology*, vol. 1 (Grand Rapids: Zondervan, 1981), pp. 521-527.

6. The blessing of grace and peace (χάρις ὑμῖν καὶ εἰρήνη) became a standard Christian greeting used by Paul in 10 of his 13 epistles (Rom. 1:7; 1 Cor. 1:3; 2 Cor. 1:2; Gal. 1:3; Eph. 1:2; Phil. 1:2; Col. 1:2; 1 Thess. 1:1; 2 Thess. 1:2; Phil. 1:3; 1 Pet. 1:2—only the pastorals omit it), by Peter (1 Pet. 1:2; 2 Pet. 1:2) and by John himself in addressing the churches in Asia (Rev. 1:4).

7. Καθὼς ἀπέσταλκέν με ὁ πατήρ, καγὼ πέμπω ὑμᾶς. Some have noticed that the verbs for "send" in Jesus' commission are different, ἀπέσταλκέν used of the Father sending Jesus and πέμπω of Jesus sending the disciples. However, in John, these words are used synonymously. The use of καθὼς makes this clear. See Leon Morris, *The Gospel according to John*, NICNT (Grand Rapids: Eerdmans, 1971), p. 846.

8. Every believer is promised the gift of the Holy Spirit upon coming to Christ in faith (Acts 2:38,39; 5:32). We are also promised the continual presence of Christ in carrying out the commission (Matt. 28:20).

9. I am indebted to John Stott for the outline of the information concerning the Great Commission in Acts. See John Stott, *The Message of Acts* (Downers Grove, IL: InterVarsity, 1990), pp. 40-45.

10. Ibid., p. 42.

11. "Times" refer to periods of great length, and "dates" refer to specific events. Stott, *The Message of Acts*, p. 43.

12. Jesus' parables concerning the nature of the growth of the kingdom (Luke 13:18-21; Matt. 13:31-33; Mark 4:30-32) display this gradual growth.

13. See Delos Miles, *Introduction to Evangelism* (Nashville: Broadman & Holman, 1983), pp. 35ff.

14. J.D. Douglas, ed., *Let the Earth Hear His Voice* (Minneapolis: World Wide Publications, 1975). p. 4.

15. However, we must point out that Niles's one-sentence description of evangelism was a part of a longer definition. See D.T. Niles, *That They May Have Life* (New York: Harper & Brothers, 1951), p. 96.

16. J.I. Packer, *Evangelism and the Sovereignty of God* (Downers Grove, IL: InterVarsity, 1961), pp. 39-40.

17. Charles H. Spurgeon, *The Soul Winner* (Grand Rapids: Eerdmans, 1963), p. 16.

18. Delos Miles examines numerous words and phrases covered in the New Testament. Miles, *Evangelism*, pp. 19-33.

19. Alan Watson, *I Believe in Evangelism* (Grand Rapids: Eerdmans, 1976), pp. 26-34.

20. Ibid., pp. 26-27.

21. Ibid., p. 29.

22. H. Friedrich, "εὐαγγέλιον" *TDNT*.

23. Watson, *I Believe in Evangelism*, pp. 32-34.

24. Vast amounts of scholarly literature deal with the tremendous issue of interpreting the exact meaning of the biblical understanding of the "kingdom of God." Several excellent studies include G.R. Beasley-Murray, *Jesus and the Kingdom of God* (Grand Rapids: Eerdmans, 1986); Herman Ridderbos, *The Coming of the Kingdom* (St. Catherines, ON: Paideia Press, 1962); and George E. Ladd, *Crucial Questions about the Kingdom of God* (Grand Rapids: Eerdmans, 1952).

25. The verb used here is κατέχω, which in this context means to hold fast, expending great energy. Compare with Heb. 3:14 (NRSV): "For we have become partners of Christ, if only we hold our first confidence firm to the end." and Heb. 10:23 (NRSV): "Let us hold fast to the confession of our hope without wavering, for he who has promised is faithful."

26. "But as for that in the good soil, these are the ones who, when they hear the word, hold it fast in an honest and good heart, and bear fruit with patient endurance" (Luke 8:15).

27. Words from the hymn "My Hope Is in the Lord" by Norman J. Clayton. *The Hymnal for Worship and Celebration*, ed. Tom Fettke (Waco: Word Music, 1986), no. 406.

28. The resurrection was at the heart of almost every apostolic sermon in the Acts of the Apostles (2:22-36; 3:12-26; 4:8-12; etc.). For a complete study see Marion L. Soards, *The Speeches in Acts* (Louisville: Westminster/John Knox, 1994).

29. Quoted in Horatius Bonar, *Words to Winners of Souls* (Phillipsburg, NJ: Puritan and Reformed Publishers, 1995), pp. 20-21.

Chapter 3

THE NEED FOR EVANGELISM: UNDERSTANDING THE BIBLICAL TEACHING ON SIN AND SALVATION

Sin is the most expensive thing in the universe. Nothing else can cost so much. Pardoned or unpardoned, its cost is infinitely great. Pardoned, the cost falls chiefly on the great atoning Substitute; unpardoned, it must fall on the head of the guilty sinner.[1]

Charles Finney

You see, our sin hurts God; hinders His plans; and spoils our lives. It is the ugliest fact in all the world. We forget that it was sin that crucified Christ. It was sin that drove in the nails and impaled Him to the tree. "Were you there when they crucified my Lord?" the old Negro spiritual asks. Yes — we were there, and we cannot deny it.[2]

Peter Marshall

Lord, I believe we're sinners more
Than sands upon the ocean shore,
Thou hast for all a ransom paid,
For all a full atonement made.

Count von Zinzendorf

A man was in the hospital close to death. A minister came to see him and asked: "Have you made your peace with God?"

"I didn't know," said the man, "that we had ever quarreled."

Most people we meet on the street would share this sentiment. The typical American today does not go to bed with the burning awareness that he is at war with God. However, this is exactly the state of the person who is outside a saving relationship with Jesus Christ. The Apostle Paul dramatically points this out in Ephesians 2:12-14a:

Remember that at that time you were separate from Christ, excluded from citizenship in Israel and foreigners to the covenants of the promise, without hope and without God in the world. But now in Christ Jesus you who once were far away have been brought near through the blood of Christ. For he, himself, is our peace.

In this context, the Lord gives one of his most solemn yet definite teachings through Scripture. The Bible declares plainly that without Christ, we are without God's promises; without Christ, we are without hope; without Christ, we are without God; without Christ, we are lost . . . *lost forever.*

The typical American today does not go to bed with the burning awareness that he is at war with God.

At this point, many today balk at the teachings of the church. "Do you mean to say," they ask, "that all those outside the church have no hope whatsoever? What about all the sincere folks who never come to Christ? What of the billions in the worlds of Islam, Buddhism and Hinduism? What of those who have never heard? What of my neighbors and friends who are good-hearted people, but who have never made Christ their Lord and Savior? **Are you saying that they are lost?** Why, if that's true, then this 'gospel' has made you Christians the most narrow-minded, bigoted people on the face of the earth."

At first, it appears difficult to respond to such claims. Perhaps, we should reply by saying, that far from being narrow-minded and bigoted, Christians are, in fact, the most loving people in the world.

Suppose you are a doctor and an individual comes to you one day and describes his symptoms. After taking a blood test you realize that this fellow has acute diabetes. You prescribe insulin injections. "Insulin!" he cries. "I don't want to take insulin." You assure him that he must take insulin.

"But, I don't want to take insulin," he complains. "Can't I take some other drug. How about penicillin? How about a double dose of Tylenol? Won't those do?" Again you reaffirm that without the insulin, he will die.

Then he exclaims, "Why, doctor, I believe you are the most narrow, closed-minded, bigoted physician I have ever met." Now, here's the question: Is the doctor narrow and bigoted or is the doctor loving, because he is telling the man the truth — the only truth which will give him life!

Christians are not narrow or bigoted. Christians are loving because we declare to the world the truth. In our sin, we are at war with God, without hope, without God in the world. But Jesus is our solution. The gospel of Christ brings us peace with God. There is no peace that can be purchased on the bargain counter. Only through Christ's victory on the cross where

God justly punishes sin and mercifully pardons the sinner, only there do we find that which brings peace. "He is our peace!" This isn't narrow or bigoted. It is the truth!

Christians are not narrow or bigoted, but rather loving because we declare to the world the truth.

What does it mean to be "saved?" Many within the church find so little zeal for evangelism because they have forgotten what it is that they have been saved from. We live in a day and age in which many churches are only concerned with support groups to help us deal with the pressures of modern living, self-esteem seminars to make us feel better about ourselves, and entertainment activities which keep our minds occupied with the trivialities inside the church instead of the trivialities outside the church.

Long ago Richard Baxter wrote:

> Ah, me! The misery of the unconverted is so great that it calls for our utmost compassion. They are in the grip of bitterness, and as yet have no part nor fellowship in the pardon of their sins nor in the hope of glory. We are therefore driven by the necessity "to open their eyes, and to turn them from darkness to light, and from the power of Satan unto God; that they may receive forgiveness of sin, and inheritance among the sanctified by faith in Christ" (Acts 26:18).[3]

To reestablish the priority of the Great Commission in our lives and our churches, perhaps we should take a look at what it means to be lost in sin. People will seldom find true joy in being saved until they realize what it is that they have been saved from.

Sin — The Ultimate Problem

Old Testament Words Describing Sin

The Old Testament is quite descriptive in words and phrases describing man's movement away from God into sin. It would take a large book just to do justice to these word studies. We will examine seven key words used in the Old Testament to describe the meaning and ramifications of sin.

The most common word for sin in the Old Testament is the Hebrew term *hata* (חטא). It occurs 595 times in the Old Testament and is the principle word for sin.[4] Its basic meaning is "to miss the mark." If the "mark" to be achieved is God's righteousness or living up to the perfect mandates of God's law, then it is easy to see why everyone is condemned by their actions.

> The next day Moses said to the people, "You have committed a great *sin*. But now I will go up to the LORD; perhaps I can make atonement for your *sin*."
> So Moses went back to the LORD and said, "Oh, what a great *sin* these people have committed! They have made themselves gods of gold. But now, please forgive their *sin* —but if not, then blot me out of the book you have written."
> The LORD replied to Moses, "Whoever has *sinned* against me I will blot out of my book" (Exod. 32:30-33, emphasis mine).

Sin has tremendous eternal ramifications. Those who miss the mark of God's holiness will be "blotted out of His book."

Another aspect of the word involves the nature of "missing the mark." It is not simply commandments which we are failing to live up to. When we sin, we destroy the relationship God intends to have with His people.[5] David's famous cry of repentance illustrates this when he writes:

> Against you, you only, have I *sinned*
>   and done what is evil in your sight,
> so that you are proved right when you speak
>   and justified when you judge
>   (Ps. 51:4, emphasis mine).

When we sin, we fall short of being like God in our thoughts and actions and thus destroy the communal relationship which God intends to have with each one of us.

When we sin, we fall short of being like God in our thoughts and actions.

Another common Hebrew word for sin is *abar* (עבר). It is found 548 times in the Old Testament.[6] Its usual meaning is that of movement or travel and can be translated "pass by or pass over." It is occasionally used of the movement of men outside of the covenant relationship with God. In the time of the Judges, Scripture records:

> Therefore the LORD was very angry with Israel and said, "Because this nation has *violated* [passed over] the covenant that I laid down for their forefathers and has not listened to me, . . . (Judg. 2:20, emphasis mine).

The theme is repeated in Hosea where the Lord declares:

> Like Adam, they have *broken* [passed by] the covenant—
> they were unfaithful to me there (Hosea 6:7, emphasis mine).

Hence, sin is a movement away from God and away from the covenant and laws which God has established between himself and mankind.

Shagag (שָׁגַג) and *shagah* (שָׁגָה) both mean to go astray and err. The noun and verb forms both emphasize the sin of ignorance and sin done inadvertently. There are many causes of this sin in Scripture: strong drink (Prov. 20:1), seductive strange women (Prov. 5:20,23), and the inability to reject evil instruction (Prov. 19:27). It can also mean the slip of the tongue (Eccl. 5:5-6) or even accidental manslaughter (Num. 35:11). At times others can take the initiative in leading people astray (Deut. 27:18). Hence sin can result in being innocently influenced by the powers of evil or those who represent evil.

Pasha (פָּשַׁע) is used frequently in the Old Testament and means "revolt or rebellion." It is used often of Israel's rebellion against God.

> But *rebels* and sinners will both be broken,
>   and those who forsake the LORD will perish (Isa. 1:28, emphasis mine).

> You have neither heard nor understood;
>   from of old your ear has not been open.
> Well do I know how treacherous you are;
>   you were called a *rebel* from birth (Isa. 48:8, emphasis mine).

> He said: "Son of man, I am sending you to the Israelites, to a *rebellious* nation that has *rebelled* against me; they and their fathers have been in *revolt* against me to this very day (Ezek. 2:3, emphasis mine).

The noun form of the word designates those who reject God's authority. It is often translated "transgression." Hence sin is a revolt against the claims of God's sovereignty.

Haneph (חָנֵף) is used often in the Old Testament and carries the basic meaning "twisted." It is usually used metaphorically of "twisting or perverting" the righteous things of God. It can refer to the land being polluted and can also refer to people's lives being polluted with sin. It is ruthless violation of that which is holy.

> Do not *pollute* the land where you are. Bloodshed *pollutes* the land, and atonement cannot be made for the land on which blood has been shed, except by the blood of the one who shed it (Num. 35:33, emphasis mine).

But now many nations
  are gathered against you.
They say, "Let her be *defiled*,
  let our eyes gloat over Zion!" (Micah 4:11, emphasis mine).

In the form of an adjective this word means a godless man or someone who forgets God.

Such is the destiny of all who forget God;
  so perishes the hope of the *godless* (Job 8:13, emphasis mine).

Hence sin is a cancer that pollutes the soul and the earth as a result.

Awa (עוה) is the verb which means to bend, twist or distort and is used 17 times in the Old Testament (Lam. 3:9; Job 33:27). The noun form (עון) is much more common (231 times in the Old Testament) and refers to infraction, crooked behavior, perversion and iniquity. Such is the lot of all humanity.

But your *iniquities* have separated
  you from your God;
your sins have hidden his face from you,
  so that he will not hear (Isa. 59:2, emphasis mine).

We all, like sheep, have gone astray,
  each of us has turned to his own way;
and the LORD has laid on him
  the *iniquity* of us all (Isa. 53:6, emphasis mine).

For I know my *transgressions*,
  and my sin is always before me.
Against you, you only, have I sinned
  and done what is evil in your sight,
so that you are proved right when you speak
  and justified when you judge (Ps. 51:3-4, emphasis mine).

Hence sin is a bending and twisting into distortion the perfection which God intends.

One last Hebrew word we need to examine is *'asham* (אשם). It is used throughout the Old Testament.[7] Its main meaning centers on being guilty and on the debt that such a sin incurs. In many places the meaning moves from the act which brings guilt to the act of punishment.

Say to the Israelites: "When a man or woman wrongs another in any way and so is unfaithful to the LORD, that person is *guilty*" (Num. 5:6, emphasis mine).

In every case that comes before you from your fellow countrymen who live in the cities — whether bloodshed or other concerns of the law, commands, decrees or ordinances — you are to warn them not to *sin* against the LORD; otherwise his wrath will come on you and your brothers. Do this, and you will not sin (2 Chr. 19:10, emphasis mine).

Hence to sin is to incur guilt which deserves and demands punishment.

In summary of the Old Testament understanding of sin we can say that:

1) To sin is to fall short of being like God in our thoughts and actions.
2) Sin is a movement away from God.
3) Sin can be innocently being influenced by the powers of evil or those who represent evil.
4) Sin is a revolt against the claims of God's sovereignty.
5) Sin is a cancer that pollutes the soul and the earth as a result.
6) Sin is a bending and twisting into distortion the perfection which God intends.
7) To sin is to incur guilt which deserves and demands punishment.

New Testament Words Describing Sin

The New Testament describes the concept of sin in very similar ways to those of the Old. In this section, we will be examining the basic meaning of several of the key concepts of what it means to stand in sin before the presence of a perfect God.

The most common Greek term for sin is ἁμαρτία (*hamartia*). It means "missing the mark" and is used throughout the New Testament, usually in reference to man's sin against God. It can refer to individual actions (Acts 2:38; 3:19) as well as the defective nature of man (especially in John's Gospel — 9:41; 15:22).[8]

Therefore no one will be declared righteous in his sight by observing the law; rather, through the law we become conscious of *sin* (Rom. 3:20, emphasis mine).

For all have *sinned* and fall short of the glory of God (Rom. 3:23, emphasis mine).

In this way they always heap up their *sins* to the limit. The wrath of God has come upon them at last (1 Thess. 2:16b, emphasis mine).

This particular word is a comprehensive expression of everything opposed to God. Hence, as in the Old Testament, sin is to fall short of being like God in our thoughts and actions.

Παράπτωμα (*paraptoma*) is used 19 times and is often translated "trespass." It indicates a lapse from godliness. It originally meant to fall by the wayside and in the figurative sense of someone deviating from one side or another. In the New Testament it usually carries the meaning of the complete abandonment of God's truth.[9]

> As for you, you were dead in your *transgressions* and sins (Eph. 2:1, emphasis mine).

> The law was added so that the *trespass* might increase. But where sin increased, grace increased all the more (Rom. 5:20, emphasis mine).

Hence, sin is forgetting the things of God.

Ἀνομία (*anomia*) is lawlessness. It is used six times in the New Testament. Literally the word means "no law." It indicates an attitude or condition of contempt for and violation of God's law.

> Everyone who sins breaks the law; in fact, sin is *lawlessness* (1 John 3:4, emphasis mine).

> Then I will tell them plainly, "I never knew you. Away from me, you *evildoers!*" (Matt. 7:23, emphasis mine).

Sin, therefore, is a willful act of rebellion against God and His laws.

Παρακοή (*parakoe*) is only used three times in the New Testament. It is the term for disobedience.

> For just as through the *disobedience* of the one man the many were made sinners, so also through the obedience of the one man the many will be made righteous (Rom. 5:19, emphasis mine).

Hence sin is turning one's back on the will of God.

Ἀσέβεια (*asebeia*) means ungodliness and sacrilege. In classical Greek, the term referred to outrage against someone whereby established laws and ordinances were broken.[10] The most common translation in the New Testament is "ungodliness or godlessness."

> The wrath of God is being revealed from heaven against all the *godlessness* and wickedness of men who suppress the truth by their wickedness (Rom. 1:18, emphasis mine).

> To judge everyone, and to convict all the ungodly of all the *ungodly* acts they have done in the *ungodly* way, and of all the harsh words *ungodly* sinners have spoken against him (Jude 15, emphasis mine).

Hence, sin is an ugliness which distorts the holiness of God.

Ἀδικία (*adikia*) is used 25 times in the New Testament and is translated by a variety of terms which carry the basic meaning of "unrighteousness." The term literally means "no justice." It usually carries the context of crimes against fellow man.

> The wrath of God is being revealed from heaven against all the godlessness and *wickedness* of men who suppress the truth by their *wickedness* (Rom. 1:18, emphasis mine).

> All *wrongdoing* is sin, and there is sin that does not lead to death (1 John 5:17, emphasis mine).

Hence, sin is the opposite of the Golden Rule in our treatment of others.

Ἔνοχος (*enochos*) is used only ten times in the New Testament and usually means guilty or in danger of punishment. In classical Greek this was a legal term which meant that a person was liable under the law.[11]

> Therefore, whoever eats the bread or drinks the cup of the Lord in an unworthy manner will be *guilty of sinning* against the body and blood of the Lord (1 Cor. 11:27, emphasis mine).

> For whoever keeps the whole law and yet stumbles at just one point is *guilty* of breaking all of it (Jas. 2:10, emphasis mine).

Sin creates a heavy liability which man must bear before the Creator. Hence, sin is a grave danger to be avoided, because in it we become liable and guilty before God.

In summary of the New Testament understanding of sin, we can say that:

1) As in the Old Testament, sin is to fall short of being like God in our thoughts and actions.
2) Sin is forgetting the things of God.
3) Sin is a willful act of rebellion against God.
4) Sin is turning one's back on the will of God.
5) Sin is an ugliness which distorts the holiness of God.
6) Sin is the opposite of the Golden Rule in our treatment of others.
7) Sin is becoming guilty before God.

The Pervasive Nature of Sin

Perhaps the most famous passage dealing with sin is in Genesis 3. From this account of the Fall, several things become obvious about the nature of sin. Sin is an act of man by which he disobeys God insofar as he transgresses a precept of God Himself (3:3,6). God had told Adam and Eve that they should not eat of the tree that was in the midst of the garden.

When they disobeyed, their actions placed them at odds with their Creator.

Besides this external act of disobedience, explicit mention is made of an internal act. Adam and Eve desired to be like God (3:5). They wished to enjoy moral autonomy. Under the direction of the serpent, Eve let certain disturbing thoughts occupy her mind. She doubted God's word! This points to the fact that the malice of sin is not found so much in the external act of disobedience as in the internal perversion that corrupts man in his innermost being.

Even before any punishment was announced, sin produced its effect. There was dramatic change in man (3:7). Adam and Eve, who had once walked with God, now fled before his presence (3:8). Sin brought about alienation. No longer was man allowed to be in the presence of his Creator and Lord. Sin had caused a disruption in the communal relationship for which God had created man. Man was cast out of Paradise.

Sin also brought about death. Man was promised that in the day he ate of the fruit he would surely die (3:3). The death which came was a death of the body and a death of the soul. Spiritually Adam and Eve died the moment they disobeyed God. Physical death was soon to follow. Sin, therefore, is a true servitude from which man cannot be freed, except by a miraculous intervention of God.

When Adam sinned, there were tremendous ramifications which entered into God's created order. Where before there had been unity, now there was separation and alienation. This alienation from sin takes place on at least four different levels.

The Multileveled Alienation of Sin

When we sin we experience **an alienation from God**. God no longer walks with us in the cool of the garden. Many people in today's world wonder why God doesn't show Himself. "If He exists and He wants us to believe in Him," they reason, "why doesn't He just appear on the Letterman Show or the evening news? That should be pretty easy if he were really God!" However, the Bible is clear that it is not God who is hiding. Isaiah wrote:

> But your iniquities have separated
> you from your God;
> your sins have hidden his face from you,
> so that he will not hear (Isa. 59:2).

It is our own sinfulness that has "hidden His face" from each one of us. Sin brings about the inescapable alienation of each of us from the Heavenly Father.

The Bible is clear that it is not God who is hiding.

In our sin, we also experience **an alienation of man from our fellow man**. On the lighter side, the first marital argument took place immediately following the first sin. Adam blamed Eve and Eve blamed the serpent. It seems that a failure to accept responsibility for one's actions and an eagerness to blame others began immediately to destroy the relationship of this first couple. In a more serious vein, not too much time elapsed before a jealous confrontation between the first two brothers resulted in Cain killing Abel. The history of the human race has been replete with the scenario of the opening chapters of Genesis being played out again and again. From the intimacy of living rooms to the broad sweeping pages of the history books, the story is the same: man is alienated from fellow man. This is the inevitable result of life lived in the pervasive power of sin.

When sin entered the world, not only was man alienated from his God and his fellow man, man also became **alienated from God's world.** The Bible records:

> Cursed is the ground because of you;
>> through painful toil you will eat of it
>> all the days of your life.
> It will produce thorns and thistles for you,
>> and you will eat the plants of the field.
> By the sweat of your brow
>> you will eat your food
> until you return to the ground,
>> since from it you were taken;
> for dust you are
>> and to dust you will return (Gen. 3:17b-19).

Not only is the discord of man's cruelty to fellow man a result of sin, but every problem within the realm of nature is seen to be a result of man altering the perfection of God's universe in his sin. Thus the universe, which God created as perfectly good, became less than God had originally intended. The universe is now "abnormal." Philosophically, this is a very important point, because Christians can explain how such a twisted fallen universe could come from the hands of a perfectly good God.[12]

The final result of sin is seen in **the alienation of man from himself**. Sin separates us from God, fellow man, our world and even ourselves.

I can remember counseling an individual who had committed a particularly heinous crime. Over and over again, he made the statement, "I just don't know why I did this." The answer of course is: sin. Augustine wrote of the pervasive nature of sin as it intertwines itself with our lives:

> There is no limit to the way in which you may sin. A man sins in looking with pleasure on what he ought not see. Yet who can restrain the speed of the eye? For it is said that the eye gets its very name from its swiftness. Who can restrain the eye or the ear? The eyes may be shut, if you will, and shut in a moment. But the ears you can stop only with an effort. You raise the hand to reach them, and if anyone should hold your hand, they remain open. Nor can you close them against abusive, impure, flattering. or deceitful words. If you hear something you ought not hear, even though you do not commit the act, are you not sinning with the ear, when you listen to something evil with pleasure? And how many deadly sins does not the tongue commit? At times it is guilty of sins of such a nature that by them a man is separated from the altar. All manner of blasphemies are a thing of the tongue, as well as a multitude of idle words which serve no purpose. But suppose the hand does nothing wrong, nor the foot run after anything evil, nor the eye glance at lewdness, nor the ear open with pleasure to filthy talk, nor the tongue utter indecent speech — yet tell me, who can control the thoughts?[13]

The final result of sin is seen in the alienation of man from himself.

The Apostle Paul repeats a similar disgust with the sinfulness of his own life in Romans 7:12-25.

Sin, also, must be recognized as more than simply individual acts against God. Sin is a mind-set that refuses to lay itself before the sovereignty of God. Just as there is personal individual sin, so also there is institutionalized national sin. A simple reading of the minor prophets points this out.[14] Hence, all the legislated prejudice and horrendous political, social and economic oppression experienced by man in the history of the human race is a direct result of sin.

It is sin which has caused the need for personal evangelism, sin which blinds men's eyes and stains men's lives. Every problem I will ever face in life is ultimately a result of sin.

God's Holy Separation from Sin

John Stott has drawn attention to five metaphors used in Scripture to describe God's holy separation from sin.[15] The first is *height*. God is called "the Most High God" (e.g., Gen. 14:18-22; Ps 7:17; 9:2; 21:7; 46:4). This "highness" of God was not understood as literal. It is not that we serve the "Big Guy up there." Rather, height is used as a symbol of transcendence. God is above and removed from sin and the sinful world.

Another metaphor used is that of *distance*. He is not only high, but also "far away" from us. God spoke to Moses out of the burning bush and told him to keep his distance (Exod. 3:5). The Israelites crossing the Jordan were told to stay at least one thousand yards away from the ark (Josh. 3:4). When Uzzah reached out to touch the ark when the cart was unsteady, "the Lord's anger burned against Uzzah" and he was struck dead (2 Sam. 6:6-7). Some commentators have difficulty explaining such an event, but it should not surprise any of us. Sinners simply cannot approach an all-holy God. Perhaps the most terrible words anyone will ever hear will be the words of Christ on the final day, "Depart from Me" (Matt. 7:23; 25:41).

The third and fourth metaphors are that of *light* and *fire*. God is light and God is a consuming fire (1 John 1:5; Heb. 12:29; 1 Tim. 6:16; Heb. 10:27,31). Both of these discourage too close an approach. One will blind and the other burn. Again, these are symbols of God's ultimate holiness and His complete incompatibility with anything sinful.

The fifth metaphor is perhaps the most graphic. Several times in Scripture, God's reaction to sin is described as *vomiting* (Lev. 18:25-28; 20:22-23; Ps. 95:10; Num. 21:5; Rev. 3:16). God warned the Israelites that if they committed the same sins as the Canaanites that the land would "vomit out its inhabitants." The most shocking use of this imagery is in Revelation 3, where Jesus threatens to "vomit" the Laodiceans out of His mouth. God simply cannot tolerate sin.

With all of this in mind, the great work of God to solve the problem of human sin must be approached with the utmost seriousness. John Stott writes:

> There is much shallowness and levity among us. Prophets and psalmists would probably say of us that 'there is no fear of God before their eyes.' In public worship our habit is to slouch or squat; we do not kneel nowadays, let alone prostrate ourselves in humility before God. It is more characteristic of us to clap our hands with joy than to blush with shame or tears. We saunter up to God to claim his patronage and friendship; it does not occur

to us that he might send us away. We need to hear again the apostle Peter's sobering words: 'Since you call on a Father who judges each man's work impartially, live your life . . . in reverent fear,' in other words, if we dare to call our Judge our Father, we must beware of presuming on him. It must even be said that our evangelical emphasis on the atonement is dangerous if we come to it too quickly. We learn to appreciate the access to God which Christ has won for us only after we have first seen God's inaccessibility to sinners. We can cry "Hallelujah" with authenticity only after we have first cried, "Woe is me, for I am lost." In Dale's words, "it is partly because sin does not provoke our own wrath, that we do not believe that sin provokes the wrath of God."[16]

Before any of us will get excited about salvation, we must realize just what it is that we have been saved from. When we share the gospel with people, we are not calling them to a heavenly good buddy they can be folksy with. We are not simply calling them to a Cosmic Psychologist who can give them personal wholeness and heightened self-esteem. We are calling them to a Redeemer, who alone can save them from their sins. If we ever forget this, we shall be guilty of distorting the gospel of Jesus Christ, and raising up a generation in the church who do not understand the basic message of what it means to be saved.

Salvation through Christ — The Ultimate Solution

For us to understand the importance of personal evangelism, just as it is important to know what it is we are saved from, so it is also important for us to know what it means to be "saved." With the effects of sin so devastating and far-reaching, the world truly is in need of the good news of Jesus Christ. Whatever the problems created by sin, the solution is found in what Christ has done for us. So far in this chapter we have taken a superficial overview of the problem of human sin. We examined the great need for evangelism from the side of the problem. Now we need to examine the need for evangelism from the side of the solution, as we see how the New Testament describes what it means to be in a personal saving relationship with Jesus Christ.

Coming to Christ Described as "Salvation"

The verb "saved" (σώζω, *sozo*) is used 106 times in the New Testament. The noun "salvation" (σωτηρία, *soteria*) is used 46 times. Originally it meant "to deliver out of immediate physical danger."[17] In the New

Testament it is most commonly used of the spiritual and eternal salvation of men and women "from their sins" (Matt. 1:21).

The new life in Christ which we possess is spoken of in three separate ways. Sometimes the Scripture speaks of salvation as an "already accomplished event" in the life of the Christian. The reality of being "saved" occurs at a specific point in time and its effects continue into the present.

> For in this hope we *were saved*. But hope that is seen is no hope at all. Who hopes for what he already has? (Rom. 8:24, emphasis mine).

> . . . made us alive with Christ even when we were dead in transgressions — it is by grace *you have been saved*. . . . For it is by grace you have been saved, through faith — and this not from yourselves, it is the gift of God (Eph. 2:5,8, emphasis mine).

And so, there is an aspect of salvation which is seen as an accomplished fact. The biblical term for this is the concept of "justification" (which we will briefly deal with in the next few sections). In other words, when a person comes to Christ, God rescues them. They are delivered "from the dominion of darkness and brought . . . into the kingdom of the Son he loves" (Col. 1:13). It is, as they say in the business world, "a done deal."

There is, however, another aspect of salvation which the text of Scripture lays before us. Salvation is also seen as a present process in the life of the saved.

> For the message of the cross is foolishness to those who are perishing, but to *us who are being saved* it is the power of God (1 Cor. 1:18, emphasis mine).

While it is true that God saves us when we come to him in faith, it is also true that this condition of being "safe" is not a static esoteric state, but rather a dynamic continual relationship.

The author of Hebrews talks of the finished and continual act of God in salvation when he writes: ". . . because by one sacrifice he has made perfect forever those who are being made holy" (Heb. 10:14). The one who promises salvation also promises to be with us to the very end of the age (Matt. 28:20). The biblical concept for this continual growth in the life of the Christian is "sanctification" (also to be dealt with later). Therefore, salvation can also be viewed as a continual growing relationship between the Christian and his Savior.

Finally, the New Testament can speak of salvation as a future hope in the consummation of all of God's promises for those in Christ at the Second Coming of our Lord.

Since we have now been justified by his blood, how much more *shall we be saved* from God's wrath through him! (Rom. 5:9, emphasis mine).

The biblical term for this aspect of salvation is "glorification." There will come a time when we will walk by "sight and not by faith," when Christ returns and receives us into the presence of the Father.

Hence in the New Testament, salvation is seen as justification (finished fact); sanctification (continual process); and glorification (final consummation). For the individual who has come into a covenant relationship with Christ, salvation is an accomplished reality at the time the individual entered into a covenant relationship to God through faith in Jesus Christ. It is a continuing present process in the daily lives of the saved as they grow to be more like Jesus. Salvation is also to be understood in its fullness as that future time of the *parousia*, when Jesus returns to establish the eternal kingdom.

The day of God's wrath is coming (Eph. 5:6; Col. 3:6). When we take part in winning people to Christ, we are taking part in God's great work of saving his beloved children from the consequences of their sins. Like a life preserver to a drowning man, like a cup of water to someone dying of thirst — this is the compassionate work to which God has called us. We, like the Apostle Peter, are to help people know how they can be "saved from this corrupt generation" (Acts 2:40).

Coming to Christ Described as "Redemption"

There are several forms of the concept of redemption used in the New Testament. In the verb form "redeem" is the translation of two Greek words, λυτρόω (*lytroo*, 3 times — Luke 24:21; Titus 2:14; 1 Pet. 1:18) and ἐξαγοράζω (*exagorazo*, 4 times — Gal. 3:13; 4:5; Eph. 5:16; Col. 4:5). The first word carries with it the concept of purchasing a slave with the view to giving him his freedom. The second word means to release an individual on the receipt of a ransom payment.

The noun "redemption" (λύτρωσις, *lytrosis*, 2 times in Luke 1:68; 2:38; Heb. 9:12; and ἀπολύτρωσις, *apolytrosis*, 10 times — Rom. 3:24; Eph. 1:7; Col. 1:14) carries the connotation of deliverance of someone held captive through the payment of a ransom price. Jesus Himself called attention to the fact that this was the very reason for His coming to earth: "For even the Son of Man did not come to be served, but to serve, and to give his life as a ransom for many" (Mark 10:45). To release the slaves of sin, he had to pay the price. We were in captivity. We were in the strong grip of sin. We could not break free. But the price was paid and the result is that we go free.[18]

Paul uses the redemption terminology in a slightly different way. He relates that, "Christ redeemed us from the curse of the law by becoming a curse for us, for it is written: 'Cursed is everyone who is hung on a tree'" (Gal. 3:13). Here, he refers to the law which speaks of capital punishment. Anyone who is hung on a tree is under God's curse (Deut. 21:23). When Jesus died on the cross, He bore the curse that would otherwise have rested on us. He suffered in our stead. He took what was coming to us. He bore the curse that sinners incurred and this is viewed as a paying of the price, an act of redemption.[19]

There is an old children's song which says:

He paid a debt He did not owe;
   I owed a debt I could not pay.
     I needed someone to take my sins away.
And now I sing a brand new song,
   Amazing grace all day long;
     Christ Jesus paid the debt that I could never pay.

Therefore, to bring people to Christ is to help them to know what it means to be redeemed by the high cost of the life of God's own Son and our Savior. When we take part in the Great Commission, we share the good news with people that the "ransom price" has been paid and they can be freed from the guilt and consequences of their sin to worship and serve the God who loved them enough to "foot the bill."

Coming to Christ Described as Justification

The concept of justification is a favorite expression used by the Apostle Paul in helping his readers understand what Christ has done for them. In the noun form (δικαίωσις, *dikaiosis*) it occurs 12 times in the New Testament.[20] It is usually translated by the term "righteous." Many people conceive of "righteousness" as a moral quality of purity. In the Gospels (Matt. 27:19) and in some places in the Epistles, it can bear this meaning (Titus 2:12; 1 Tim. 6:11). But when Paul uses this word in reference to what Christ has done for those who turn to him, the word carries the concept of the state of acquittal. It is a legal term. Men are declared as "not guilty" (righteous) on the basis of meeting the conditions of the acquittal.

The verb form, "to justify" (δικαιόω, *dikaioo*), means to be declared right or righteous.[21] This justification is given by God to men who meet His condition, which is faith. God justifies, or in other words, He declares "not guilty" the life of the individuals who place their faith and trust in Jesus. Perhaps the key passage of Scripture in the entire New Testament on this subject is found in Romans 3:21-26. Jesus is spoken of as the "atoning sacrifice." This is the redemption price which God had to pay for our forgiveness. The sacrifice of his own Son is the means whereby he can call guilty sinners "justified." Paul concludes his discussion of the atonement by stating:

> God presented him as a sacrifice of atonement, through faith in his blood. He did this to demonstrate his justice, because in his forbearance he had left the sins committed beforehand unpunished — he did it to demonstrate his justice at the present time, so as to be just and the one who justifies those who have faith in Jesus (Rom. 3:25-26).

Many wonder how God can be just if he punishes sinners. "How could a just and loving God possibly send anyone to hell?" is the question that is often put to evangelical Christians today. For Paul in Romans 3, the exact opposite seems to be his concern. "How could God be just and at the same time forgive sinners?" Leon Morris discusses this issue when he writes:

> Paul is arguing that sinners deserve to be punished for their sins; but in the past God has not invariably punished sin. Sinners have gone on living, just as they were. Now you can argue that this shows God to be merciful, or compassionate, or kind, or forbearing, or loving, but you cannot argue that it shows him to be just. Whatever else the absence of punishment of sins shows, it does not show us justice. Because God had not invariably punished sinners, people might be tempted to think that he is not a just God.
> Not any more, Paul is saying. The cross demonstrates the righteousness, the justice of God. In the very act by which sin is put away decisively, the death of Christ on the cross, God is seen to be just. It is not the fact that God forgives that shows him to be righteous, but the fact that he forgives in a certain way, the way of the cross. It is the cross that shows God to be righteous in the very act of forgiveness.[22]

The cross of Christ makes it possible for a perfect God to perfectly punish sin and at the same time perfectly forgive sinners. Because of what Christ has done, God can "justly" declare sinners who place their faith in Christ as "not guilty." When we take part in carrying out the Great Commission, we tell the joyous news of how sinners can stand in the presence of an all-holy God uncondemned.

Coming to Christ Described as Being Sanctified

The concept of sanctification (ἁγιασμός, hagiasmos) finds its root in the word for holiness (ἅγιος, hagios).[23] To be "holy" is to be "set apart" as special and unique. While it is true that the word itself stands for the difference between God and man; holiness refers positively to what God is and what belongs to Him rather than negatively to what man is not.[24] In the New Testament it is used of the concept of the believer being separated to God for a special service (2 Thess. 2:13), as well as the believer being separated from evil things and ways (1 Thess. 1:3ff).

The verb "to sanctify" (ἁγιάζω, *hagiazo*, 28 times in the New Testament) is used in a variety of ways in the New Testament. In respect to the Christian life it describes the effect on the believer of the death of Christ: "And by that will, we have been made holy through the sacrifice of the body of Jesus Christ once for all" (Heb. 10:10). To be sanctified at times refers to the setting apart of the believer for God: "Now I commit you to God and to the word of his grace, which can build you up and give you an inheritance among all those who are sanctified" (Acts 20:32). Other times, the concept is used to show the separation of the believer from worldly behavior: "Sanctify them by the truth; your word is truth," and "For them I sanctify myself, that they too may be truly sanctified" (John 17:17,19). Finally, the concept of the believer being sanctified involves the acknowledgement of the Lordship of Christ: "But in your hearts set apart Christ as Lord. Always be prepared to give an answer to everyone who asks you to give the reason for the hope that you have. But do this with gentleness and respect" (1 Pet. 3:15). Notice that the first three uses of "sanctify" refer to the work of God upon our lives, while the final use refers to an action of faith taken by the believer to grow in the grace which God has made available.

One of the key passages on sanctification is in Paul's letter to the Thessalonians. He writes:

> It is God's will that you should be sanctified: that you should avoid sexual immorality; that each of you should learn to control his own body in a way that is holy and honorable, not in passionate lust like the heathen, who do not know God; and that in this matter no one should wrong his brother or take advantage of him. The Lord will punish men for all such sins, as we have already told you and warned you. For God did not call us to be impure, but to live a holy life (1 Thess. 4:3-7).

It seems that there are two aspects to the Christian concept of sanctification. When an individual comes to faith in Christ, the merits of Christ's death are applied to the life of the believer. When this occurs, God "sets the new Christian apart" as a new creation and a new member of His kingdom. The new Christian then continually "sets God and the things of God apart" in his heart and life. This is a process in which the Christian continually strives to become more and more like Jesus (Phil. 3:12-14).

And so, when we call people to faith in Christ, we are calling them to allow God to set them apart to a life of loving service — daily becoming more like Jesus in their thoughts and actions.

Coming to Christ Ends the Alienation which Sin Brings

Earlier in this chapter we examined four great areas of alienation which sin brings to distort and destroy our lives and our world. Each of these areas of alienation are conquered through the work of Christ.

The alienation between man and God is removed through the work of Christ on the cross.

> [God] wants all men to be saved and to come to a knowledge of the truth. For there is one God and one mediator between God and men, the man Christ Jesus, who gave himself as a ransom for all men — the testimony given in its proper time (1 Tim. 2:4-6).

When a person comes to Christ, the fellowship between God and man is restored (1 John 1:3). We look forward to the final consummation of that relationship at the Second Coming of Christ.

The alienation between man and fellow man is removed through the Cross by the new fellowship which is established in the church:

> He came and preached peace to you who were far away and peace to those who were near. For through him we both have access to the Father by one Spirit. Consequently, you are no longer foreigners and aliens, but fellow citizens with God's people and members of God's household (Eph. 2:17-19).

This new community of fellowship and unity is signified in the partaking of the Lord's Supper:

> Is not the cup of thanksgiving for which we give thanks a participation in the blood of Christ? And is not the bread that we break a participation in the body of Christ? Because there is one loaf, we, who are many, are one body, for we all partake of the one loaf (1 Cor. 10:16-17).

Whenever Christian's gather to partake of the Communion Meal, we declare that God has begun to remove the alienation of man from fellow man. Paul writes of this new "oneness" that is found in Christ:

> You are all sons of God through faith in Christ Jesus, for all of you who were baptized into Christ have clothed yourselves with Christ. There is neither Jew nor Greek, slave nor free, male nor female, for you are all one in Christ Jesus. If you belong to

Christ, then you are Abraham's seed, and heirs according to the promise (Gal. 3:26-29).

Of course, the alienation will be completely and finally removed when Christ returns. The Church is to provide a visual aid to a watching world of the type of peaceful fellowship which is possible for those who come under the Lordship of Christ.

The alienation that separates us from the fallen world shall be removed when Christ returns. Christians are to be good stewards of God's creation, but the final removal of the effects of sin from the created universe lies in the future consummation of all things. Paul writes:

> The creation waits in eager expectation for the sons of God to be revealed. For the creation was subjected to frustration, not by its own choice, but by the will of the one who subjected it, in hope that the creation itself will be liberated from its bondage to decay and brought into the glorious freedom of the children of God (Rom. 8:19-21).

Finally, **the alienation that blinds our eyes concerning the truth about ourselves is removed in Christ:**

> All of us also lived among them at one time, gratifying the cravings of our sinful nature and following its desires and thoughts. Like the rest, we were by nature objects of wrath. But because of his great love for us, God, who is rich in mercy, made us alive with Christ even when we were dead in transgressions — it is by grace you have been saved (Eph. 2:3-5).

And so the Scripture speaks the truth when it says, "Therefore, if anyone is in Christ, he is a new creation; the old has gone, the new has come!" (2 Cor. 5:17).

Leading People to Jesus Is the Ultimate Solution to the Ultimate Problems Facing Our World

When an individual comes into a covenant relationship with Jesus Christ, he is saved from the sin which alienates him from God, the world, his fellow man, and himself. The purchase price of that salvation is the atoning death of Jesus on the cross. The saved person is a purchased person. Whereas once he was guilty, because of his faith in the sacrifice of Christ, now he is declared "not guilty" by the mercy of God. He is set apart from sin and set apart to God for a life of loving service and joy.

For those committed to Christ and His great plan, this is the most exciting news the universe has ever heard:

Finally, God wants volunteers to help on this great work. God has given Himself, and given His Son and sent His Spirit, but more laborers still are needed; and what will you give? Paul said, I bear in my body the marks of the Lord Jesus. Do you aspire to such an honor? What will you do — what will you suffer? Say not, I have nothing to give. You can give yourself — your eyes, your ears, your hands, your mind, your heart, all; and surely nothing you have is too sacred and too good to be devoted to such a work upon such a call! How many young men are ready to go, and how many young women? Whose heart leaps up crying — Here am I! Send Me?[25]

Charles Grandison Finney

---

1. Charles Grandison Finney, "God's Love for a Sinning World" in *Twenty Centuries of Great Preaching* , vol 3, ed. Clyde Fant, Jr. and William Pinson (Waco: Word, 1974), p. 330.

2. Peter Marshall, "The Robe, the Ring and the Fatted Calf" in *Great Preaching*, vol 12, p. 25.

3. Richard Baxter, *The Reformed Pastor* (Portland: Multnomah, 1982), p. 73.

4. The verb is used 237 times and the noun 356 times. Ernst Jenni and Claus Westermann, eds., "חטא," *Theological Lexicon of the Old Testament* (Peabody, MA: Hendrickson, 1997).

5. Ibid.

6. "עבר," Ibid.

7. Willem A VanGemeren, ed., s.v. "אשם," *New International Dictionary of Old Testament Theology and Exegesis* (Grand Rapids: Zondervan, 1996).

8. Gerhard Kittel, ed., "ἁμαρτάνω," *Theological Dictionary of the New Testament (TDNT)*.

9. Colin Brown, ed., "sin," *The New International Dictionary of New Testament Theology (NIDNTT)*.

10. "godliness," ibid.

11. "guilt," ibid.

12. For an overview of the implications of the fallen universe being abnormal, see Francis A. Schaeffer's *He Is There and He Is Not Silent* in *The Complete Works of Francis Schaeffer*, Vol. 1 (Westchester, IL: Crossway Books, 1982), pp. 293-304.

13. Augustine, "The Lord's Prayer Explained," in *Great Preaching* , vol. 1, pp. 131-132.

14. For a good brief overview of the "corporateness of sin" see the chapter on "Structural Evil and World Hunger" in Ron Sider's *Rich Christians in an Age of Hunger* (Downers Grove, IL,: InterVarsity, 1977), pp. 131-167.

15. John Stott, *The Cross of Christ* (Downers Grove, IL: InterVarsity, 1986), pp. 106-108.

16. Stott, *The Cross of Christ*, pp. 108-109.

17. "redemption," *NIDNTT*.

18. Leon Morris, *The Atonement: It's Meaning and Significance* (Downers Grove, IL: InterVarsity, 1983), p. 121.

19. Ibid.

20. δικαίωσις, 2 times — Rom. 4:25; 5:18; and δικαίωμα, 10 times — Luke 1:6; Rom. 1:32; 2:26; 5:16,18; 8:4; Heb. 9:1,10; Rev. 15:4; 19:8.

21. δικαίοω, 39 times in the New Testament.

22. Morris, *Atonement*, p. 195.

23. ἁγιασμός, 10 times in the New Testament — Rom. 6:19,22; 1 Cor. 1:30; 1 Thess. 4:3,4,7; 2 Thess. 2:13; 1 Tim. 2:15; Heb. 12:14; 1 Pet. 1:2.

24. Norman H. Snaith, *Distinctive Ideas of the Old Testament* (New York: Schocken Books, 1964), pp. 19-50, esp. 30.

25. Charles Grandison Finney, "God's Love for a Sinning World" in *Great Preaching* , vol. 3, p. 341.

Chapter 4
Evangelism in the Ministry of Jesus

> The work of conversion is the first and most vital part of our ministry . . . . It seems to me that he who will let a sinner go to hell simply by not speaking to him gives less place to hell than the Redeemer of souls does. So whoever you pass over, do not forget the unsaved. I say it again. Focus on the great work of evangelism, whatever else you do or leave undone.[1]
>
> Richard Baxter
>
> For the Son of Man came to seek and to save what was lost."
>
> Luke 19:10

Before we can examine how to carry out the Great Commission in our own day and time, we would do well to examine the life of Jesus. All the aspects of Jesus' ministry revolve around this one central theme: "He came to seek and save the lost." His finished work on the Cross is the means by which salvation is brought to those lost in the darkness of sin. However, much can be learned from Jesus' lifestyle about the manner in which he went about "seeking" the lost. This chapter will briefly overview the evangelistic ministry of Jesus. We will take note of the main message which He proclaimed as well as the overall strategy by which He intends to save the world. We will finish the chapter by viewing his specific instructions to the Twelve when He sent them out on their first "evangelistic effort." From this we hope to glean several principles to be applied in our own evangelistic efforts.

An Overview of Jesus' Evangelistic Ministry

Shortly after His baptism, Jesus returned to Galilee "to fulfill" the words of Isaiah 9:2 by beginning His preaching ministry (Matt. 4:14-17).

Mark records an incident that occurred early in Jesus' ministry. Simon and others of the disciples found Jesus, who had departed from the house before daylight to pray, and gave Him this message, "Everyone is looking for you!" But Jesus' response was that they come with Him to nearby villages so He could preach in them also, for "that is why I have come" (1:35-39). Some time later, while preaching in the synagogue in Nazareth, Jesus said He was fulfilling the prophecy concerning preaching good news to the needy (Luke 4:17-21). Late in Jesus' ministry, at the conclusion of His encounter with Zacchaeus, Jesus stated that "the Son of Man came to seek and to save what was lost" (Luke 19:10). While the "saving" certainly referred to His anticipated work on the cross, the "seeking" undoubtedly referred to His evangelistic endeavors. Thus we see that throughout His ministry, Jesus saw His mission as one of evangelism.

Throughout His ministry, Jesus saw His mission as one of evangelism.

Jesus' evangelistic ministry included two phases, one public and the other private. The public ministry began in Nazareth. Luke gives the most complete account of this in 4:14-30. Several aspects which were to characterize all of Jesus' public evangelistic efforts are evident in this passage and much can be learned by close examination of the incident. As He proclaimed the good news, the Master Evangelist went first to those closest to Him, the folk of His hometown. Certainly, Jesus would later state that "only in his hometown and in his own house is a prophet without honor" (Matt. 13:57), yet He began His preaching ministry by relating to those with whom He would have held the most in common. Some three years later He gave instructions to His disciples prior to His ascension. At that time He directed them to adopt the same evangelistic strategy by beginning in Jerusalem and then working in ever expanding circles proceeding to Judea and Samaria and ultimately to the ends of the earth (Acts 1:8). His preaching was not done in His own strength and power, but in the power of the Spirit of God.

Jesus began His evangelistic ministry in the synagogue, the Jewish center of worship, on the Sabbath day, the Jewish day for worship, thus evangelizing within the prevailing cultural norms. Jesus based His evangelism on the Word of God, which He first read and then explained to His listeners. Jesus brought the scriptural application home to the lives of His audience, and as He did so, He encountered strong opposition. Even in the face of persecution, Jesus did not alter His evangelistic message, nor did He stop proclaiming it. He merely changed locations and audiences. In their parallel accounts of this same incident, Matthew and Mark give some additional information concerning the content of Jesus' evangelistic message. He called for His listeners to repent and believe the gospel message because the kingdom of heaven (God) was near (Matt 4:12-17; Mark 1:14-15).

Jesus' evangelistic efforts were by no means limited to the public sphere. Indeed, some of the most tender glimpses of Jesus' life were those involving His evangelism in one-on-one or small group situations, a case in point being His conversation with the Samaritan woman recorded in John 4. Just as Luke 4 is instructive as a model for Jesus' public evangelism, John 4 serves as a picture of Jesus' private evangelism. For Jesus, personal evangelism was a priority; thus we see that, in a day in which most Jews would walk many miles out of their way to avoid passing through despised Samaria, John records that Jesus "had to go" through Samaria, a likely reference to His divine foreknowledge concerning this woman and her need.[2] Jesus initiated a conversation with the woman of Samaria, a needy person, who was looked upon as an outcast and a misfit. He did this by making Himself vulnerable to her and expressing a need that she could meet. He very adeptly looked for opportunities to steer the conversation from the immediate and the physical to the eternal and the spiritual. He used language calculated to pique the curiosity of His listener and skillfully guided the discussion back to the subject at hand when the woman tried to divert the conversation. Jesus utilized a mixture of the pastoral (4:13-14) and the confrontational (4:16-18) as He told the woman the good news of the kingdom, and He presented Himself to her as the Christ, the ultimate answer to all of her needs (4:25-26). Jesus made use of the occasion to instruct His disciples concerning the priority of the evangelistic endeavor and their need to, along with Him, be involved in evangelism, noting that it is a process which may include several different participants.

Jesus "had to go" through Samaria.

The importance Jesus attached to evangelism was underscored by events which transpired during the final few days of His earthly life. Just as the beginning of His public ministry had been characterized by both public and private evangelism, so the culmination of His earthly life was marked by the same. Matthew 21 and 22 are filled with examples in which Jesus proclaimed the good news to an increasingly hostile audience, alternately confronting (21:40-46) and tenderly calling (22:37-40) His listeners in efforts to lead them into the kingdom. On the last night of His earthly life, standing before a group of powerful religious leaders determined to put Him to death, Jesus never hesitated to proclaim to them, one last time, the gospel. In response to the impassioned query of the high priest to tell them if He was the Christ, Jesus replied, "Yes, it is as you say . . . . In the future you will see the Son of Man sitting at the right hand of the Mighty One and coming on the clouds of heaven" (Matt. 26:64). A few hours later, Jesus again testified of the gospel, this time to the most powerful political figure in the land (1 Tim. 6:13; John 18:36-37). And with His dying breath, He spoke to the thief on the cross "today you will be with me in paradise" (Luke 23:40-43). It is impossible to examine the life of Jesus Christ without recognizing that, from beginning to end, His priority was to proclaim, to many or to few, the good news of the coming kingdom.

What was the good news that He proclaimed? What was the message that He preached which made it such "good news"? It may have come as somewhat of a shock to His listeners that, in spite of their sin and wickedness, God still loved them (John 3:16) and wanted to save them (3:17) and give them eternal life (3:36). That salvation was offered to any who would believe in God's Son (3:16) and be born again, of water and the Spirit (3:3,5). The good news was that, although Jesus' kingdom was not of this world (John 18:36), God did care deeply about mankind — so deeply that He was able and willing to meet man's every need (Matt. 6:31-33). God was in the process of ushering in His kingdom, and that kingdom would be at least partially realized in the church, which would not be overcome even by the gates of Hades (Matt. 16:18). Jesus' message called for men to turn from their wicked ways (Mark 1:15) and confess Him before men (Luke 12:8-9), after which they were to be baptized (Matt. 28:19). He assured His followers that, although He was going away (John 13:33), He would return to take them to be with Him where He was going (John 14:3; Matt. 24:42,44). Until that time came, He would send another Counselor, who would literally live in them (John 14:16-17). The Lord was very careful to stress to would-be followers that any decision to follow Him was not to be entered into lightly (Luke 9:57-62). Yet at the same time, He assured those who would come to Him that they would find rest for their souls, for His yoke was easy and His burden light (Matt. 11:29-30). Whatever Jesus' followers would ask for in prayer would be granted them (Mark 11:24; John 14:13). With promises such as these, it is no wonder that Jesus' message was called the gospel — good news.

Jesus' evangelistic proclamation was accompanied not only by an exemplary lifestyle, but also by miraculous signs and wonders calculated to reinforce His message in such a way that persons might believe the gospel and thereby have life in His name (John 20:30-31). Each miracle also had individual and immediate importance in meeting people's needs or in relieving their suffering. So the four thousand were fed from seven loaves and a few small fish, not only to instill faith in Jesus' disciples (Matt. 16:8-10), but also to prevent hungry people from collapsing on their way home (Matt. 15:32). Jesus always made it very clear that every miraculous sign was done in answer to prayer and in the power of God (John 11:41-42; Mark 7:34-35). The Lord demonstrated His power over the elements (Mark 4:39), over demonic forces (Mark 5:1-13), and over sickness (Matt 8:14-17). Neither nature (John 2:6-10) nor leprosy (Mark 1:40-42) nor death (Luke 7:14-15) was any match for Jesus' marvelous power. And certainly the ultimate verification of His message came when, as He had repeatedly foretold, He Himself rose victorious from the grave (Luke 24:5-7).

Each of Jesus' miracles had individual and immediate importance in meeting people's needs.

Since evangelism was so central to the ministry of Jesus, it is not surprising that He made provision for the continued proclamation of the good news after He departed this earth. So included in the three year preparation of the apostles were at least two practice preaching missions as well as extensive instruction in the manner in which they were to evangelize (Matt 10; Luke 10:1-17). Jesus gave the keys to the kingdom of heaven first to Peter and then to all the apostles so that when they proclaimed the gospel, whatever they bound on earth would have already been bound in heaven and whatever they loosed on earth would have already been loosed in heaven (Matt 16:19; 18:18).[3] On the shore of the Sea of Galilee, Jesus directed Peter to feed His sheep, to teach and shepherd Christians, helping them to mature spiritually. This maturation process was an essential aspect of the proclamation of the good news (John 21:15-17). And the final recorded instruction of our Lord to His followers was the specific directive to evangelize all ethnic groups (Matt 28:18-20).

The Ultimate Nature of Jesus' Message

The New Testament Gospels lay great emphasis on the fact that Jesus came preaching the good news of the Kingdom (Matt 4:23; 9:35; Luke 4:42; 8:1; 16:16; also see Mark 1:14,15; Luke 4:18; 7:22). We have already given a basic overview of the flow of Jesus' evangelistic ministry. We now need to turn our attention to the heart and kernel of His central message. In his book *Living Proof* Jim Petersen has aptly pointed out that Jesus' message never wavered.[4] Whether He spoke to His opponents or to the multitudes or to His innermost circle of disciples, His message was always the same. His message was Himself — His own person and the work He came to perform.

When Jesus addressed His enemies, His message was HIMSELF. Jesus' discussions with them seldom dealt with intellectual difficulties over His claims. Rather the focus was on the subjective nature of their resistance to Him. No matter what obstacles presented themselves to Jesus' opponents, His message never changed. Jesus understood HIMSELF to be the main issue at hand. When public opinion and concern for social status was the barrier, Jesus pointed His opponents to consider who He was.

> You diligently study the Scriptures because you think that by them you possess eternal life. *These are the Scriptures that testify about me, yet you refuse to come to me to have life . . . .* How can you believe if you accept praise from one another, yet make no effort to obtain the praise that comes from the only God? (John 5:39-40,44).

At times, misinformation stood in the way of Jesus' enemies. They mistakenly believed Him to have been born in Nazareth (John 7:41-43). Yet Jesus' message in the midst of the debate continued to be centered upon Himself. He preached, "If anyone is thirsty, let him come to me and drink. Whoever believes in me, as the Scripture has said, streams of living water will flow from within him" (John 7:37b-38).

Self-sufficiency also proved to be a problem. In the account of Jesus' healing the man born blind in John 9:35-41, the Pharisees proved to be blind to their own spiritual blindness. Jesus pointed out that the reason for their blindness was their unwillingness to recognize Him for who He was. Hence excessive faith in self is often a barrier to belief. Yet to the man who had been healed, Jesus continued to proclaim what the Pharisees had rejected. John records the moving interaction between the two:

> Jesus heard that they had thrown him out, and when he found him, he said, "Do you believe in the Son of Man?"
> "Who is he, sir?" the man asked. "Tell me so that I may believe in him."
> Jesus said, "You have now seen him; in fact, he is the one speaking with you."
> Then the man said, "Lord, I believe," and he worshiped him (John 9:35-38).

In the final drama of Jesus' confrontation with His enemies at His trial, the heart of Jesus' teaching comes front and center. When asked directly,

"'Tell us if you are the Christ, the Son of God.' 'Yes, it is as you say,' Jesus replied. 'But I say to all of you: In the future you will see the Son of Man sitting at the right hand of the Mighty One and coming on the clouds of heaven'" (Matt. 26:63-64). Upon hearing this the members of the High Council went into a frenzy of hatred and abuse as they lowered themselves to the level of a street gang and assaulted Jesus before turning Him over to the Roman authorities (Matt. 26:65-68). In the face of His enemies, Jesus only had one message: HIMSELF.

When Jesus found Himself preaching to the multitudes, He did not alter His message in the least. In the sixth chapter of John's Gospel, this point is driven home again and again. The masses were drawn to Christ for two basic reasons. They were amazed at His teaching (Matt. 7:28-29; John 7:46), and they were amazed at His power (Luke 11:29). In John's account of the feeding of the 5,000 and the subsequent teaching in His famous "Bread of Life Discourse," Jesus challenged the multitudes to accept the implications to which His miracles pointed, that being His own deity.

> Then they asked him, "What must we do to do the works God requires?"
>
> Jesus answered, "The work of God is this: to believe in the one he has sent" (John 6:28-29).

> Then Jesus declared, "I am the bread of life. He who comes to me will never go hungry, and he who believes in me will never be thirsty" (John 6:35).

> "I am the living bread that came down from heaven. If anyone eats of this bread, he will live forever. This bread is my flesh, which I will give for the life of the world" (John 6:51).

Again, Jesus' message is unmistakably clear. Jesus told the multitudes, either accept the full implications of His identity or go home. On this occasion, Scripture sadly records, "From this time many of his disciples turned back and no longer followed him" (John 6:66).

The same thread — Jesus' identity — runs through everything He taught His disciples. In fact, His most significant teaching on His identity was to those who followed Him most closely. In explaining the "Parable of the Soils" in Mark 4, Jesus declared that "The secret of the kingdom of God has been given to you. But to those on the outside everything is said in parables" (Mark 4:11). In a study of the Gospels it becomes clear that the true disciples of Jesus understood the dimensions of His authority and brought themselves, step by step, under that authority.

It didn't happen all at once. For instance, early in His public ministry, in Matthew 8, we see the story of Jesus calming the storm. After He rebuked the winds and the waves, Matthew records that the disciples were amazed and asked, "What kind of man is this?" (Matt. 8:27). Later, in Matthew 14, we see a similar scenario in the account of Jesus' walking on the water. When Jesus finally entered the boat, again the winds died down. Only this time the disciples did not have to ask what kind of man Jesus was. They had discovered in their close association with Him that He was not a mere man at all. On this occasion Matthew records that those who were in the boat "worshiped him, saying, 'Truly you are the Son of God'" (Matt. 14:33). The culmination of this growing understanding of Jesus would come in Peter's great confession recorded in all four Gospels (Matt. 16:16; Mark 8:29; Luke 9:20; John 6:68-69), "You are the Christ, the Son of the Living God."

In considering Jesus' teaching Petersen writes:

> The continuity of this theme of Jesus' identity as it runs through all his relationships demonstrates that it is an issue of ultimate importance! Every other theme is subordinate to this one. He is the gospel. He is our message. Everything else we Christians believe and hold dear is an outworking of this one truth. If we are to be effective among the people of this generation, our own understanding of Christ — the implications of His identity, His death and His resurrection — must be dynamic and growing.[5]

The Master's Plan for Evangelism

Robert Coleman's classic study *The Master Plan of Evangelism* outlines an eightfold strategy which can be traced from the Gospels, by which Jesus set the groundwork for the evangelization of the world.[6] A quick overview of these eight guiding principles reveals the wisdom of our Lord in preparing His followers to be able to carry out the Great Commission.

The first principle employed by Jesus was that of **SELECTION.** Men were Jesus' method. The Gospels record that Jesus began to gather His disciples before He began His public ministry or even preached a sermon (John 1:35ff). The only qualification was that the men had to be willing to learn. The disciples were not intellectuals (Acts 4:13), but they were teachable. Because of the early disciple association with John the Baptist, it appears that they were fed up with the established Jewish institutionalism. So Jesus concentrated on a "few good men." He understood that the world will be transformed only as men within the world are transformed. Jesus therefore selected a group small enough to work with (Luke 6:13-17).

Jesus did not neglect the masses or a broader group of disciples (Luke 10:1). It is clear that Jesus proportioned His life to those He wanted to train. Why did Jesus concentrate His life upon so few people? He wanted to demonstrate that before the world could ever be permanently helped, men would have to be raised up who could lead the multitudes in the things of God. Though He did what he could for the multitudes, He devoted Himself primarily to a few men, rather than the multitudes, in order that the multitudes could ultimately be saved.

Jesus proportioned His life to those He wanted to train.

In developing an overall strategy of evangelism this is where we must begin today. In the church, while ministry must extend to all, training of a few key leaders in the work of evangelism is an absolute necessity. Coleman writes that "a few people so dedicated in time will shake the world for God. Victory is never won by the multitudes. . . . Everything that is done with the few is for the salvation of the multitudes."[7]

The second principle employed by Jesus was that of **ASSOCIATION.** The most elementary reading of the Gospels reveals one simple point: Jesus stayed with His disciples. His disciples were not distinguished by outward conformity to certain rituals, but by being with Him, and thereby participating in His doctrine (John 18:19). It was by association with Jesus that knowledge was gained, before it was understood by explanation. The Twelve were chosen so that "they might be with Him" (Mark 3:14; Luke 6:13). Therefore, in order for us to carry out the Great Commission, we must build associations with those who come to Christ and are in turn trained to do the work of evangelism.

The next principle we see in the ministry of our Lord is that of **CON- SECRATION.** Simply stated, Jesus required obedience. He expected the men He was with to obey Him. They were not required to be smart, but they had to be loyal. In fact, this became the distinguishing mark by which they were known. The disciples did not have to accept a statement of faith, they simply had to follow Jesus.

The disciples were not required to be smart, but they had to be loyal — the distinguishing mark by which they were known.

Jesus replied, "If anyone loves me, he will obey my teaching. My Father will love him, and we will come to him and make our home with him. He who does not love me will not obey my teaching. These words you hear are not my own; they belong to the Father who sent me (John 14:23-24).

Jesus did not apologize about demanding obedience (Luke 14:26-35). He needed no apology because He was the perfect example of obedience (Phil. 2:8). A father must teach his children to obey him if he expects his children to be like him.

The great need for the church today is obedience to the Cross and the commands of Christ. Coleman writes that

> the great tragedy is that little is being done to correct the situation, even by those who realize what is happening. . . . It is high time that the requirements for membership in the church be interpreted and enforced in terms of true Christian discipleship. But this action alone will not be enough. Followers must have leaders, and that means that before much can be done with the church membership, something will have to be done with the church officials. If the task seems too great, we will have to begin the way Jesus did by getting with a few chosen ones and instilling into them the meaning of obedience.[8]

The fourth principle used by Jesus was **IMPARTATION.** Jesus gave Himself away. His life was spent giving away what the Father had given Him (John 15:15; 17:4,8,14). He gave away all He had. Love is like that. In giving Himself to God, Jesus gave Himself to those about Him so that they would come to know through His life a similar commitment to God's great mission to save the world. His whole evangelistic plan hinged on this dedication and, in turn, upon the faithfulness by which His disciples would pour themselves out in order to save the lost world.

Those who have freely received from Christ must make the "giving of themselves" the hallmark of their ministry. This is made possible through the Spirit-filled life. One of the main emphases in the Acts of the Apostles is the Holy Spirit's work in the lives of those who made up the early church (Acts 4:8,31; 6:3,5; 7:55; 9:17; 11:24; 13:9,52). The whole evangelistic enterprise revolved around the character of Jesus. Basically His way was His life. And so it must be with His followers. We must have His life in us by the Spirit if we are to do His work and practice His teaching.

The next principle displayed in Jesus' life is that of **DEMONSTRATION.** Jesus showed people how to live. His disciples learned spirituality from their association with the One to whom the Spirit was given "without measure" (John 3:34). Jesus showed His followers the power of a life of prayer. The Gospels call attention to the prayer life of Jesus over twenty times.[9] Jesus also taught His disciples the importance of using Scripture.[10]

The Gospels call attention to the prayer life of Jesus over twenty times.

Yet as important as the above-mentioned elements were in Jesus' life, the chief aspect of Jesus' ministry was "soul winning." Practically everything Jesus did had something to do with the work of evangelism. When it is all boiled down, those of us who are seeking to train men must be prepared to have them follow us, even as we follow Christ (1 Cor. 11:1). Disciples will do the things they see and hear in their leader (Phil. 4:9).

The sixth principle we see in the life of our Lord is that of **DELEGATION.** Jesus assigned His disciples work in greater and greater degrees. He allowed them to baptize converts (John 4:2). He also reminded them that they were to be fishers of men (Mark 1:17; Matt. 4:19; Luke 5:10). When He felt like they were ready for bigger responsibilities, He sent them out on preaching missions (Mark 6:7; Matt. 10:5; Luke 9:1-2). In those times when He sent them out, He gave them brief instruction. In the following section of this chapter, we will examine this more closely, but briefly stated, He told them to spend the bulk of their time on the most promising prospects (Matt. 10:11). He also told them to expect hardship (Matt. 10:17ff). Jesus warned them that, at times, His gospel would be divisive (Matt. 10:34-38).

This principle of delegation must be given tangible expression by those who are following the Savior. The best way to be sure that this is done is to give practical work assignments to those we are training in evangelism and expect them to be carried out.

The seventh guideline employed by Jesus is the principle of **SUPERVISION.** Jesus always made it a point to follow up after His disciples had gone out on their preaching/evangelistic tours (Mark 6:30; Luke 9:10; 10:17-24). He shared with them concerning their attempts at healing a young boy (Mark 9:17; Matt. 17:14-20; Luke 9:37-43). He also reviewed their work in the feeding of the 5,000 (Mark 6:30-44; 7:31–8:9,13-21). This was on-the-job-training at its best. Here is a key principle of personal evangelism — it cannot simply be learned in a classroom. It usually is only learned in the living room.

The final principle shown in Jesus' eightfold plan of evangelistic training is that of **REPRODUCTION.** Jesus expected His disciples to produce His likeness in and through the Church as it was gathered throughout the world. The Great Commission was clear (Matt. 28:18ff) and, although the task was vast, Jesus knew that the Church would be victorious in the end (Matt. 16:18). This ultimate victory would be built upon the witness that

Jesus was the Christ, the Son of the Living God (Matt. 16:16, Mark 8:29; Luke 9:20).

After the victory of the cross and the empty tomb, the true test of Jesus' ministry remained upon the question: Would the disciples carry on after He had gone? The existence today of the worldwide influence of the Church is evidence that they were indeed faithful. The Acts of the Apostles tells the earliest story of the miraculous empowerment of the Holy Spirit in the lives of Jesus' followers. Today, we must continue their same work through the same empowerment of the Holy Spirit.

We are here today because the early Church and Jesus' disciples proved that the Master's plan for world conquest is successful. Coleman writes:

> This is why we must say with E.M. Bounds that "men are God's method." Until we have men imbued with His Spirit and committed to His plan, none of our methods will work. This is the new evangelism we need. It is not better methods, but better men — men who know their Redeemer from something more than hearsay — men who see His vision and feel His passion for the world — men who are willing to be nothing in order that He might be everything — men who want only for Christ to produce His life in and through them according to His own good pleasure. This finally is the way the Master planned for His objective to be realized on the earth, and where it is carried through by His strategy, the gates of Hell can not prevail against the evangelization of the world.[11]

Jesus Teaches "Evangelism 101"

Matthew 9 ends with a dramatic appeal from our Lord on behalf of His evangelistic mission. We see Jesus give an appeal to pray for laborers to be sent into the harvest fields.

> Jesus went through all the towns and villages, teaching in their synagogues, preaching the good news of the kingdom and healing every disease and sickness. When he saw the crowds, he had compassion on them, because they were harassed and helpless, like sheep without a shepherd. Then he said to his disciples, "The harvest is plentiful but the workers are few. Ask the Lord of the harvest, therefore, to send out workers into his harvest field" (Matt. 9:35-38).

In Matthew 10, we see an extensive amount of teaching as Jesus instructed the Twelve what to do and expect out in that harvest field. While this information is directed to them (almost exclusively in Matthew

9–10), we can learn several principles that will help prepare us to carry out the Great Commission commanded at the end of Matthew's Gospel.

In Matthew 10:1 we first see a divine commissioning as Jesus gives the Twelve the authority over both demons and disease. There is no mistake about to whom this very specialized information is addressed as Matthew lists for us the names of the Twelve (10:2-4). In the remainder of the chapter (Matt 10:5-42) we see Jesus' divine instructions to the apostles on how to do evangelism. Again, we must point out that many of the specific instructions of Jesus were only applicable to the Twelve, but the principles which lay behind the instructions are applicable to all Christians in sharing the good news of the Kingdom.

Evangelism 101

We could call Matthew 10:5-25 "Evangelism 101." Here Jesus gives the basic instructions to the disciples on where to go and what to do. First, the Twelve were instructed to go only to the lost sheep of the Israel (10:5-10).

> These twelve Jesus sent out with the following instructions: "Do not go among the Gentiles or enter any town of the Samaritans. Go rather to the lost sheep of Israel. As you go, preach this message: 'The kingdom of heaven is near.' Heal the sick, raise the dead, cleanse those who have leprosy, drive out demons. Freely you have received, freely give. Do not take along any gold or silver or copper in your belts; take no bag for the journey, or extra tunic, or sandals or a staff; for the worker is worth his keep (Matt. 10:5-9).

For them, the time was not right to begin to work with anyone other than their own countrymen. Their vision was too narrow and their hearts too cold toward those outside of the nation of Israel. It would take the coming of the Holy Spirit (Acts 2); the direct leading of the Spirit (Acts 10); and the commissioning of the Spirit (Acts 13) for God's final desire for worldwide evangelism to begin.[12] The instructions concerning what they were to take along with them was unique and intended for the apostles on this mission alone. Also the content of their preaching was quite different from what we share today.

A.B. Bruce correctly writes:

> As regards the preaching, on the other hand, there was not only reason, but necessity, for restriction. The disciples could do no more than proclaim the fact that the kingdom was at hand, and bid men everywhere repent, by way of a preparation for its

advent. This was really all they knew themselves. They did not as yet understand, in the least degree, the doctrine of the cross; they did not even know the nature of the kingdom. They had, indeed, heard their Master discourse profoundly thereon, but they had not comprehended his words. Their ideas respecting the coming kingdom were nearly as crude and carnal as were those of other Jews, who looked for the restoration of Israel's political independence and temporal prosperity as in the glorious days of old. In one point only were they in advance of current notions. They had learned from John and from Jesus that repentance was necessary in order to have citizenship in this kingdom. In all other respects they and their hearers were pretty much on a level. Far from wondering, therefore, that the preaching program of the disciples was so limited, we are rather tempted to wonder how Christ could trust them to open their mouths at all, even on the one topic of the kingdom.[13]

The disciples could do no more than proclaim the fact that the kingdom was at hand, and bid men everywhere repent.

The main principle for us to glean from all of this can be stated in the phrase, *"target your audience."* We need to know whom it is we are trying to reach so that we can ensure that our presentation of the gospel message will have the best chance of being heard and understood.

Next Jesus instructs the Twelve to "look for some worthy person" (Matt. 10:11-16):

> Whatever town or village you enter, search for some worthy person there and stay at his house until you leave. As you enter the home, give it your greeting. If the home is deserving, let your peace rest on it; if it is not, let your peace return to you. If anyone will not welcome you or listen to your words, shake the dust off your feet when you leave that home or town. I tell you the truth, it will be more bearable for Sodom and Gomorrah on the day of judgment than for that town. I am sending you out like sheep among wolves. Therefore be as shrewd as snakes and as innocent as doves (Matt 10:11-16).

For us this could be interpreted as: *Center on the most receptive people groups.* All harvest fields need to be brought into the storehouse, but some are more "ripe" than others. Long ago Jesus instructed the Twelve to center their attention on those most open to receiving the message. In later chapters we will learn a lot more about this principle.

Finally, Jesus warned the Twelve against the inherent dangers of being God's messengers in a lost world (Matt 10:17-25). He tells them to be on guard against men.

> Be on your guard against men; they will hand you over to the local councils and flog you in their synagogues. On my account you will be brought before governors and kings as witnesses to them and to the Gentiles. But when they arrest you, do not worry about what to say or how to say it. At that time you will be given what to say, for it will not be you speaking, but the Spirit of your Father speaking through you.
>
> Brother will betray brother to death, and a father his child; children will rebel against their parents and have them put to death. All men will hate you because of me, but he who stands firm to the end will be saved. When you are persecuted in one place, flee to another. I tell you the truth, you will not finish going through the cities of Israel before the Son of Man comes.
>
> A student is not above his teacher, nor a servant above his master. It is enough for the student to be like his teacher, and the servant like his master. If the head of the house has been called Beelzebub, how much more the members of his household! (Matt 10:17-25).

For us the message can be the same. *We are to be aware of the hazards to evangelism.* These dangers can come from two distinct sources. Persecution may come from outsiders (10:17-20). It may also come from insiders (10:21-23). For the apostles, this meant that persecution would arise from the ranks of supposedly faithful Jews who would be opposed to the messianic message of Jesus. For us, as strange as it may seem, this could mean that opposition to evangelism could even come from within the walls of the local congregation of believers. Not everyone is excited about a serious call to carry out the Great Commission. Finally in this section, Jesus taught His disciples and us today that persecution is the true badge of faithfulness (10:24-25).

An Overarching Command — Have NO FEAR

After giving the Twelve the basic instructions for carrying out their preaching mission, He gave them an overarching command — have **NO FEAR**. There are three reasons shared by Christ why we can be obedient in carrying out the Lord's commands in the face of persecution. First, Jesus declares that *we have the truth.*

> So do not be afraid of them. There is nothing concealed that will
> not be disclosed, or hidden that will not be made known. What I
> tell you in the dark, speak in the daylight; what is whispered in
> your ear, proclaim from the roofs (Matt. 10:26-27).

The secular world of our day seems to have a monopoly on both the mind
and heart of our society. The arts, the sciences, education and the media
are all at the beck and call of the secular mind. The secularist would ask
those who follow Jesus, "Look at the complete triumph of the secular mind
here at the beginning of the 21st Century. How can you argue with such
success?" We tend to forget that Christianity began in a world which was
much more in control of a godless mind-set than we are today in Western
culture. Yet these early Christians literally transformed their world. They
knew what we must learn. *The only way to argue with success is with the
truth.* It is this truth that Christ has given us in complete supply.

The only way to argue with success is with the truth.

Next, Jesus states that we know that *the ultimate persecution —
death — is not a final act.*

> Do not be afraid of those who kill the body but cannot kill the
> soul. Rather, be afraid of the One who can destroy both soul and
> body in hell (Matt 10:28).

Jesus had already shared that persecution is the badge of true discipleship
(10:24-25). Now he encourages the Twelve, that even in the face of life's
ultimate persecution — death — there needs to be no fear. Quite the contrary. It is God whom we must fear, respect, and obey. True followers of
Christ in every age have borne testimony to this truth. It has been said
that the church has been built on the blood of its martyrs (with Jesus
being the first and foundation). It is no accident that our English word
"martyr" was derived from the Greek word μάρτυς (*martys*) which means
"WITNESS." Those who laid down their lives in the great work of the
gospel bear the ultimate witness of their love and devotion to the Lord
Jesus Christ. Jesus said, "Greater love has no one than this, that he lay
down his life for his friends" (John 15:13). One of my seminary professors
once said that for the Christian, death is not terminal, it is only hazardous
to your health.

The Apostle Paul would write that as Christians we have already suffered death. Upon coming to Christ, we have been "buried with him in baptism" (Rom. 6:4). "I have been crucified with Christ," Paul writes elsewhere,

"and I no longer live, but Christ lives in me. The life I live in the body, I live by faith in the Son of God, who loved me and gave himself for me" (Gal. 2:20). It is only when we lose our lives for the sake of the gospel that we will find true life (Mark 8:35). And so we who would "witness" for Christ must learn what Martin Luther so long ago lived by and put to song:

> Let goods and kindred go,
> > This mortal life also.
> The body they may kill:
> > God's Truth abideth still.
> His Kingdom is forever![14]

Finally, Jesus shares that in carrying out his instructions that *God promises His continued providence.*

> Are not two sparrows sold for a penny? Yet not one of them will fall to the ground apart from the will of your Father. And even the very hairs of your head are all numbered. So don't be afraid; you are worth more than many sparrows (Matt. 10:29-31).

God never calls a man or a woman to do a job and then leaves him unequipped. The Spirit indwells His people and grants them gifts for carrying out His tasks (1 Cor. 12). God will not leave unattended those who labor in His great task of evangelism. Jesus promised the Twelve that they were of tremendous value to the Father. And the same promise is made to those who labor for the cause of Christ in carrying out the Great Commission. The pledge, "I am with you always, to the very end of the age" (Matt. 28:20), is made by the one to whom all authority is given. Whether from the pulpit of a vast megachurch or on a dirty street corner in a third-world slum, the promise is the same. Christ is with us. It is in the knowledge and power of this promise that we labor in the harvest field.

Two Universal Traits of All Evangelists

After describing the ultimate command to the evangelists — have no fear — Jesus displays two universal traits that will be a part of the life of all true evangelists (10:32-39).

First, Christ declares that all true evangelists will *acknowledge Jesus before men no matter what the cost.*

> Whoever acknowledges me before men, I will also acknowledge him before my Father in heaven. But whoever disowns me before men, I will disown him before my Father in heaven.
> Do not suppose that I have come to bring peace to the earth. I did not come to bring peace, but a sword. For I have come to turn

"a man against his father,
   a daughter against her mother,
a daughter-in-law against her mother-in-law —
   a man's enemies will be the members of his own household"
(Matt. 10:32-36).

Jesus meant his disciples to understand at the very beginning of their labor that being faithful to His cause would carry, at times, a very high price tag. When people come to Christ, the alienation between man and God is removed — they are reconciled to God (2 Cor. 5:17-21). But it is also true that they become alienated from the sinful world (John 17:14). This sometimes takes the form of becoming alienated from those immersed in a sinful, Christless lifestyle. This is why Jesus was very forceful in the high requirements of becoming His true disciple. Jesus must come before family and friends. Jesus must come before life itself. Those who would make such a commitment should consider the cost (Luke 14:26-35). Yet in comparison with the privilege of sharing Christ, all our meager sacrifices grow small in comparison. Years later, the Apostle Paul would write the truth that every true evangelist has come to know: "What is more, I consider everything a loss compared to the surpassing greatness of knowing Christ Jesus my Lord, for whose sake I have lost all things. I consider them rubbish, that I may gain Christ" (Phil. 3:8).

Second, Jesus related that all true evangelists *place obedience to Christ above all else.*

Anyone who loves his father or mother more than me is not worthy of me; anyone who loves his son or daughter more than me is not worthy of me; and anyone who does not take his cross and follow me is not worthy of me. Whoever finds his life will lose it, and whoever loses his life for my sake will find it (Matt 10:37-39).

The Promise of Fruit and Blessing

Matthew 10 concludes with the promise of fruit from the labors of those who carry out the plans of the Lord Jesus. Not only will the good news produce converts to the Kingdom — God has promised to bless and receive those who care for Christ's messengers.

He who receives you receives me, and he who receives me receives the one who sent me. Anyone who receives a prophet because he is a prophet will receive a prophet's reward, and anyone who receives a righteous man because he is a righteous man will receive a righteous man's reward. And if anyone gives even a cup of cold water to one of these little ones because he is my disciple, I tell you the truth, he will certainly not lose his reward (Matt. 10:40-42; see a parallel in Matt. 25:31-46).

The greatest life in the world is one poured out in love and service to God. Late in his life the Apostle Peter would write of this when he said,

> Praise be to the God and Father of our Lord Jesus Christ! In his great mercy he has given us new birth into a living hope through the resurrection of Jesus Christ from the dead, and into an inheritance that can never perish, spoil or fade — kept in heaven for you, who through faith are shielded by God's power until the coming of the salvation that is ready to be revealed in the last time (1 Pet. 1:3-5).

The Apostle Paul also understood fully the blessing of being a part of God's great work to redeem the world through Christ. He could write, while in the depths of prison, "Rejoice in the Lord always. . . . the Lord is near (Phil. 4:4-5). The blessing for all who come to Christ is to take part in His great work. We are to make the things of the Kingdom top priority in our lives. When we do, the greatest blessing in all the world will be ours, for we shall see the face of God in the people we bring to Christ.

Christ's Work Must Be Our Work

The Lord came to "seek and to save that which was lost." His work must be our work. He has called out the church, equipped the church, and placed the church in the world to carry out His great task of worldwide conquest. Wherever the gospel of Christ is shared faithfully by witnesses called and empowered by their Master, the most amazing results occur. Why? Because in evangelism people come face to face with Jesus. James S. Stewart preached of this in his great sermon, "The Wind of the Spirit."

> There is no citadel of self and sin that is safe from Him, no unbelieving cynic secure beyond His reach. There is no ironclad bastion of theological self-confidence that is immune, no impregnable agnosticism He cannot disturb into faith, no ancient ecclesiastical animosities He cannot reconcile. And blessed be His name, there is no winter death of the soul that He cannot quicken into a blossoming springtime of life, no dry bones He cannot vitalize into a marching army.[15]

1. Richard Baxter, *The Reformed Pastor* (Portland: Multnomah, 1982), p. 73.

2. William Hendriksen, *John*, New Testament Commentary (Grand Rapids: Baker, 1953), p. 155.

3. Craig L. Blomberg, *Matthew*, The New American Commentary (Nashville: Broadman, 1992), p. 255.

4. Jim Petersen, *Living Proof: Sharing the Gospel Naturally* (Colorado Springs: NavPress, 1992), pp. 39-45.

5. Petersen, *Living Proof*, p. 45.

6. Coleman states that the eight "steps are not to be understood as invariably coming in this sequence, as if the last were not initiated until the others had been mastered. Actually all of the steps were implied in each one, and in some degree they all began with the first. The outline is intended only to give structure to His method and to bring out the progressive logic of the plan." Robert Coleman, *The Master Plan of Evangelism* (Old Tappan, NJ: Fleming H. Revell, 1980), p.19.

7. Ibid., pp. 34-35.

8. Ibid., p. 60.

9. At his baptism, Luke 3:21; selection of the 12, Luke 6:12; Mount of Transfiguration, Luke 9:29; the confession of His Messiahship, Luke 9:18; after hearing the reports on evangelism, Luke 10:21ff; healing the multitudes, Mark 1:35; feeding the 5,000, Mark 6:41; Matt. 14:19; Luke 9:16; John 6:11; feeding the 4,000, Mark 8:6; Matt. 15:35; healing the deaf-mute, Mark 7:34; raising of Lazarus, John 11:41; before the conflict with religious leaders, Luke 5:16; after sending away the 5,000, Mark 6:46; Matt. 14:23; blessing the little children, Mark 10:16; Model Prayer, Luke 11:1-11; Matt. 6:9-13; Last Supper, Matt. 26:27; High Priestly prayer, John 17:6-9; His loving concern for Peter, Luke 22:32; in Gethsemane, Luke 22:39-46; for those who nailed him to the cross, Luke 23:34; on the cross, Luke 23:46; at the home of the two from Emmaus, Luke 24:30.

10. Called the words of the Holy Spirit, Mark 12:36; Matt. 22:43; called the Word of God, John 10:35; Mark 7:13; Matt. 15:6; Luke 8:12; Scriptures bore witness to Jesus, John 5:39; Matt. 5:17-18; called attention to the fact that his life was a fulfillment of Scripture, Matt. 5:18; 8:17; 13:14; 26:54; Mark 14:49; Luke 4:21; 21:22; John 13:18; 15:25; 17:12; the Word fortified Jesus against temptation, Matt. 4:4,7,10; Luke 4:4,8,12; it was Jesus' textbook for public and private teaching, Luke 4:17-21; 24:27,32,44,45. For a fine study on Jesus' understanding and use of Scripture, see John W. Wenham, *Christ and the Bible* (Grand Rapids: Baker, 1984).

11. Coleman, *The Master Plan of Evangelism*, pp. 113-114.

12. "The time would come when Jesus might say to His chosen ones, 'Go ye into all the world, and preach the gospel to every creature;' but that time was not yet. The twelve, at the period of their first trial mission, were not fit to preach the gospel, or to do good works, either among Samaritans or Gentiles. Their hearts were too narrow, their prejudices too strong: there was too much of the Jew, too little of the Christian, in their character. . . . Suppose these raw evangelists had gone into a Samaritan village, what would have happened? In all probability they would have been drawn into disputes on the religious differences between Samaritans and Jews, in which, of course, they would have lost their temper; so that, instead of seeking the salvation of the people among whom they had come, they would rather be in a mood to call down fire from heaven to consume them, as they actually proposed to do at a subsequent period (Luke 9:54)." A.B. Bruce, *The Training of the Twelve* (Grand Rapids: Kregel, 1971), p. 101.

13. Ibid., p. 102.

14. From the final stanza of "A Mighty Fortress Is Our God."

15. James S. Stewart, *The Wind of the Spirit* (Grand Rapids: Baker, 1984), p. 14.

Chapter 5
EVANGELISM IN THE MINISTRY OF THE EARLY CHURCH

"King Agrippa, do you believe the prophets? I know you do."

Then Agrippa said to Paul, "Do you think that in such a short time you can persuade me to be a Christian?"

Paul replied, "Short time or long — I pray God that not only you but all who are listening to me today may become what I am, except for these chains."

Acts 26:27-29

Christianity grew because Christians constituted an intense community . . . . And the primary means of their growth was through the united and motivated efforts of the growing number of Christian believers, who invited their friends, relatives and neighbors to share the "good news."[1]

Rodney Stark

Its beginnings were quite humble — eleven disciples, a few women, and Jesus' recently converted half-brothers (Acts 1:13-14). Added to this core group was a wider, unorganized company of 500 others (1 Cor. 15:6) with very few notable citizens.[2] The association was composed of one small ethnic minority within the Roman Empire — the Jews.[3] And this tiny group of believers were even considered outcasts by the vast majority of their own countrymen. They were located in Jerusalem, in the provincial Roman state of Judea, far outside the main cultural centers of the day. And yet within 30 short years these believers in Jesus would spread the faith with such urgency and power that they would find representation in nearly every major metropolitan area in the Empire. By the end of the second century A.D., the Christian church would become a closely organized and well-knit federation of communities extending from one end of the Mediterranean world to the other. By the end of the third century, the church would become the single most important religious force in most of

the Empire, challenging the age-old supremacy of the Greco-Roman pantheon of gods. And by the early portion of the 4th century, under Emperor
Constantine, Christianity would be declared the "official religion" of all the
lands.[4] As sociologist Rodney Stark puts it:

> Finally, all questions concerning the rise of Christianity are one:
> How was it done? How did a tiny and obscure messianic move-
> ment from the edge of the Roman Empire dislodge classical
> paganism and become the dominant faith of Western civilization?[5]

Historians and sociologists have been trying to answer that question
for many years. For our purposes, perhaps the place to begin is simply by
examining the historical record of these earliest Christians as recorded in
the *Acts of the Apostles*. We cannot duplicate the sociological climate of
the first few centuries of Christianity's expanse. We can, however, emulate
the dynamic nature of their faith and adopt the spiritual priorities which
allowed for such a dramatic spread of those who had become "disciples of
the Lord Jesus Christ."

The Place of Prayer in Evangelism — A Study from Acts

The Events Surrounding Pentecost (Acts 1–2)

As the Gospel of Luke comes to an end, we see the apostles continually in the temple area praising God. Luke continues the story in the Acts of
the Apostles with a brief description of Jesus' instructions to His disciples.

> After his suffering, he showed himself to these men and gave
> many convincing proofs that he was alive. He appeared to them
> over a period of forty days and spoke about the kingdom of God.
> On one occasion, while he was eating with them, he gave them
> this command: "Do not leave Jerusalem, but wait for the gift my
> Father promised, which you have heard me speak about. For
> John baptized with water, but in a few days you will be baptized
> with the Holy Spirit." . . . But you will receive power when the
> Holy Spirit comes on you; and you will be my witnesses in
> Jerusalem, and in all Judea and Samaria, and to the ends of the
> earth" (Acts 1:3-5,8).

We can hardly imagine the magnitude of the task that stretched out
before this small group of men. By evidence of the resurrection, Jesus had
proven Himself to be the divine Son of God and the Messiah of all the Old
Testament Scriptures. And with all the authority of heaven and earth at
His disposal (Matt. 28:18) He has now informed these men that they
would, beginning at Jerusalem and moving in ever-widening circles, bear

the responsibility of carrying His message to the very ends of the earth. And to further display His authority in these matters, the apostles witness Jesus' ascension into heaven itself!

If the task of worldwide evangelism looks daunting to us, imagine how it must have looked to them.

If at times the task of worldwide evangelism looks daunting to us, imagine how it must have looked to them. They did not have 2,000 years of Christian history and experience upon which to draw for support. They did not have millions of churches and hundreds of millions of believers stretching out across the globe. They did not have publishing houses and libraries filled with Christian literature and resources. They simply had Jesus, and Jesus was enough! They had their faith in the resurrected Jesus and the truth of that faith as outlined in the Old Testament Scriptures. They also had the promise of the imminent coming of the Holy Spirit upon their lives.

It is paramount to realize that to which the apostles gave their immediate attention after receiving the Great Commission. In modern America, we would expect the disciples to have returned from the Mount of Olives and continually devoted themselves to the formation of committees! Peter, of course, could have been in charge of the pulpit committee. Matthew would have been the obvious choice for the finance committee. And so the list would go on. While we do see them take the time to put forth a replacement for Judas Iscariot (Acts 1:15-26), the text of Acts 1 is clear. These men, along with a few others, made PRAYER their chief priority. "They all joined together constantly in prayer, along with the women and Mary the mother of Jesus, and with his brothers" (Acts 1:14).

Before they appointed a committee — before they preached a sermon — before they made a single plan for exactly how they would carry out the Great Commission — they "joined together constantly in prayer." And just how long did this early extended prayer meeting last? Acts 2 begins with the apostles together in one place on the Day of Pentecost.[6] This means that from the Ascension to Pentecost — a ten day stretch — these men were "joined together constantly in prayer."

The events which occurred at Pentecost describe, in majestic fashion, how God brought His Church into existence. The Spirit came with power upon the apostles just as Jesus had promised. The attending miraculous signs of wind and fire would have brought to the immediate remembrance how God's Spirit was revealed in the past (2:2-4).[7] They also spoke in languages they had never learned (2:5-12).[8] A large crowd gathered, and Peter took the opportunity to preach the very first gospel message of the death, burial, and resurrection of Jesus Christ (2:14-40). In response, Luke records that 3,000 people accepted the Lordship of the Messiah into their lives through repentance and baptism (2:41).

Luke immediately describes what this first messianic community devoted themselves to: the apostles' teaching, fellowship, breaking of bread, and prayer. The wording here is very important. The NIV misses the phrasing at this point. The exact word used in 1:14 translated "joined together constantly" is the word used here translated "devoted themselves to."[9] *Luke seems to be intentionally hedging in the entire Pentecost event with prayer.* It began with a continual devotion to prayer, and it ended with a continual devotion to prayer. God saw fit to pour out His Spirit upon the apostles and indwell through His Spirit those who responded to the gospel message. And thus, the church was born with a tremendous surge of evangelism within the attitude and atmosphere of prayer.

Peter's Second Sermon and the Outcome (Acts 3–4)

The second great evangelistic thrust recorded in Acts surrounds the story of Peter and John at the temple's Beautiful Gate. Once again Luke begins his story with an emphasis on the place of prayer in the lives of the Apostles."One day Peter and John were going up to the temple *at the time of prayer* — at three in the afternoon" (Acts 3:1). The following story of Peter healing a crippled man (3:2-10) is told in simplicity. Again a large crowd gathered in the temple area because of the obvious miracle which had occurred. As on the Day of Pentecost, Peter took the opportunity to proclaim a simple gospel message centering on the death, burial, and resurrection of Jesus (3:12-26). But unlike the events which unfolded at Pentecost, Peter and John were arrested before they had an opportunity to finish all their teaching (4:1-3). Yet, as a result of their faithful witness to Christ, Luke records that 5,000 more were added into the new community of the church. Acts 4:1-22 relates Peter and John's encounter with the Jewish authorities. After repeated threats, the two apostles were released. Luke chooses to end the account with Peter and John gathering with the whole church in an intensive time of prayer.

What follows in Acts 4:22-31 is the longest recorded prayer in the New Testament outside of the Gospels. The church began (4:24a) by addressing God as Sovereign Lord (Δέσποτα, despota). The highest council in the land might stand against them, but they recognized that they served the true Sovereign who was on their side. Next, the church was filled with praise as they acknowledged God's sovereignty in creation (4:24b). If God could

call the universe into existence with His very word, surely He could handle
this present crisis. Following this, the believers acknowledged in praise
that God was Lord through revelation (4:25-26). Here they used Scripture
in prayer quoting Psalm 2:1-2, which was regarded as Messianic even by
first-century Jews. What they were enduring had already been foretold by
God in Scripture and had been preached by the Jews for centuries. These
early Christians rejoiced in the fact that this persecution firmly established
their place in God's ultimate plan!

If God could call the universe into existence with His very word, surely He could handle this present crisis.

Their prayer subsequently turned to recognizing that God was the
Sovereign Lord of history (4:27-28). The great men of their ancient world,
Herod and his dynasty, Pilate and the Roman power he represented, the
events surrounding Jesus' death (which seemed so out of control at the
time) — ALL OF THESE THINGS WERE UNDER GOD'S GUIDANCE AND
POWER! If God could guide and use the events surrounding Calvary, surely
He could work his purpose in this present predicament.

Finally the church made its petition to the Lord (4:29-30). This petition
was threefold in its nature. First, God was asked to "consider their threats."
They were not asking God to remove the threats, nor even to judge the
threats; only that they would be on His mind. Second, God was asked to
grant that the church be strengthened to *speak God's word with boldness*.
This is a prayer which God will always grant, when it is made in absolute
sincerity. Third, God was asked to continue to extend His hand to heal and
perform miraculous signs and wonders through the name of His holy
Servant, Jesus. These signs had garnered two vast audiences which provided great harvest fields for the first two bold proclamations of the gospel
(Acts 2 and 3). The miracles were not requested for their own sake, but
rather to provide themselves as "signs" of divine authentication of the
apostolic witness.

So often in today's church, the purpose of our prayers revolve around
our own personal peace and safety. The purpose of this prayer, in Acts 4,
was to PRAISE GOD AND ASK FOR THE BOLDNESS AND EMPOWERMENT
TO CARRY OUT THE GREAT COMMISSION! In Acts 4:31 we see that God
granted a dramatic response to the prayers of His people. First, the place
of their meeting was shaken. They were filled with the Holy Spirit. Finally,
their prayer was answered. They spoke the Word of God boldly. And so
the second main evangelistic endeavor of the church recorded in Acts 3–4

began with an emphasis on prayer in the lives of Peter and John (3:1) and it ended in an emphasis on prayer in the life of the early church (4:24-31) with the dramatic results of 5,000 conversions and the whole of the Jerusalem church "boldly" carrying out the Great Commission.

A Social Problem Solved and a Surge of Evangelism (Acts 6:1-7)

At the beginning of Acts 6, Luke records for us another instance of difficulty within the life of the early church. The Hellenistic Jewish widows were being neglected in the daily distribution of food. The Apostles recognized that they could not neglect the ministry of the word of God even for something as important at this. They gave instructions for men to be chosen who could faithfully carry out this domestic ministry. What Luke records next, again shows the emphasis on prayer in the life of the early church and its leaders.

> "Brothers, choose seven men from among you who are known to be full of the Spirit and wisdom. We will turn this responsibility over to them and will give our attention to prayer and the ministry of the word." . . . So the word of God spread. The number of disciples in Jerusalem increased rapidly, and a large number of priests became obedient to the faith (Acts 6:3-4,7).

Notice that the apostle's mention prayer as preceding the ministry of the word. Why? Because that is right where it belongs! In Acts, devotion to prayer always seems to precede evangelism. Here the case is the same. When the leadership gave themselves over to correct spiritual priorities, the result was tremendous evangelism: "The number of disciples in Jerusalem increased rapidly, and a large number of priests became obedient to the faith" (Acts 6:7).

Notice that the apostle's mention prayer as preceding the ministry of the word.

A complete study of the place of prayer in Acts is not possible here. We should, though, observe that Paul was praying as Ananias came to baptize him (9:11). Prayer surrounded both Peter (10:9) and Cornelius (10:30-31) as the gospel crashed through the centuries-old boundary between Jew and Gentile. As the gospel spread out into the "ends of the earth" through the ministry of the Apostle Paul, prayer was continually mentioned by Luke. It was while the church was fasting and praying that the Holy Spirit set Saul and Barnabas apart for the first great evangelistic tour in Cyprus and Asia (Acts 13:1-3). As the gospel traveled to Europe for the very first time during Paul's second evangelistic tour, prayer was at the center of the outreach at Philippi. Lydia was converted at a place of prayer (Acts 16:13). Paul and Silas were heading toward a place of prayer when they healed the demon-possessed girl (Acts 16:16). And it was the singing and prayer of these evangelists that apparently made such a great impression on the Philippian jailer, leading to his conversion (Acts 16:25).

When the church acted in Acts, it was almost never without bathing their plans in prayer. Contemporary Christians may wonder why they haven't done many great things for God. God would probably ask: "How much have you prayed?" For many Christians, the typical amount of time spent in prayer each day is about five minutes. Yet five minutes is less than thirty-five one hundredths of one percent of all the time we have at our disposal in a single day. Historians tell us that the great reformer, Martin Luther, spent the best four hours of every day in prayer. He only ripped half of Christendom out of a pagan pope's hands and reestablished political boundaries that stood in Europe for a hundred years. How much have we prayed?

God might also ask, "What have we prayed for?" Simply treating prayer as a celestial shopping list to be poured out on behalf of our own ease and comfort can hardly be expected to accomplish the great plans of God. Remember, the early church did not pray for ease and comfort. They prayed for the boldness and power to carry out the Great Commission. When this becomes the centerpiece of all our prayer life, then God will act in the providential blessing of our own evangelistic labors. An old evangelist once said, "Friend, don't expect a $1,000 answer to a 10 cent prayer." The great Reformed theologian, John Owen, once said, "He who prays as he ought, will endeavor to live as he prays."

The Book of Acts begins with Jesus giving His apostles the commission to be His witnesses throughout the whole world (1:8). The church in Acts prayed for boldness to carry out our Lord's instructions (4:24-31). And the Book of Acts ends with the Apostle Paul in Rome carrying out the Commission with the boldness made possible through prayer.

> For two whole years Paul stayed there in his own rented house and welcomed all who came to see him. Boldly and without hindrance he preached the kingdom of God and taught about the Lord Jesus Christ (Acts 28:30-31).

In the first century or the twenty-first century, the emphasis must be the same — God's people must pray for the Lord to equip us to carry out the Commission.

The Evangelistic Work of the Early Church Was Carried on through the Power of the Holy Spirit

It has been pointed out that "The Acts of the Apostles" is probably misnamed as the title for the history book of the early church in our New Testament. A more appropriate title would be "The Acts of the Holy Spirit," since the Holy Spirit is mentioned specifically 57 times in the book while the apostles are mentioned specifically only 33 times. It was only through the direction of and the power of the Holy Spirit that the apostles carried on their ministry.

A detailed study of the work of the Holy Spirit in The Acts of the Apostles is outside the scope of our study. However, even a simple reading of the text reveals the dramatic role the Holy Spirit played in the evangelistic efforts of these early Christians. Consider the following:

☞ Jesus' instructions to the apostles for the evangelization of the world were given through the Holy Spirit (1:2).

☞ The Holy Spirit played the key role in the birth of the Church. Jesus promised that the apostles would be baptized with the Holy Spirit, and that this would enable them to carry on their witness to the world through the power of the Holy Spirit. The apostles, then, received the promised baptism of the Holy Spirit at Pentecost and proclaimed that this new dispensation of the Spirit had been prophesied in the Old Testament. Peter went on to promise that the indwelling presence of the Holy Spirit would be a gift to all those who accepted Christ by faith (1:5,8; 2:4,17,18,33,38).

☞ The Holy Spirit empowered Peter to be a bold witness before the Jewish high council (4:8).

☞ In the face of persecution, after praying for boldness, the Holy Spirit filled the whole church and enabled them to, indeed, speak God's word with boldness (4:31).

☞ The deceit of Ananias and Sapphira involved lying to and testing the Holy Spirit. Because of this, extreme discipline was administered by God Himself. The result of such a cleansed church was great evangelism (5:3,9,14).

☞ The Holy Spirit was a witness to the truth of the gospel which the apostles preached. All those who obeyed God's gospel were promised that they would receive the Spirit (5:32).

☞ The Holy Spirit filled the life of Stephen to such an extent that those arguing with him could not stand against his wisdom or the Spirit by which he spoke. Stephen accused those who rejected the gospel of "resisting the Holy Spirit." Through the Holy Spirit, Stephen was allowed a glimpse of heaven at the time of his execution (6:5,10; 7:51,55).

☞ The Holy Spirit played a key role in the events surrounding the Samaritan revival under Philip's preaching. Peter and John were called to pray and lay hands on the new converts to impart the Holy Spirit in a manner which could be seen. Simon the Sorcerer was cursed for attempting to purchase the apostle's power to give the Holy Spirit through the laying on of hands (8:15,16,17,18,19).

☞ Through the Holy Spirit's prompting, Philip evangelized the Ethiopian treasurer, and the Spirit sent Philip off in another direction after the Ethiopian's baptism (8:29,39).

☞ The Holy Spirit was promised to Saul of Tarsus by Ananias. God had revealed that Saul would play a key part in the evangelization of the Gentile world. "This man is my chosen instrument to carry my name before the Gentiles and their kings and before the people of Israel." Ananias was sent to help him "see again and be filled with the Holy Spirit" (9:15,17).

☞ The Holy Spirit encouraged the church throughout Palestine resulting in an emphasis on evangelism and holiness (9:31).

☞ The Holy Spirit played a vital role in the spread of the gospel to the first Gentile, the Roman Centurion Cornelius. The Holy Spirit instructed Peter that the centurion's men were looking for him. When Peter preached to Cornelius and his household, he emphasized the power of the Holy Spirit in the ministry of Jesus. As Peter preached, the Holy Spirit fell on all the Gentiles in a similar manner as the apostles had experienced at Pentecost. Peter commanded their baptism and then related the story to the Jerusalem church, emphasizing the similarity to Pentecost as well as the fact that Jesus had spoken of this very thing (10:19,38, 44,45,47; 11:12,15,16).

☞ Barnabas was described as a good man full of the Holy Spirit, and through his ministry in Syrian Antioch "a great number of people were brought to the Lord" (11:24).

☞ The Holy Spirit set apart and sent out Paul and Barnabas on the first evangelistic tour (13:2,4).

☞ Filled with the Holy Spirit, Paul leveled a curse on the sorcerer Elymas after he had tried to hinder the spread of the gospel (13:9).

☞ The Holy Spirit ensured that the decisions of the Jerusalem Council did not burden the Gentile evangelism with the mandates of ceremonial Judaism (15:28).

☞ The Holy Spirit guided Paul and Silas on their travels during the second evangelistic tour (16:6-7).

☞ On the third evangelistic tour, Paul confronted former disciples of John the Baptist at Ephesus who had come to believe in the Messiahship of Jesus. However, it became apparent that their conversion was incomplete. These 12 men had never received or even heard of the Holy Spirit. Paul saw to it that they were baptized in Jesus' name. Then, he laid his hand's on them to impart a miraculous spiritual gift to verify that they now had indeed received the Spirit (19:2,6).

☞ The Holy Spirit compelled Paul to return to Jerusalem after the third evangelistic tour, and warned him that prison and hardship were waiting for him there (20:22,23).[10]

Perhaps we could summarize the wide variety of information shared in *The Acts of the Apostles* with the following ten observations:

(1) The command to carry out the Great Commission was given by our Lord through the prompting of the Holy Spirit.

(2) The apostles were to carry out their evangelistic ministry through the power of the Holy Spirit.

(3) The birth of the church at Pentecost was carried out in its completeness through the power of the Holy Spirit.

(4) All those who yielded up their lives in faith to Christ were promised the indwelling gift of the Holy Spirit.

(5) The Holy Spirit worked in the lives of committed believers to produce bold witnesses who would give bold proclamation.

(6) The Holy Spirit worked in guiding the circumstances which would place bold witnesses in the presence of those who needed to hear the good news.

(7) Evangelism was always the direct result whenever the Holy Spirit produced faithfulness to Christ within the life of the church.

(8) The great "racial" barriers which had existed in all human history up to this point were brought crashing down by the work of the Holy Spirit as "all men" were incorporated into the body of Christ, the church.

(9) The great evangelists mentioned in Acts (particularly Paul) were commissioned and sent out by the Holy Spirit.

(10) The great evangelistic enterprises chronicled in Acts were guided and empowered by the Holy Spirit.

Evangelism was always the direct result whenever the Holy Spirit produced faithfulness to Christ within the life of the church.

Considering the emphasis given to the guiding role of the Spirit in the evangelistic outreach of the church in Acts, it would be difficult to overestimate our present need to rely on His continuing ministry within our lives. Oswald Hoffman was correct when he said:

(Luke's) story is one of action, not so much by the Apostles . . . but by the Holy Spirit, teaching, reminding, guiding, showing, convict-ing, convincing and producing a new people for a new age — all through witness to the man Christ Jesus who has been declared by resurrection from the dead to be the Son of God with power.[11]

Any evangelistic efforts in the first or the twenty-first centuries will only come about through the work of the Holy Spirit within the lives of those committed in faith to the Lord Jesus.

The Key Elements of Spiritual Power in the Early Church

When we turn our attention to the body life of the church in Acts, we are confronted by a unique company of individuals from a variety of back-grounds, bound together in a dynamic community of service and witness. Christians have continually turned their attention to the very first church described in Acts 2:42-47. This community formed the basis for the spread of the gospel, ultimately throughout the entire world. Every Christian today can trace their spiritual roots back to the "First Christian Church of Jerusalem." When we examine Luke's description of their activities, four aspects of the body life of the church jump out at us from this page of Scripture. These four aspects are the key elements of spiritual power in the life of that very first church.

Devotion to the Apostles' Teaching

Our postmodern generation would rather feel something than learn something.

First, we see that the church devoted themselves to the apostles' teaching (Acts 2:42). Today we live in a very experience-oriented culture. Our postmodern generation (see chapters 6 and 7) would rather feel some-thing than learn something. And yet the very first church made it their chief priority to devote themselves to the apostles' teaching (τῇ διδαχῇ τῶν ἀποστόλων, tē didachē tōn apostolōn). Of course, in Jerusalem, A.D. 30, that involved listening to the apostles teach the message of Jesus and give the divinely inspired interpretation of the Old Testament as Jesus and the Holy Spirit revealed it to them. Today, we must continually devote our-selves to the same form of teaching which captivated the hearts and souls of these early Christians as we read and study the Bible, especially the

New Testament. No aspect of the Christian life can be substituted for faithfulness to the apostolic message of Christ.

This means that the church of Christ on earth must see itself as a *learning center.*[12] Our purpose is to present the message of Jesus in a way which is both consistent with the apostolic testimony revealed in the New Testament, and also culturally relevant to those who have been won to Christ. Those Christians and churches who refuse to devote themselves to a steady diet of spiritual food run the risk of starvation. Many die to spiritual growth at age twenty and are buried sixty years later.

I remember attending a rural church and visiting before the morning service with one of the older members. When I asked, "Have you been here with this church family for a long time?" he proceeded to unbutton his suit coat and display on the inner lining a series of perfect attendance Sunday School pins that would have put General Patton's dress uniform medals to shame. I remember commenting on how impressed I was. Then I said, "You must be one of the adult teachers or church leaders by now, with all your years of study."

"Oh no!" he replied, almost shocked. "I couldn't do anything like that. But I sure have been here."

Simply being in the vicinity of the teaching of the Bible does not guarantee spiritual growth. There must be a "continual devotion" to that teaching. Where this is not present, the church will not become what God intends it to become. Evangelism to the Jesus revealed in the New Testament becomes impossible where there is not a continual devotion to that teaching. First and foremost in the atmosphere of the spiritual growth leading to evangelism is a continual devotion to the apostles' teaching.

Devotion to Fellowship

Next, we see the church devoted to fellowship (Acts 2:42). Fellowship (κοινωνία, *koinonia*) in the New Testament has both a vertical and horizontal aspect. Our fellowship is primarily with God the Father and with His Son, Jesus Christ. "God, who has called you into fellowship with his Son Jesus Christ our Lord, is faithful" (1 Cor. 1:9). For Paul, the basis for genuine fellowship between people is found only in the new community of faith created by Jesus. It is only because our relationship to God has been restored by the sacrifice of Christ on the cross that we can ever hope to have fellowship with our fellow man. Hence, when Paul talks about fellowship, he often centers on the restored fellowship that exists between God and man through faith in Christ. And so he speaks of "the fellowship of His Son" (1 Cor. 1:9), "the fellowship of the Holy Spirit" (2 Cor. 13:13) and "fellowship in the gospel" (Phil. 1:5). In Galatians 2:9, when Peter, James and John extend to Paul and Barnabas "the right hand of fellowship," it is not just a handshake of social grace but rather a mutual recognition of being "in Christ."

It is our fellowship with Christ which makes fellowship with other Christians possible.

We also have fellowship with one another.

> We proclaim to you what we have seen and heard, so that you also may have fellowship with us. And our fellowship is with the Father and with his Son, Jesus Christ (1 John 1:3).

It is our fellowship with Christ which makes fellowship with other Christians possible. When we are obedient to Jesus, the avenue of true fellowship between man and fellow man opens up. John writes, "But if we walk in the light, as he is in the light, we have fellowship with one another, and the blood of Jesus, his Son, purifies us from all sin" (1 John 1:7).

Although the word "fellowship" is used sparingly in the New Testament, the expression of fellowship is graphically displayed in the "one another" passages of the New Testament (emphasis below is mine).

John 13:34 A new command I give you: *Love one another.* As I have loved you, so *you must love one another.*

John 13:35 By this all men will know that you are my disciples, if you *love one another.*

Rom. 12:10 *Be devoted to one another in brotherly love.* Honor one another above yourselves.

Rom. 12:16 *Live in harmony with one another.* Do not be proud, but be willing to associate with people of low position. Do not be conceited.

Rom. 13:8 Let no debt remain outstanding, except the continuing debt to *love one another,* for he who loves his fellow man has fulfilled the law.

Rom. 14:13 Therefore *let us stop passing judgment on one another.* Instead, make up your mind not to put any stumbling block or obstacle in your brother's way.

Rom. 15:7 *Accept one another, then, just as Christ accepted you,* in order to bring praise to God.

Rom. 16:16 *Greet one another with a holy kiss.* All the churches of Christ send greetings.

1 Cor. 1:10 I appeal to you, brothers, in the name of our Lord Jesus Christ, that *all of you agree with one another so that there may be no divisions among you* and that you may be perfectly united in mind and thought.

---

1 Cor. 16:20 All the brothers here send you greetings. *Greet one another with a holy kiss.*

2 Cor. 13:12 *Greet one another with a holy kiss.*

Gal. 5:13 You, my brothers, were called to be free. But do not use your freedom to indulge the sinful nature; rather, *serve one another in love.*

Eph. 4:2 Be completely humble and gentle; be patient, *bearing with one another in love.*

Eph. 4:32 *Be kind and compassionate to one another, forgiving each other*, just as in Christ God forgave you.

Eph. 5:19 *Speak to one another with psalms, hymns and spiritual songs.* Sing and make music in your heart to the Lord.

Eph. 5:21 *Submit to one another* out of reverence for Christ.

Col. 3:13 *Bear with each other and forgive whatever grievances you may have against one another.* Forgive as the Lord forgave you.

Col. 3:16 Let the word of Christ dwell in you richly as you *teach and admonish one another* with all wisdom, and as you sing psalms, hymns and spiritual songs with gratitude in your hearts to God.

1 Thess. 5:11 Therefore *encourage one another and build each other up,* just as in fact you are doing.

Heb. 3:13 But *encourage one another daily,* as long as it is called Today, so that none of you may be hardened by sin's deceitfulness.

Heb. 10:24 And *let us consider how we may spur one another on toward love and good deeds.*

Heb. 10:25 Let us not give up meeting together, as some are in the habit of doing, but *let us encourage one another* — and all the more as you see the Day approaching.

Jas. 4:11 Brothers, *do not slander one another.* Anyone who speaks against his brother or judges him speaks against the law and judges it. When you judge the law, you are not keeping it, but sitting in judgment on it.

1 Pet. 1:22 Now that you have purified yourselves by obeying the truth so that you have sincere love for your brothers, *love one another deeply,* from the heart.

1 Pet. 3:8 Finally, all of you, *live in harmony with one another;* be sympathetic, love as brothers, be compassionate and humble.

1 Pet. 4:9 *Offer hospitality to one another* without grumbling.

1 Pet. 5:5 Young men, in the same way be submissive to those who are older. All of you, *clothe yourselves with humility toward one another*, because, "God opposes the proud but gives grace to the humble."

1 Pet. 5:14 *Greet one another with a kiss of love.* Peace to all of you who are in Christ.

1 John 1:7 But if we walk in the light, as he is in the light, *we have fellowship with one another,* and the blood of Jesus, his Son, purifies us from all sin.

1 John 3:11 This is the message you heard from the beginning: We should *love one another.*

> 1 John 3:23 And this is his command: to believe in the name of his Son, Jesus Christ, and to *love one another* as he commanded us.
>
> 1 John 4:7 Dear friends, let us *love one another*, for love comes from God. Everyone who loves has been born of God and knows God.
>
> 1 John 4:11 Dear friends, since God so loved us, we also ought to *love one another*.
>
> 1 John 4:12 No one has ever seen God; but if we *love one another*, God lives in us and his love is made complete in us.
>
> 2 John 5 And now, dear lady, I am not writing you a new command but one we have had from the beginning. I ask that we *love one another*.

Part of continually devoting themselves to the apostle's teaching of necessity would have meant a continual devotion of their lives to the Lord Jesus and to one another in fellowship. This would have shown the first church to be a *healing community* in which the alienating power of sin so evident all around them was in the process of being conquered through the power of Christ creating this new community of fellowship.

If ever there is to be a place on Planet Earth where people can live in peace and harmony, God intends for it to be in the church which he purchased with his own precious blood. A local church which continually displays a lack of fellowship with one another is, in effect, denying the power of Christ and the gospel itself.

If ever there is to be a place on Planet Earth where people can live in peace and harmony, God intends for it to be in the church.

I belong to a church tradition which has chosen to argue about the strangest things. Some, in the history of the tradition of the Restoration Movement, have decided it is best to worship and sing without the aid of instrumental music. Others, see instrumental music as a great aid in helping to express love and devotion to God. I heard of a small rural church one time whose members were caught up in a tremendous argument whether or not to keep musical instruments as a part of their worship service. All this small church had was one old upright piano. One group became convinced that the piano needed to be removed from the sanctuary. Another group was equally convinced that the piano must stay. One Sunday everyone showed up to the morning worship service and the piano was gone. They looked everywhere for it. Two years later, someone found it. It was in the baptistery!

When biblical fellowship is missing from the body life of any congregation, evangelism becomes next to impossible. God is not in the habit of putting healthy spiritual babies in sick incubators. When the members of a local church body develop a living fellowship with God through Christ, they will live out that fellowship in their interaction with one another. This creates the spiritual climate necessary for evangelism to take place and for the Great Commission to be carried out.

Devotion to Worship

Next, we see that the first church was continually devoted to worship (Acts 2:42). Luke records that they devoted themselves to "the breaking of bread and prayer" (2:42). We have already discussed the great theme of prayer throughout the Book of Acts. Most scholars understand the "breaking of bread" (τῇ κλάσει τοῦ ἄρτου, *te klasei tou artou*) to be an allusion to the celebration of the Lord's Supper.[13] Luke records,

> Every day they continued to meet together in the temple courts. They broke bread in their homes and ate together with glad and sincere hearts, praising God and enjoying the favor of all the people (Acts 2:46-47a).

From the above, several key aspects concerning worship seem to be apparent. The church which God desires must be seen as a *worship center.* Worship in the early church contained both a *corporate* and *personal* aspect. The corporate nature of worship is seen in the ceremony of celebrating the Lord's Supper (breaking of bread). Paul discusses the fact that part of the celebration of the Supper involves recognizing the unity of all believers in Christ (1 Cor. 10:16-17). This was to be brought out and experienced as the believers participated in this corporate ceremony together. Worship also had a personal aspect in the prayer life of the believers. While it is obvious that they often prayed together (Acts 4:24ff; etc.), the nature of prayer is extremely personal in its nature (Matt. 6:6). Hence worship is to be the heartfelt interaction of a believer with his God, but this is to be experienced within the life of the Christian community. The embodiment of what Jesus did and who He has made us to be is seen in the Lord's Supper. Worship is always to be personal but *never* simply private.

Worship in the early church contained both
a *corporate* and *personal* aspect.

We also see that the worship of these early Christians was experienced in *large groups* (in the temple courts) and in *small groups* (house to house). There is an aspect of spiritual growth which is available only in a group small enough where individual needs can be shared and cared for.[14] The most common image of the church in the New Testament is that of "family" (see chapters 12 and 13).[15] God, through His Word, is calling His church to experience interaction; not simply in the context of community, but in the context of the closest community known in this life: the community of the family. In order to accomplish this, the local congregation, no matter how large, will have to provide the opportunity for Christians to grow in a family type of setting. This implies small group interaction. While family reunions may run into the hundreds, families grow normally in smaller cell groups.

Most people would rather sing praises with 3,000 than with 3.

However, there is also an aspect of worship that is available only in a larger corporate group. Most people would rather sing praises with 3,000 than with 3. The large group contains a dynamic and excitement that is a prelude to the vastness of the worship to be experienced in heaven (Rev. 5:11-14). We see both aspects displayed by the first church in Jerusalem. The temple courts were the only areas of the city large enough to contain the large numbers of people that made up this first church (Acts 2:41; 4:4). And yet they obviously divided themselves into smaller groups which would allow for the type of fellowship commanded by the Lord and His apostles. C. Peter Wagner has written about this very dynamic structure of the early church in his famous definition of a local congregation. Wagner writes that "cell group" plus "celebration/congregation" (large group worship) equals "church."[16]

A church without dynamic worship of the nature described in Acts 2 will find it very difficult to carry out the Great Commission. A large group that is basically devoid of personal inner devotion to God is little more than a club, reflecting the surrounding culture rather than transforming it. A small group that refuses to grow is probably not living out the dynamic of New Testament fellowship or the Savior's command to "make disciples." But when a group of believers experiences a dynamic inner relationship with Jesus Christ which displays itself in the corporate body life of the church, when they experience the power of large group worship as well as the intimacy of small group spiritual growth, that church will provide the soil out of which tremendous evangelism can grow.

Devotion to Sacrificial Service

The fourth and final aspect of the very first church is seen in its devotion to sacrificial service (Acts 2:43-47). Luke records the practical outcome of lives joined in community which are devoted to the apostles' teaching, fellowship and worship.

Everyone was filled with awe, and many wonders and miraculous signs were done by the apostles. All the believers were together and had everything in common. Selling their possessions and goods, they gave to anyone as he had need. Every day they continued to meet together in the temple courts. They broke bread in their homes and ate together with glad and sincere hearts, praising God and enjoying the favor of all the people (Acts 2:43-47a).

In the context of the apostles' ministry, the early believers exhibited a selflessness that seemed to be a hallmark of the early church (Acts 4:34-37; 11:29-30; Rom. 15:25-26; 1 Cor. 16:1-3). In a day and age in which hardship was often viewed as the displeasure of God upon sinners, the loving, self-sacrificial lifestyle of these early Christians immediately set them apart from not only the Greek culture but also from much of the Jewish culture. This allowed the early church to be as popular with the common people as Jesus, Himself, had been.

This sacrificial service proved to be the demonstration of the gospel, which we spoke about in chapter 1. Joe Aldrich calls these works of good deeds, "the music of the gospel."[17] The secular world might not be ready to listen to our doctrine, but they simply cannot ignore the loving care that forms the heart of the lifestyle of followers of Jesus. The secular world can disregard doctrine. It can turn its back on the trappings of religion. It can shun the mandates of the moralists. But no one can ignore love — true self-giving, self-denying, self-sacrificing, self-crucifying love. Francis Schaeffer once said, "Love is the final apologetic." After every philosophical and theological argument has run its course, love will ultimately convince the world of the truthfulness of the claims of Christ. Evangelism will be possible in the life of the church which translates its theology into practical Christian living displayed through love.

The secular world can disregard doctrine, turn its back on the trappings of religion, and shun the mandates of the moralists, but no one can ignore love.

The Ultimate Result of the Church Being the Church

It has at times been noted that there is very little reference in the Epistles to encourage believers to share their faith. The giving of the Great Commission is basically confined to the Gospels and the Book of Acts. However, this should not be interpreted as a lack of emphasis on the part of the first-century church toward evangelism. Rather, the Epistles were written to help encourage Christians with a correct interpretation of the saving event of the atonement provided by the Lord Jesus and to display the lifestyle that faith in such a Redeeming God demands. When the church actually lives out the theology of the cross, evangelism is the ultimate by-product.

As it was in the very first church, so it must be in every church until the Lord Jesus returns: Christians, in an attitude of prayer, must live their lives in total reliance on the Spirit's power. There must be a continual devotion to apostolic teaching, fellowship, worship and sacrificial service. When this occurs in our own day as it did in theirs, then the result will be the same:

> And the Lord added to their number daily those who were being saved (Acts 2:47b).

When the church actually lives out the theology of the cross, evangelism is the ultimate by-product.

---

1. Rodney Stark, *The Rise of Christianity: A Sociologist Reconsiders History* (Princeton: Princeton University Press, 1996), p. 208.

2. It is likely that Nicodemus and Joseph of Aramethea would be numbered among this early group (John 19:38-39).

3. Adolph Harnack suggested that out of a population of 54-60 million in the Roman Empire, up to 4.5 million may have been Jews. Most contemporary historians rely on Harnack's conclusions. The Jews, therefore, probably made up no more that 7% of the population of the Empire. See Adolf Harnack, *The Expansion of Christianity in the First Three Centuries*, Vol 1, trans. James Moffett (New York: Books for Libraries Press, 1904), pp. 1-24.

4. Nearly all historians, both secular and Christian recognize that Constantine's edict was not the cause of Christianity's triumph, but rather merely the natural response to rapid Christian growth within the Empire. For a thorough account of the early expansion of the church see W.H.C Frend, *The Rise of Christianity* (Philadelphia: Fortress Press, 1984).

5. Stark, *The Rise of Christianity*, p. 3.

6. While some say that this was the "upper room" mentioned in Acts 1:13, it is more likely that this was one of the porticos of the temple (Luke 24:53). This would explain how a crowd would have immediately gathered which numbered in the thousands. Also the immediate context of the beginning of Acts 2 requires us to understand that only the Twelve were

together on this particular occasion since they are the last specific group mentioned in Acts 1:26 and the group mentioned specifically involved in the Pentecost preaching (Acts 2:14).

7. A sound *like* the blowing of a violent wind was the first sign. Wind is often used as a reference to the Spirit of God. In the OT the word for wind and spirit is the same — "*ru'ah.*" The second sign was *what seemed to be* tongues of fire that separated and came to rest on each of them (sense of sight). In the OT fire was also associated with the presence of God, Exod. 2:2-3; 13:21-22.

8. There are 15 different language groups/nationalities mentioned here in Acts. Luke lists them and we can perhaps organize them into 5 groupings: 1) Parthians, Medes, Elamites, and residents of Mesopotamia (east of Judea); 2) Judea; 3) Cappadocia, Pontus, Asia, Phrygia, and Pamphylia (provinces of Asia Minor); 4) Egypt, parts of Libya near Cyrene (north Africa); 5) Visitors from Rome (both Jew and proselytes); and 6) Cretans and Arabs. All 15 different groups heard the Apostles declaring the wonders of God in their own language.

9. The word προσκαρτεροῦντες (*proskarterountes*) in this exact form (pres., act., part., masc., pl., nom.) is used in 1:14 and 2:42.

10. Other instances of the Holy Spirit's work in Acts include: (1) The Holy Spirit's voice was heard in the church through the Old Testament Scriptures. (4:25; 28:25); (2) The seven men selected to solve the meals crisis in the Jerusalem church had to show evidence of being "full of the Spirit." (6:3,5); (3) The early Christian prophet, Agabas, made his predictions through the Holy Spirit, as did other unnamed prophets. (11:28; 21:4,11); (4) After Paul and Barnabas planted the church at Pisidian Antioch, the believers were "filled with joy and the Holy Spirit" even in the face of persecution. (13:52); (5) At the Jerusalem Council, Peter again recounted the fact that God had poured out the Holy Spirit upon Cornelius and his household in a manner similar to that of Pentecost. (15:8); (6) The Holy Spirit was even responsible for the selection of the elders of the church at Ephesus (20:28).

11. Oswald Hoffman, "The Work of the Holy Spirit in Acts," in *One Race, One Gospel, One Task* (Berlin World Congress on Evangelism), vol. 1, ed. Carl F.H. Henry and W. Stanley Mooneyham (Minneapolis: World Wide Publications, 1967), p. 66.

12. The four images of the church in Acts 2 as being a learning center, healing community, worship center and deploying agency have been borrowed from Joe Aldrich. See Joe Aldrich, *Life-Style Evangelism* (Portland: Multnomah, 1981), p. 116.

13. Both liberal and conservative scholars are in basic agreement about this. See Ernst Hänchen, *The Acts of the Apostles*, trans. Basil Blackwell (Philadelphia: Westminster, 1971), p. 119; and F.F. Bruce, *The Acts of the Apostles: The Greek Text with Introduction and Commentary* (Grand Rapids: Eerdmans, 1990), p. 132.

14. In the past 15 years a wealth of material has been published in the area of small group development as a display of biblical growth and worship. For an historical overview see C. Kirk Hadaway, et al., *Home Cell Groups and House Churches* (Nashville: Broadman, 1987), pp. 38-54. For an overview see Julie A. Gorman, *Community That Is Christian* (Wheaton: Victor Books, 1993); also see my unpublished doctoral project, Terry A. Bowland, *The Establishment of Care Groups* (Deerfield: Trinity Evangelical Divinity School, 1989), pp. 13-56.

15. While the actual phrase "the family of God" (πατρία τοῦ θεοῦ, *patria tou theou*) is not used in the New Testament, family terminology abounds. The most common address for God is the term "Father" (259 times in the NT). The most important phrase in the study of the self-disclosure of Jesus is the "Son of God." Christians are addressed by the apostolic witness as "brethren" (30 times in Acts; 130 times in Paul), making it the most common designation for believers used in the New Testament.

16. C. Peter Wagner, *Your Church Can Grow* (Ventura, CA: Regal Books, 1976), pp. 97-109.

17. Aldrich, *Life-Style Evangelism*, pp. 77-96.

Chapter 6
Understanding Our Postmodern Culture

We are approaching a major turning point in history. I can compare it only with the turning point from the Middle Ages to the modern era, a shift of civilizations. It is the sort of turning point at which the hierarchy of values to which we have been dedicated all our lives is starting to waver, and may collapse.[1]

Aleksandr Solzhenitsyn

There is one thing a professor can be absolutely certain of: almost every student entering the university believes, or says he believes, that truth is relative. If this belief is put to the test, one can count on the students' reaction: they will be uncomprehending. That anyone should regard the proposition as not self-evident astonishes them, as though he were calling into question 2 + 2 = 4. These are things you don't think about. The students' backgrounds are as various as America can provide. Some are religious, some atheists; some are to the Left, some to the Right; some intend to be scientists, some humanists or professionals or businessmen; some are poor, some rich. They are unified only in their relativism and in their allegiance to equality.[2]

Allan Bloom

It's not that the men and women graduating from our seminaries do not know the answers. They do know the answers. They just don't know the questions.[3]

Francis Schaeffer

Thus far in our study, we have examined the biblical material showing the great importance of carrying out the Great Commission. However, if we only exegete the text of Scripture, we will probably be very frustrated in our attempts to share the good news of Christ with the people around us. We must have a thorough knowledge of two indispensable issues if we can ever hope to share the gospel with the world. We must know the gospel; this is first and foremost our chief priority. But *we must also know the world to which we would take the gospel.* This is why Francis Schaeffer's quote above is so revealing. Many in our churches and in our theological schools are quite knowledgeable when it comes to understanding the finer points of the gospel, but often Christians are totally ignorant about the mind-set of the culture which we wish to challenge with that gospel. It is never enough to simply exegete the Bible message. If we are serious about communicating that message to the world in which we live, we must also become experts in exegeting our current cultural setting.

We must know the gospel and also know the world to which we would take the gospel.

The World Has Changed

Much of the evangelism done in past generations was what we might term "Argument-Based Evangelism." This methodology used two basic tools: (1) rational argument, and; (2) an appeal to biblical authority. On the American scene prior to the 1950s, most people at least gave lip service to the belief that the Bible was the Word of God. If you could simply show the chapter, book, and verse of your position, that was enough to convince most people that at least your position was what the Bible said. However, if that method is attempted today, the typical response would be: "Who cares!" Biblical authority has ceased to be a source of influence in the lives of typical Americans. However, that is only the beginning of the problem.

Prior to the mid-1960s rational arguments, based upon accepted authority, were enough to gain people's attention and convince them of the validity of a certain position or claim. However, today an individual can be given a flawless argument for anything from why they should buy a particular brand of laundry detergent to why they should believe that Jesus is the Christ, the Son of the living God. After the argument is laid out in all its technical precision, a typical response from many would be: "Whatever!" And they would go off on their merry way. This is not simply a problem with "religious truth." It is a problem with any type of truth.

The brilliant legal theorist, Robert Bork, shares an encounter with this type of antirationalism in an exchange with a student while teaching at Yale Law School.

> In the first year course on constitutional law, I led one student through a conventional analysis of an aspect of the Fourteenth Amendment to the Constitution, in which he reached the only coherent and legally non-controversial conclusion possible. (I

think it was that the amendment prohibited only official and not private action.) About ten minutes later he raised his hand, was recognized, rose from his front-row seat, turned to his fellow students, and said, "I want to apologize to the class for reaching the conclusion I did. I must have sounded like Attila the Hun." He resumed his seat and waited for me to proceed with whatever topic was then under discussion. The class showed no sign that anything unusual had happened. Neither then nor afterward did he explain what was wrong with the reasoning that led to the conclusion; the latter was just not acceptable politically, and that was that. When last heard of, he was a professor of law.[4]

Today an individual can be given a flawless argument for virtually anything and simply respond, "Whatever!"

Can we begin to see the problem — sharing the biblically authoritative message of Jesus as He makes His claims of absolute Lordship over every avenue of life with those who not only reject the authority of the Bible, but also are not initially swayed by any form of rational argumentation which would make a claim of absolute truth? This is why "argument-based evangelism" is generally not an effective starting point in developing a method of sharing the good news of Christ with the non-Christians living in our society. We are indeed commissioned by God to share the biblical message of Christ in all its fullness. But simply shouting out Bible verses and expecting to make disciples by outarguing people will not prove effective in today's culture.

The End of the Enlightenment Paradigm[5]

Before we begin looking at a more fruitful methodology of carrying out the Great Commission, we need to take some time to exegete our culture, to see how these tremendous changes have come about and why we can be hopeful in our efforts to win people to Christ, in spite of the challenges.

David Bosch and Hans Kung have done an extensive amount of work examining the ebb and flow of Western Culture from the time of Christ to the present.[6] They have categorized six major "paradigm shifts" that have occurred throughout the centuries that have marked entire new avenues of cultural understanding. We could list these paradigms as follows:

1.   The Apocalyptic Paradigm of Primitive Christianity (AD 30-100)
2.   The Hellenistic Paradigm of the Patristic Period (AD 100-600)

3. The Medieval Roman Catholic Paradigm (AD 600-1500)
4. The Protestant Reformation Paradigm (AD 1500-1700)
5. The Modern Enlightenment Paradigm (AD 1600-2000)
6. The Postmodern Paradigm (1960s-present)

Paradigm is used to give meaning and organization to the world in which we live. Some philosophers call this a "worldview." These major paradigms have served as a lens through which we view and make sense of our life and times. A paradigm shift is when one major view of life replaces another as the main interpretive framework through which people view their world. The dates provided above are somewhat arbitrary. Generally, these paradigm shifts take place gradually over the course of many decades.

In the Apocalyptic Paradigm of the Early Church (AD 30-100), the small but growing group of Christians were primarily involved in evangelism as they urgently spread the good news of Christ, expecting the imminent return of the Lord Jesus. In the Hellenistic Paradigm (AD 100-600), the evangelistic zeal of the church continued and, as the church grew, Christians sought to legitimize their faith before their pagan neighbors as Christianity carved out for itself a major place in society. The Medieval Roman Catholic Paradigm (AD 600-1500) saw the church replace the fallen Roman Empire as the preserver of culture in Western Europe. So successful was the church that society virtually became Christian, at least in its universal profession. However, the excesses of an increasingly unspiritual hierarchy brought the need for change within Christendom. The Paradigm of the Protestant Reformation (AD 1500-1700) sought to maintain Christ at the center of society while restoring a more heartfelt and personal view of salvation with the Bible replacing church tradition as the sole source of authority. Many events occurred in the time of the Reformation which gave rise to the Modern Enlightenment Paradigm (AD 1700-2000). We will examine several of these changes in greater detail later in this chapter. The Enlightenment was characterized by an elevation of human reason over every other aspect of life. God was replaced by man's attempts to adequately explain the entire universe with no reference to deity or the supernatural.

The Enlightenment was characterized by an elevation of human reason over every other aspect of life.

The arrogance of the Enlightenment can be capsulized in a conversation between Napoleon, emperor of France, and Pierre Simon de LaPlace (1749-1827), the famous French astronomer and mathematician. LaPlace had written a book on celestial mechanics, dealing with the orbit of the planets in the solar system. He presented his book in honor of the emperor. In those days heads of state were also conversant in the scientific theories of the day. When LaPlace was given an audience with the Emperor, Napoleon said, "Dr. LaPlace, I was fascinated by your theories about the motion of the planets. But I find it strange that in your entire work you make no reference to God." To this, came LaPlace's famous reply, "Sire, I no longer have need of that hypothesis."

The Enlightenment began in the development of a systematic examination of the universe which God had created. Almost all of the early scientists were devoted Christians. However, as the great success of the scientific method brought technological advances on every side, God was seen as an unnecessary belief, left over from the unenlightened days of the Dark Ages.

There were four pillars of Enlightenment thought which became the grid through which all human knowledge was evaluated. The first pillar can be stated as the "ultimate reality of nature." Carl Sagan stated this most eloquently in the opening word of his famous work *Cosmos*: "The Cosmos is all that is or ever was or ever will be."[7] Under this assumption, all reference to the supernatural was removed from public discourse. Not only did "God talk" become absent from the halls of the universities, but finally all serious consideration of God was eventually removed from every public school.

The second pillar of the Enlightenment was the "ultimate animality of man." If the physical universe is all that could exist, then man can only be a part of that physical world and nothing more. Hence, any reference to the "soul" of man was removed from serious consideration. If you would study "anthropology" at the university, man would be examined in the same manner as any other animal species. Darwin's theory gave this pillar scientific credence. All of human behavior could be explained by an appeal to social conditioning or genetic determination. No longer was man to be viewed as a special creation in the image of God, but rather, only as the highest rung on the evolutionary ladder.

The third pillar of the Enlightenment was the "inherent goodness of man." It was believed that man was the measure of all things. Since God was out of the picture, so was any concept of sin. Before the Enlightenment reprehensible human behavior was always blamed upon the fact that man had transgressed the absolute standards and laws of God. He was in need of repentance and salvation. However, with no recourse to the laws of God, Enlightenment Man was not viewed as evil but merely illiterate or uneducated in the true nature of human character. No longer was the church to provide salvation through the offer of repentance and forgiveness. Education would become the vaunted savior of society. If people were simply "taught the right thing," then they would "do the right thing." Higher education was expected to help us solve all our social, political, economic and psychological problems.

With no recourse to the laws of God, Enlightenment Man was not viewed as evil.

The final pillar of the Enlightenment was the "inevitability of progress." No longer did people need to hope for the coming of a future messianic age in which, as Handel (and the Scripture) proclaimed, "The kingdom of this world will become the kingdom of our Lord and of His Christ. And He will reign forever and ever."[8] With human reason alone and the inherent goodness of human character, man would forge out a society in which all the solutions of human pain and problems would be found. Society was seen as progressing on an upward spiral toward the achievement of these goals.

The Enlightenment swaggered into Europe with immense confidence in human reason and man's ability to become his own savior. However, we are currently experiencing the collapse of the period of the Enlightenment. Both secular and Christian thinkers all agree. Christian philosopher, Diogenes Allen writes:

> A massive intellectual revolution is taking place that is perhaps as great as that which marked off the modern world from the Middle Ages. The foundations of the modern world are collapsing and we are entering a postmodern world. The principles that forged the Enlightenment, which formed the foundations of the modern mentality, are crumbling.[9]

Allen and many others have outlined how all of the pillars of the Enlightenment Paradigm have been shown to be lacking.

The first pillar of the Enlightenment to come crashing down is the concept of the ultimate reality of nature. Enlightenment thinking had taken for granted that the idea of God is superfluous. We were told that we do not need God to account for anything. Subject after subject is studied in our universities without any reference to God, so that anyone educated outside church schools or colleges, is given the impression that religious questions are irrelevant. But today there are fundamental developments in philosophy and cosmology that actually point toward God. The greatest physicist since Einstein, Stephen Hawking, makes dozens of references to God in his popular book *A Brief History of Time*.[10]

It can no longer be claimed that philosophy and science have established that we live in a self-contained universe. Questions like "Why does the universe have this particular order, rather than another possible one?" or "Why does the universe exist?" point toward God as an answer. As we shall see, it is beyond the capacity of Enlightenment thinking to make a positive pronouncement on the matter. All scientists can say is that the order and existence of the universe pose real questions that they cannot answer and secular intellectuals are recognizing that God is a truly possible answer. Diogenes Allen writes:

> This is a complete about-face. Both science and philosophy have been used for several centuries to exclude even the possibility of God. On strictly intellectual grounds, this can no longer rightly be done. This is a fundamentally different cultural situation.[11]

The second Enlightenment pillar, "the ultimate animality of man," has also been widely discarded by people of our day. While biology departments continue to teach that man is nothing more than the product of evolution, most people are unwilling to live with the consequences of that belief. If animal species evolve upwardly through the survival of the fittest, the natural social deduction would be the concept that "might makes right." However, wherever man has most consistently employed the evolutionary theory within society, the results have been disastrous and repulsive to all thinking people. If evolutionary theory is indeed how "man" is to live, then anything from violent crime to the mass execution of the Jews in Nazi Germany can be rationalized by an appeal to the laws of evolution. And yet, wherever men have most acted like "animals" within the last hundred years, their actions have continually been held up to public contempt and ridicule. Man can be taught to believe that he is an animal. But man continually refuses to accept the results when he consistently acts like an animal.

The concept of "the inherent goodness of man" has also fallen on hard times. Enlightenment thinking failed to find a basis for morality and society. A major project of the Enlightenment was to base traditional morality and society on the character of man and his ability to reason instead of upon the revealed teaching of the Christian faith. But it has been argued widely at the end of the twentieth century, as we face a new millennium, that all attempts to give morality and society a secular basis are bankrupt. Man, with no recourse to God, has produced two world wars, Hitler, Auschwitz and Buchenwald, Korea, Vietnam, the killing fields of Cambodia, the gulags of Stalinist Russia, the mustard gas of the trenches, biological warfare, ethnic cleansing, hydrogen bombs, euthanasia, and the mass abortion of the human race — just to name a few of our more notable accomplishments. All of the acts of man's inhumanity to fellow man throughout history pale into insignificance when compared to the results of Enlightenment morality.

All of the acts of man's inhumanity to fellow man throughout history pale into insignificance when compared to the results of Enlightenment morality.

The final pillar of the Enlightenment, "the belief in inevitable progress," has also been discarded by most thinking people today. It is true that modern science and technology became so successful in improving the quality of life that people came to believe that science coupled with the power of education would completely free us from social bondage and vulnerability to nature. However, few, if any, thinking people truly believe that serious social and economic problems such as crime, pollution, poverty, racism, and war will ultimately be solved by science. In fact, today science is often viewed as the villain instead of the savior of society. Most future visions portrayed in novels and the cinema are apocalyptic and extremely pessimistic. The world is often pictured as a burned out shell where technology has devoured all natural resources and society is mechanistic, with human life viewed as being as meaningless as it is worthless.

The cultural paradigm which has held sway in Western society for the past 300 years is coming to an end. A new paradigm of thought is upon us. This paradigm has been termed as "Postmodern." In order to take the gospel of Jesus Christ to our generation, we are going to have to understand some of the basic principles of this new paradigm. Before we examine these principles, we need to take a closer look at one of the chief elements that led to the collapse of Enlightenment thinking. This will help us understand the flow of postmodern thinking.

The Death of Truth and the Rise of Postmodern Thinking

Children of the Enlightenment believed that man could adequately explain the entire universe, himself included, with absolutely no reference to God. Yet, as we have already seen, when God was left out of the equation, man became a "zero," merely a cog in the cosmic machine of the universe. This presented tremendous problems for the secular philosophers who were attempting to develop an optimistic view of mankind in a cold impersonal universe. Rationally, it seemed impossible to give mankind real value and worth when we viewed ourselves simply as a part of a valueless material universe. Human traits like love, compassion, and the desire for meaning and self-worth transcend the physical world. How could man rationally, on the one hand, believe in the ultimate reality of nature and, on the other hand, believe that men and women were special and had intrinsic value and ultimate meaning and purpose. It was this inability to find a place for the dignity of man in a mechanistic universe that lead to the collapse of Enlightenment thought and the rise of postmodernism.

Francis Schaeffer was the first evangelical thinker to see the Enlightenment worldview in collapse. Millard Erickson is correct when he writes that Schaeffer was ahead of his time.[12] To go into a thorough discussion of Schaeffer's analysis of our age would be outside the scope of our present work.[13] However, Schaeffer recognized the dilemma of modern man's attempting to find a place for himself in an impersonal, materialistic universe. Schaeffer understood that in the late nineteenth century, Enlightenment thinkers ceased their attempt to find a rational meaning for the existence of man. In Schaeffer's words, thinkers crossed "the line of despair."[14] They admitted that rational thought could give no meaning and purpose to man's existence. However, every man feels as though such meaning and purpose do indeed exist. Hence if man is to find meaning and purpose, it will have to be done "IRRATIONALLY." Schaeffer writes:

> The line of despair indicates a titanic shift at this present time within the unity of rationalism. Above the line, people were rationalistic optimists. They believed they could begin with themselves and draw a circle which would encompass all thoughts of life, and life itself, without having to depart from the logic of antithesis. They thought that on their own, rationalistically, finite people could find a unity within the total diversity — an adequate explanation for the whole of reality. . . .
>
> But at a certain point this attempt to spin out a *unified* optimistic humanism came to an end. The philosophers came to the conclusion that they were not going to find a unified rationalistic circle that would contain all thought, and in which they could live. It was as though the rationalist suddenly realized that he was trapped in a large round room with no doors and no windows, nothing but complete darkness. From the middle of the room he would feel his way to the walls and begin to look for an exit. He would go round the circumference, and then the terrifying truth would dawn on him that there was no exit, no exit at all! In the end the philosophers came to the realization that they could not find this unified rationalistic circle and so, departing from the classical methodology of antithesis, they shed the concept of truth, and modern man was born.[15]

Schaeffer saw the beginning of this movement in the writings of George Wilhelm Fredrich Hegel (1770-1831). His system of accepting contradictory positions in a form of synthesis was the beginning of the end of rational thought being seen as the avenue of helping man discover meaning and purpose in his life. Søren Kierkegaard (1813-1855) was a Danish philosopher, the son of a wealthy Lutheran, who retired early to devote his life to piety and writing. He is called the "Father of Modern Thought." Kierkegaard developed the concept of the "leap of faith." He believed that rational thought only lead to pessimism and to find meaning and purpose in life involved an irrational leap of faith. A professor explained it to me once like this. Suppose you are being chased by a wild hungry tiger through the jungle. You come to a cliff, and when you look over the edge, all you see is a thick fog. You have no rational reason for knowing whether or not there is a ledge below the cliff where you can jump to safety. But the tiger is getting closer and so you jump because THERE MUST BE A LEDGE THERE! This is what modern man means when he talks about a leap of faith. Modern man believes that the world is a machine and yet there must be meaning and purpose for man. Rational thought cannot give him the answers he needs and so modern man must leap into the area of irrationality to discover real purpose and meaning in life.

Reality is seen as follows: (1) The Rational/Logical — this is naturalism studied by science. There is no purpose, no meaning, in a totally mechanistic world. The result is extreme pessimism when we think about man. However, there is also (2) The Nonrational/Nonlogical — this is existential experience. It is not logical or rational. Hence, it is not even rationally communicable. We know it to be true through our FEELINGS! The result is optimism. But it is an optimism that is irrational!

The result of Existentialism is an optimism, but one that is irrational!

Schaeffer traces how this irrational search for meaning has spread throughout our entire culture. The first to write about it were the philosophers.[16] Three of the most influential were Karl Jaspers, Jean-Paul Sartre, and Martin Heidegger. Karl Jaspers (1883-1969) was born in Germany but taught at Basel. He believed that man could find meaning and purpose in what he called a noncommunicatable final experience. Jean-Paul Sartre (1905-1980) was a French author and philosopher. He believed that rationally the Universe was absurd, and yet men could authenticate themselves through what he called an act of the will. The German Martin Heidegger

(1889-1976) believed that man could authenticate himself through a feeling of "angst" or dread. On a more popular level philosophers like Aldous Huxley and Timothy Leary believed that man could find the irrational experience which would give meaning and purpose to their lives through the use of psychedelic drugs.

After the philosophers, Schaeffer shows that this new way of searching for meaning was displayed in Western art.[17] Many Christians find themselves at a loss when going through a contemporary art museum. Most of the time, we stare at a shapeless sculpture or a bizarre canvas and exclaim, "I don't understand what this is." Were the modern artist present, he would simply shake his head and state that we are missing the point. The artist has not produced his work so that we will "understand it" with our minds, but rather, he created his work to produce in us a FEELING! Modern artists have adopted the belief that the true answers for man are not in the area of rational thought, but in the area of feelings.

Many would not like to recognize the extent of this move toward the irrational in our culture. After all, no one really reads philosophers or takes modern art seriously, do they? That is why Schaeffer then moves on to show how this view of life has filtered down into the avenues of general culture.[18] Today all things from music to movies are judged, not by the message that they convey, but rather by how they make us feel. It is interesting to listen to young people talk about the newest movie they have seen. If they really liked it, just ask them what it was they liked about it. Do they like the view of morality or honesty which the movie promoted? Was it the vocabulary of the main character which caused them to give the movie high reviews? No! They judged the movie to be good or bad by HOW IT MADE THEM FEEL! The same can be said for anything from a favorite song to a favorite food. Meaning and value are determined by how something makes us FEEL.

Unfortunately, this view of truth has even made its way into our churches.[19] Truth is not seen in the propositional content of Scripture but in the experience a person has in worship or in the life of the congregation. Therefore, for many Christians in our Western culture today, faith has become an optimistic leap based on subjective experience without verification or communicable content.

For many Christians in our Western culture today, faith is an optimistic leap based on subjective experience without verification or communicable content.

The Results of the Postmodern Mind on Evangelism

This is where the collapse of the Enlightenment has left us culturally. This is where the Postmodern Generation is in the way it views life. It is this "death of truth" and the elevation of "how one feels about something" that has lead to such an impasse in the way we attempt to do evangelism. How can we share the absolute message of the Bible with a generation which has abandoned any concept of absolute truth? In the coming chapters, we will be attempting to give an answer to this imperative question which will take seriously both the unchanging gospel message and our turbulent cultural setting. But before we proceed, let's take one last overarching look at the culture which Jesus has called us to evangelize.

Seven Symptoms of Postmodernism

There have been several attempts to evaluate the major tenets of our current postmodern culture. Most of them approach the subject from a purely philosophical or theological viewpoint.[20] I would propose a list of seven symptoms that will help us to get a handle on our current cultural climate with a view of seeing the relevance of these symptoms to the manner in which we approach carrying out the Great Commission.

Symptom #1: Relativism

We have already noted at the beginning of this chapter the loss of any sense of absolute standards within our culture. George Barna has surveyed Americans on the question, "Is there absolute truth?" Among the elderly who still live with their Enlightenment worldview, only 46% (less than half) strongly believe that absolute truth exists. Among the Baby Buster generation (Generation X — born between 1961-1981) only 28% maintain such truth possible.[21] In the Millennial Generation (those born after 1981) the numbers are even lower. As Postmodernism establishes itself in our culture, total relativism has become the standard way of thinking.

As Postmodernism establishes itself in our culture, total relativism has become the standard way of thinking.

Patterson and Kim write:

So who are our moral leaders now? Well, the overwhelming majority of people (93 percent) said that they, and nobody else, determine what is and what isn't moral in their lives. They base their decisions on their own experience, even on their daily whims. In addition, almost as large a majority confessed that they would violate the established rules of their religion (84 percent), or that they had actually violated a law because they thought that it was wrong in their view (81 percent). We are the law unto ourselves. We have made ourselves the authority over church and God. We have made ourselves the clear authority over the government. We have made ourselves the authority over laws and the police.[22]

Hence, any attempt at evangelism in the new millennium will have to assume that those we are seeking to reach will initially reject any claim of absolute truth on our part, as Christians.

Symptom #2: Experientialism

Because people today reject outside authority and absolutist claims does not mean that they have no way of making decisions. As we have already seen, experience — through sense and feeling — is the ultimate source of authority in most people's lives. In his book *Culture Shift*, David W. Henderson has characterized our generation by three striking models.[23]

First, we are *consumers*. America's favorite tourist attraction, beating out Disney World and drawing nearly ten times as many people as the Grand Canyon, is the Mall of America outside of Minneapolis, Minnesota. Is there any rationale behind purchasing hundreds of times the number of items we need to live and scores of times more items than we need to live comfortably? No, but the accumulation of wealth gives the momentary *experience* of well-being.

Next, Henderson points out that in Western contemporary society, we are a culture of *spectators*. The average person in the United States watches more than four hours of television a day. That translates into 28 hours, more than one full day, every week, 1500 hours in a single year, spent staring at a tube.[24] And what is the purpose? To have the *illusion of experiencing* life on every possible level. Most Americans live a rather mundane daily existence. Yet the television and the cinema allow us the illusion of living as a private detective, or a starship captain, or in the perpetual state of romance (complete with full orchestration).

Finally, Henderson notes that we have become a culture of *self-absorbed individuals*. Henderson writes:

> We drive alone, make life's hardest decisions alone, raise our
> children to stand alone, and lay down to die alone. Boil any one

of us down and what remains stuck to the sides of the pot is simply this: my concern for me. "Self-" has become the modifier of choice as we approach the year 2000: self-image, self-actualization, self-concept and self-help are all newcomers to the English language, products of a culture that has the individual as its primary concern.[25]

Henderson notes that we have become a culture of self-absorbed individuals.

Of course, all of this is what we would expect from a culture which has elevated experience to the highest level of importance. Any attempt to reach people with the gospel of Christ will have to take into account that people in today's postmodern world want to experience what we have to offer. If they cannot experience it, chances are they will never accept it.

Symptom #3: Pluralism

Because absolute truth has been discarded by the majority of the non-Christians in our society, it stands to reason that pluralism has become the standard trend of the day. Simply stated, pluralism is the belief that all viewpoints and positions not only be given equal consideration, but that they also ALL HAVE EQUAL VALIDITY! All individual beliefs, values, lifestyles and truth claims are of equal value. Josh McDowell quotes a *Newsweek* article which stated that our universities must teach our students to be multiethnic and multicultural, and that every citizen will be demanded to understand, appreciate and respect pluralism.[26] This has led McDowell and others to proclaim that "tolerance" is the #1 virtue in America. In the absence of any culturally recognized absolute truth, pluralism is the only possible conclusion for a generation which has jettisoned their brains.

Pluralism is the only possible conclusion for a generation which has jettisoned their brains.

To a rational, thinking person, the concept of two mutually contradictory viewpoints being given not only equal consideration but equal validity is irrationality at its highest level. This would place the vilest pornographer's work on the same level as that of Rembrandt and Michelangelo. It would place the ignorant, disease-ridden culture of the stone-age tribes of Papua New Guinea living in squalor on the same level as that of the culture of the most sophisticated westerner who is using his mind and technology to improve mankind's lot and explore God's universe. And yet this is the very thing we see happening all around us.

If we are to hope to reach our present generation with the gospel, we will have to deal with individuals who will initially reject our claims that Christianity is the only true way to God and that the Christian lifestyle is the highest form of life that can be lived on planet earth.

Symptom #4: Deconstructionism

One of the most bizarre results of postmodern thinking is what philosophers call "deconstructionism." Its roots are based in communication and literary criticism. Deconstructionists reject the basic, historically accepted rules concerning communication and understanding in language. Harold O.J. Brown has written:

> The hermeneutics of thinkers such as Jacques Derrida and Michel Foucault challenges the concept of objective meaning of a text. In order to interpret it, a reader must deconstruct it, identifying the dominant conceptual structures that underlie it and interpreting it according to his or her own perspective. This does not mean that a text has no meaning at all but rather that the meaning is dependent on the perspective of the reader. Such an approach makes intellectual inquiry and the communication of learning and meaning so difficult that its appeal is usually limited to a small circle; many simply give up seeking truth.[27]

The deconstructionist does not believe that there is an objective reality "out there" in the "real" world. Reality is only that which we create in our minds through language. Knowledge is not so much found as it is made. The words we use can take on different shades of meaning depending upon who is speaking, who is listening, and the context in which it is spoken. Therefore, words do not have objective meanings.

Corresponding to this idea is the belief that every interpretation is just as valid as the next, even if they are contradictory, because there are no absolutes in any area, only personal experience. The meaning of any piece of literature (including the Bible) is then dependent upon the reader, upon what the reader brings with him to the text. Reality is reduced to a matter of perspective. This means that there is no one meaning of the world, no transcendent center to reality as a whole, but only individual interpretations of it.[28]

Reality is reduced to a matter of perspective, leaving no one meaning of the world.

Postmodern man is no longer committed to the concepts of real truth and objective reality as was the case only a few decades ago. Today there is a growing trend to dismiss even assured facts and scientific evidence as interpretations that will naturally vary from observer to observer. No longer sure of the truths of even the natural sciences, postmodern Western man sees everything as dependent on his own understanding and interpretation of reality. A few decades ago Western man showed virtually unlimited confidence in the ability of science to lead him into all truth. Now he has come to doubt that there is such a thing as truth or, if it exists, that it can be known.[29]

In an age of deconstructionism, being applied especially to literature and communication, those who would communicate the gospel of Christ recorded in the sacred literature of Scripture must recognize the unique setting of our day. To simply display the obvious meaning of the Bible in its original context may not initially be enough to convince a postmodern pagan of the main message of the Bible. The gospel message must be communicated in its original biblical context. In fact to do anything less would be to distort the divinely revealed Word of God. Logical communication must be the vehicle we use to share the unchanging truth of Christ; however it may not be the best place to start in our evangelistic efforts.

Symptom #5: Nihilistic Fatalism

If it is up to each individual to define reality with no foundation of absolute truth upon which to stand, is it any wonder why the pervasive attitude of our generation is PESSIMISM? The optimistic worldview of the Enlightenment, with its infinite trust in human reason, could not produce adequate meaning and purpose in the life of modern man. The cynical worldview of the postmodern man, with its perpetual doubt about everything, can produce nothing but nihilistic pessimism. Nihilism is the philosophy that everything is absolutely meaningless. Fatalism is the philosophy that the future is set and there is nothing we can do about it. Hence, nihilistic fatalism is the ultimate pessimistic view of the future. Anyone, even remotely aware of contemporary thought, can plainly see this viewpoint in every direction. Jean-Paul Sartre caught the sense of this in his play *No Exit*, where the characters carry out meaningless conversation in a drab room from which there is no escape. Others, like Albert Camus in his novels *The Fall* and *The Plague*, display a life with neither meaning nor hope.

Today's headlines revolve around senseless mass executions in our nation's public schools by frustrated students who have been crushed by the meaninglessness of our culture. Woody Allen captured the spirit of our age when he said, "Civilization stands at the crossroads. Down one road is despondency and despair, and down the other is total annihilation. Let us pray that we choose the right road."

Nihilistic fatalism is the ultimate pessimistic view of the future.

The only meaning available to postmodern man is to be found in the experience of the moment. I heard one young person say that life was simply traveling from one experience to another and nothing lasted longer than the time it took to experience it. That "experience" might be helping in a homeless mission, or it might be in having a sexual affair. For postmodern man, the source of the experience is not as important as the experience itself.

It is to people floundering in the cesspool of nihilistic fatalism, that we are sent to declare good news. There is meaning! There is hope! What they have given up on, is exactly what we have to offer in a personal relationship with Jesus Christ. However, when we attempt to carry out the Great Commission in our present age, we must find a way to demonstrate that our message can produce what many believe simply does not exist.

Symptom #6: Fraternalism (Search for Community)

Because the lonely contemporary individual standing in a meaningless world is unable to provide what is necessary for his existence, this sixth trait of Postmodernism has arisen — fraternalism. I define fraternalism as the search for a community where an individual can find identity and significance. The model of the isolated enlightened individual has been replaced by a community-based model. Truth is defined by and for the community and all knowledge occurs within some community.[30]

It is because of the narcissistic fatalism which assails each individual that individuals are forced to search for meaning and identity within a group. Traditionally, people found their place in society through their family, their church, and their nation. However, today with the breakdown of the family (especially in minority groups), the fractured impotency of many churches and the general distrust of national leaders, many are driven to find community in alternative associations. Multiculturalism is the watchword of the day, with people finding their "place" by returning to their ethnic roots. Aberrant sexuality forms a strong community for the homosexual population. Athletes bond together, as does everyone from musicians to bodybuilders. Gangs provide this source of community for many youth in the inner cities.

Gangs provide the source of community for many youth in the inner cities.

Concerning this trait in the younger generation, Gary Zustiak has written:

> Without a doubt the most popular sitcom with the Generation X crowd is "Friends." A curious observation about the program is that the characters are hardly ever doing anything of substance. We rarely see them at work or involved in some cause. The entire program consists of their hanging out at a coffee shop or in one of their apartments eating and dealing with some aspect of their interpersonal relationships with each other, former spouses or lovers.
>
> Eating together has almost become a sacred activity with Generation X. It doesn't have to be at a fancy restaurant and it doesn't have to be a gourmet meal. It is the time spent together in bonding, sharing problems, and supporting one another that is pursued by this generation. I believe it is an attempt to create a spirit of family which most of them never had because their families were either dysfunctional or fragmented by divorce. Their friends have become their substitute family. With their special group of friends, they can say anything, do anything, and be anything — and they know they will still be accepted. Meal times are when the members of a family share the events of the day, work out problems and support one another. Generation X missed that and they are making up for that loss with their friends.[31]

The truly great thing about this particular trait of Postmodernism is that authentic biblical Christianity provides EXACTLY what our present generation is seeking. But it must be authentic, biblical Christianity. If the church is simply a stuffy formal place where people come once a week wearing their religious masks, we can kiss reaching our current generation good-bye. But if the church displays the genuine community of the biblical model in Acts 2 and the biblical theology of the New Testament, then we can truly offer our lost generation the community they are so desperately seeking. For the church to truly be the church is perhaps the greatest tool God has placed at our disposal to aid us in carrying out the Great Commission at the beginning of the new millennium.

Authentic biblical Christianity provides *exactly* what our present generation is seeking.

Symptom #7: Spirituality

The final trait of postmodernism is found in its deep search for spirituality. As we noted in a previous chapter, John Naisbitt has defined the "Religious Revival of the Third Millennium" as one of the most influential trends of our day.[32] With the collapse of Enlightenment skepticism concerning the supernatural, people are increasingly open to discussions of spirituality. The problem is, with the concept of pluralism and tolerance firmly entrenched, spirituality may be anything from orthodox Christian faith to strange occultic spiritualism — and everything in between. Any night of the week on our televisions we are invited to call an "on-line psychic" for a free "reading." Series and documentaries on the paranormal and supernatural abound — and people (even educated, literate people) are taking them seriously. That the views of these different "spiritualities" are contradictory presents no problem for the postmodern mind. Each individual determines his own view of truth and then enters into a community which promotes such a view. The only thing at issue is the experience to be gained from the spiritual journey.

On the one hand, Christians need to rejoice that culture in general is increasingly open to discussions on the need for spirituality. However, we must be clear that Christianity is not true simply because it gives us an "emotional experience." Rather, we experience the living Christ in our daily lives precisely because CHRISTIANITY IS THE ABSOLUTE TRUTH OF THE UNIVERSE! It is only when our postmodern world sees us experience, on a daily basis, the presence of Christ in our lives, that they will begin to take our message seriously.

We must be clear that Christianity is not true simply because it gives us an emotional experience.

The Contemporary Church's Great Opportunity

Diogenes Allen in his *Christian Belief in a Post-Modern World* suggests that the Christian Church is now reaching an unprecedented opportunity.[33] Dr. Allen argues that due to 20th-century revolutions in science and philosophy, the Enlightenment is now a spent force. Allen makes five observations about the postmodern world where scientists and philosophers have abandoned their Enlightenment roots.[34]

First, human beings are not as good and reasonable as the Enlightenment ideology taught. The coming of the atomic age and the evils of the 20th century have taught us this. Second, the Enlightenment teaching about a common "natural religion" in human nature has not survived examination. There is no common element in the world's major religions. Third, society has proven incapable of developing, by reason alone, a consensus of morality. Fourth, science and education have not liberated humanity from entrenched problems like crime, pollution, poverty, racism and war; and this failure has crippled the notion of the "inevitability of progress." Fifth, as the 20th-century scientists probed the mystery of the atom, the Newtonian view of the universe as a machine was not confirmed; indeed, nature at its core now appears random and mysterious. Consequently, many leading scientists and philosophers now admit the limits and fallibility of science, and the myth of complete scientific objectivity. Many scientists and philosophers are no longer closed to the possibility of God, and they now pursue it as an open and important question. They recognize that God is one possible answer to the greatest questions posed by man.

This means that the pillars of "modern" Western Civilization — erected during the Enlightenment — are now crumbling. Allen observed that we are now in a period of culture lag — in which most people in the Western world are not yet as aware as scientists and philosophers that the Enlightenment is over. Allen predicts "when the dust settles" we will see that the "fields are ripe for the harvest."[35]

Even a physicist like Stephen Hawking recognizes the need for a centralizing message which will give structure and hope to our shattered world. Hawking writes:

> However, if we do discover a complete theory, it should in time be understandable in broad principle by everyone, not just a few scientists. Then we shall all, philosophers, scientists, and just ordinary people, be able to take part in the discussion of the question of why it is that we and the universe exist. If we find the answer to that, it would be the ultimate triumph of human reason — for then we would know the mind of God.[36]

For those of us within the Christian community, we can only rejoice at the openness of such a statement, because we know that we already possess that which Hawking and others are seeking. It is only up to us to share the good news in such a way that it can be heard.

Dietrich Bonhoeffer once said, "The way which the Son of God trod on earth . . . (is) the way we too must tread as citizens of two worlds on the razor edge between this world and the kingdom of heaven."[37] This is the call of the Lord upon the life of every Christian seeking to win the lost world to Christ. For those seeking true spirituality, we must live His life in a pure and genuine way, so they will turn their attention to the "Greatest Story Ever Told."

> When he saw the crowds, he had compassion on them, because they were harassed and helpless, like sheep without a shepherd. Then he said to his disciples, "The harvest is plentiful but the workers are few. Ask the Lord of the harvest, therefore, to send out workers into his harvest field" (Matt. 9:36-38).

---

1. Quoted in Carl Wilson, *With Christ in the School of Disciple Building* (Grand Rapids: Zondervan, 1979), p. 18.

2. Allan Bloom, *The Closing of the American Mind* (New York: Simon & Schuster, Inc., 1987), p. 25.

3. Commonly quoted; source unknown.

4. Robert Bork, *Slouching toward Gomorrah* (New York: Harper Collins, 1996), pp. 36-37.

5. A paradigm is a view of life which becomes accepted by the majority of people within a culture.

6. Their work is summarized in Jimmy Long, *Generating Hope* (Downers Grove, IL: InterVarsity, 1997), pp. 60-63.

7. Carl Sagan, *Cosmos* (New York: Random House, 1980), p. 4.

8. Rev 11:15; quoted in Handel's *Messiah*.

9. Diogenes Allen, *Christian Belief in a Postmodern World* (Louisville: Westminster/John Knox Press, 1989), p. 2.

10. Hawking refers to God no less than eleven times in the final five-page chapter of his book. Stephen Hawking, *A Brief History of Time* (New York: Bantam Books, 1990), pp. 171-175.

11. Allen, *Christian Belief,* p. 3.

12. Millard Erickson, *Modernizing the Faith: Evangelical Responses to the Challenge of Postmodernism* (Grand Rapids: Baker, 1998), p. 64.

13. See Millard Erickson's evaluation of Schaeffer's thought in reference to postmodernism in ibid., pp. 63-80.

14. Francis A. Schaeffer, *The God Who Is There* contained in *The Complete Works of Francis A. Schaeffer,* vol. 1: *A Christian View of Philosophy and Culture* (Westchester, IL: Crossway Books, 1982), pp. 5-12.

15. Ibid., p. 10.

16. Ibid., pp. 13-25.

17. Ibid., pp. 27-34.

18. Ibid., pp. 35-47.

19. Ibid., pp. 51-55.

20. See Millard Erickson, *Postmodernizing the Faith*, pp. 18-19; also J. Richard Middleton and Brian J. Walsh, *Truth Is Stranger than It Used to Be: Biblical Faith in a Postmodern Age* (Downers Grove, IL: InterVarsity, 1995), pp. 7-84.

21. George Barna, *What Americans Believe* (Ventura, CA: Regal, 1991), p. 83.

22. James Patterson and Peter Kim, *The Day America Told the Truth* (New York: Prentice Hall, 1991), p. 27.

23. David W. Henderson, *Culture Shift: Communicating God's Truth to Our Changing World* (Grand Rapids: Baker, 1998), pp. 20-95.

24. Ibid., p. 72.

25. Ibid., p. 97.

26. Kenneth S. Stern, "Battling Bigotry on Campus," *USA Today Magazine* (March, 1995), p. 64. Quoted in Josh McDowell's *Tolerating the Intolerable: A Mandate to Love* (Campus Crusade for Christ Staff Conference Handout).

27. Harold O.J. Brown, *The Sensate Culture* (Dallas: Word, 1996), p. 54.

28. Gary Zustiak, *The Next Generation: Understanding and Meeting the Needs of Generation X* (Joplin, MO: College Press, 1996), p. 137.

29. Brown, *The Sensate Culture*, p. 54.

30. Erickson, *Postmodernizing the Faith*, p. 19.

31. Zustiak, *The Next Generation*, p. 167.

32. Naisbitt, *Megatrends 2000*, pp. 270-297.

33. Allen, *Christian Belief*, pp. 1-19.

34. These are summarized by George G. Hunter, III, *How to Reach Secular People* (Nashville: Abingdon, 1992), pp. 37-38.

35. Ibid., p. 38.

36. Hawking, *A Brief History of Time*, p. 175.

37. Dietrich Bonhoeffer, *The Cost of Discipleship* , trans. R.H. Fuller (New York: Macmillan, 1961), p. 212.

Section 2
"BAPTIZE"

"We must employ the very best methodology to help bring those we meet to display saving faith in Jesus Christ."

Chapter 7
RECOGNIZING POSTMODERN TRAITS IN OUR FRIENDS AND NEIGHBORS

> For most people, religion plays virtually no role in shaping their opinions on a long list of important public questions. . . . On not one of those questions did a majority of people seek the guidance of religion in finding answers. Most people do not even know their church's position on the important issues. That, perhaps, is the true measure of Americans' indifference to the teachings of organized religion: We don't follow what our church says because we're not interested enough to find out what it's saying.
>
> *The Day America Told the Truth*[1]

> Suppose one of you has a hundred sheep and loses one of them. Does he not leave the ninety-nine in the open country and go after the lost sheep until he finds it? And when he finds it, he joyfully puts it on his shoulders and goes home. Then he calls his friends and neighbors together and says, "Rejoice with me; I have found my lost sheep." I tell you that in the same way there will be more rejoicing in heaven over one sinner who repents than over ninety-nine righteous persons who do not need to repent.
>
> Luke 15:4-7

In the first section of the book, we have attempted to examine both the content of Scripture dealing with the Great Commission and the culture to which we would share the good news of Christ. To misunderstand Scripture is to be unfaithful to the mind and heart of God. To misunderstand the culture in which we live, is to guarantee less than fruitful labor as we attempt to win people to Christ.

In this section of our study, we will seek to combine our understanding of God's Word with our understanding of the present postmodern cultural predicament as we work toward developing a methodology for evangelism.

In many ways our current time in history presents many parallels with the situation in which the early church found itself during its first few centuries of existence. In the first 300 years of its existence, the church realized four objectives in its task to communicate the Christian message.[2] First, the church faced a population with no knowledge of the gospel. It had to *inform* people of the story of Jesus. This is the scenario facing the church of the 21st century. The ancient church also faced a hostile population. It had to *influence* people to develop a positive attitude toward the message of Christ and the movement of Christianity. Today, most non-Christians have negative attitudes toward the institutional church. The church must look for new ways to break down the barriers of distrust and animosity which many non-believers have toward the church. The church in the first three centuries had to face an empire with an established complex of religious beliefs. Therefore, it had to *convince* people of Christianity's truth. Today, in a world of relativist pluralism, we face an even more complex task. We must help people come to recognize, not only that absolute truth exists, but that such truth is found only in the teaching of Jesus Christ as recorded in the Bible. Finally, the early church faced a vast unconverted population. It had to *invite* people to adopt their faith and join the community of those who followed Jesus as Lord. This remains our task, as well, today. A church that does not extend an invitation to come to Christ is a church which is being unfaithful to the Christ it claims to serve.

In many ways our current time in history parallels
the first few centuries of the early church.

Identifying Postmodern Traits in Our Unchurched Friends and Neighbors

In the last chapter, we examined the great shift in our present culture as we have moved from an enlightenment to a postmodern worldview. We identified seven symptoms or traits of our current postmodern society. We gave a brief definition and description of each of these traits. At times, philosophical definitions lose some of their meaning if we fail to identify how those traits have indeed filtered into the mainstream of the world in which we live.

In the area of evangelism, several individuals have done an excellent job in identifying the traits of our current generation. Lee Strobel in his work, *Inside the Mind of Unchurched Harry and Mary*, has identified fifteen traits of the typical unchurched American.[3] George G. Hunter, III, has also identified ten characteristics of secular people in his book *How to Reach Secular People*.[4] A number of other concerned Christian scholars have also examined the current cultural trademarks on the contemporary American scene.[5] Perhaps it would be good to see how several of these cultural traits fit into the postmodern framework of our society, with a view to gaining a better understanding of how to reach such people with the gospel message.

Relativism

We need to remember that relativism is the belief that there are no absolute values for anything in the world around us. Lee Strobel has pointed this out when he notes that the unchurched are morally adrift but secretly want an anchor.[6] In the 1950s and to some extent in the 1960s there was something of a moral consensus in America. In the 1990s and beyond, there is absolutely NO MORAL CONSENSUS whatsoever. Sixty-nine percent of Americans declare there are no moral absolutes and that ethics are determined by the situation.

Gary Zustiak has written about this trait in Generation X (those born between 1961 and 1981):

> Christians, especially fundamentalists, are difficult for Xers to accept because of their exclusive doctrinal claims. Christians believe that Jesus Christ is the *only* way to heaven, the *only* religion that offers true salvation, and the *only* source of spiritual truth. The relativism and tolerance of Generation X finds that unacceptable. They see all religions as having equal authority and validity and anyone who claims to have exclusive insight to spiritual truth or God is intolerant. For the Xer, no one person has the right to make a judgment concerning another's spiritual experience or their methodology at arriving at spiritual truth.[7]

Unchurched Americans today seem to be far more conscious of doubt than guilt. Dr. J. Ernest Rattenbury observed that, "in the late nineteenth century, you could count on a general sense of guilt. Now (by the 1930s) the only thing you can count on is a general sense of doubt."[8] Because of the total relativism of our age, they have been encouraged to think very largely in terms of doubt. The more authoritatively we claim to speak, the more likely we are to produce a negative reaction in many postmodern Americans.

In the late nineteenth century, you could count on a general sense of guilt; by the 1930s all you could count on was a general sense of doubt.

At first, this may seem devastating to the proclamation of the gospel message. However, Strobel notes that an Associated Press article on June 2, 1992, declared that many baby boomers are "not turned off by religion, just indifferent to churches that do not stand out from the surrounding culture."[9] It is a fact that the only churches growing in the United States are biblically conservative churches who preach a message that confronts the moral decay we see in much of the culture around us.

Theologically liberal churches are losing members at an alarming rate. My friend, Mark Scott, the academic dean of Ozark Christian College, was traveling in Indiana recently when he passed by the church building of a denomination notorious for its weak stand on biblical truth. The sign in front of the church had a message placard that read, "Such-and-Such-a-Church: Where Men Are Not Promise Keepers and Women Are Not Submissive!"

It is no wonder that churches which merely reflect the culture around them attract so little attention. Moths are not drawn to the darkness, but rather to the light which pierces the darkness. So the non-Christian, entrenched in his relativism, will only be attracted by that which stands apart from the moral relativity that surrounds him. The unchurched may have adopted the relativism of the culture, but secretly they are searching for a moral anchor.[10] It's up to the church to provide such an anchor.

Another trait of the unchurched in our culture is their resistance to rules. The unchurched don't like to be told what to do, but they are generally open to reasoning.[11] They want to see the wisdom behind changing their ways, which opens up terrific opportunities for Christians to explain how God's guidelines for our lives are reasonable, practical and just; and how they are motivated by His great concern for us. When this is coupled with a lifestyle that truly reflects the gospel in daily life, we will be like Jesus described, "A city on a hill [which] cannot be hidden" (Matt. 5:14b).

Experientialism

Because people today reject outside authority and absolutist claims, experience — through sense and feeling — becomes their ultimate source of authority. Strobel has observed this when he notes that the unchurched don't ask, "Is Christianity true?" Rather, they ask, "Does Christianity work?"[12] The typical unchurched American doesn't care where a suggestion comes from — Hinduism, Buddhism, the occult, or Christianity. His main question is, "Does it work?"

Again, writing about Generation X, Gary Zustiak notes:

Xers are not as cognitive oriented as they are affective oriented. By that, I mean that they don't concern themselves as much with ideas and arguments as they do with experiences and feelings. To them, God is basically a concept — a nontangible idea.[13]

Because this is where the unchurched will be in the way they determine truth, one of our top evangelistic strategies should be explaining how Christ is available to help in the practical arena of everyday life. Our challenge is to help this new generation understand that Christianity does work!

Some may balk at the above statement, claiming that to do this alone is a retreat into pure utilitarianism — whatever works is the truth. However, as Christians, we know that the reason Christianity works is because it is THE TRUTH. We are not saying that it's true because it works, but rather because it is true, it therefore works. We understand that even if no one ever applied a single Christian principle to their lives, the Christian faith would stand true because of what God has done in history through the finished work of Christ on the cross.

As Christians, we know that Christianity is not true because it works, rather Christianity works because it is true.

However, we cannot expect our postmodern, unchurched neighbor to be able to start with that assumption. He does not initially care about such things as the vicarious atonement or the sanctifying power of the Holy Spirit. He only wants to know if what we possess in Christ will help keep his kids off of drugs, or put his marriage back together, or give him a reason for getting out of bed in the morning. And the glorious opportunity in all of this is that the living Lord Jesus can do all these things — and more! We simply must demonstrate that our faith has practical outworkings which the seeker can see and hope to experience in his own life.

Along these same lines, Strobel notes that most non-Christians don't just want to know something; they want to experience it.[14] George Hunter has noted that secular people are seeking life before death.[15] Many postmodern non-Christians are aware of their mortality, but most of them fear extinction more than they fear hell or seek heaven. The thought of themselves as no longer existing is the frightening thought. Consequently, they generally do not ask about life after death so much as they ask about real life this side of death. While seeking to salvage this life, they struggle to make sense of their life, to find meaning and purpose, to attain significance, and to make a contribution while they live.

For most of the unchurched on their spiritual journey, experience — not evidence — is their method of discovery. The postmodern heart, like every human heart, has always cried out for a personal experience with God. Sixteen hundred years ago, Augustine wrote, "Thou awakest us to delight in Thy praise; for Thou madest us for Thyself, and our heart is restless until it repose in Thee."[16] The objective of evangelism should be to bring our unchurched friends into a personal encounter with God, not merely to pass on information about God.

For most of the unchurched on their spiritual journey, experience is their method of discovery.

Many of the unchurched will determine whether or not they can experience God with us by what they discover when they visit our worship services. Strobel notes that if Christ is alive, His church shouldn't be dead. If we keep our church services tuned to God, prayerfully encourage the Holy Spirit to be active, and endeavor to connect with God in creative ways, we're more likely to create a climate conducive to the unchurched individual's quest for a personal experience with HIM.[17]

Pluralism

We need to remember that pluralism is the belief that all viewpoints and positions not only be given equal consideration, but that they all have equal validity! This may seem to be an insurmountable barrier for those interested in the spread of biblical Christianity. After all, didn't Peter say, "Salvation is found in no one else, for there is no other name under heaven given to men by which we must be saved" (Acts 4:12). How can we ever hope to take such a message to a postmodern generation who believes in the equal validity of every religious claim, no matter how contradictory those claims may be? When churches preach the exclusive claims of Christ, will this not produce resentment in the tolerant (if not irrational) hearts of our postmodern audience?

George Hunter concurs with this when he notes that secular people have a negative image of the church. If many secular people have doubts about Christianity's truth claims, they also have a negative image of the church. Specifically, they doubt the intelligence, relevance, and credibility of the church and its advocates.[18] Yet, in spite of this animosity, Hunter observes a reason for hope from the writings of German theologian, Helmut Thielicke. Concerning Thielicke, Hunter writes:

Writing from experience with secular people in Germany, Helmut Thielicke saw how supremely important is the Church's credibility with secular people. In *The Trouble with the Church,* Thielicke observed several credibility gaps in western societies. People, rightly, question the credibility of politicians making campaign promises and athletes advertising soft drinks. People, likewise, ask questions about the credibility of the Church and its advocates. They do not ask whether we in fact drink the soft drink we commend to others — they assume we probably do. "The question is rather whether [we] quench [our] own thirst with the Bible." Does believing it make any difference in our lives? Or are preachers just paid propagandists for the institutional church? Thielicke believed that the perceived "credibility of the witnesser" is the crucial variable in communicating Christianity in secular Europe today.[19]

It is the consistency of the message and the messenger which will garner a hearing from our non-Christian audiences. Only when we display the power of the message we preach will we arrest the attention of pluralistic, postmodern Americans. Or, as a famous preacher once said, "There is nothing so powerful as the gospel of Christ preached through the life of a truly redeemed man."

Lee Strobel agrees when he notes that the unchurched have rejected the institutional church, but that doesn't necessarily mean they have rejected God.[20] While it is true that most non-Christians do see church as archaic and irrelevant (91% of the unchurched believe the church is not sensitive to their needs), yet it is equally true that most Americans do have a belief in God. Only 13% of Americans are atheists or agnostics. A recent survey showed 91% of American women and 85% of American men prayed.[21]

We call people to Christ; not to a church family, a theological position, or a faith tradition.

In fact, a majority of the unchurched in America — 52% — say they have made a personal commitment to Jesus Christ that is important in their lives. This sends two distinct messages to those of us who are serious about sharing the gospel with our generation. First, it tells us that most Americans are open and even sympathetic, at least to the "image" of Jesus Christ. John Stott was correct when he wrote: "The unchurched are hostile to the church, friendly to Jesus Christ."[22] This is a source of tremendous optimism, because Christ is the center and heart of our message. We do not call people to a church family, or to a theological position or even to a faith tradition. We call people to Him! The tolerance created by our pluralistic society has guaranteed a sympathetic hearing by most people when they come to trust the one sharing the message.

The second message we receive from the above information is less optimistic. If over half of the unchurched believe they have made some meaningful decision concerning Jesus Christ, this is pretty sound evidence that the typical unbeliever doesn't have a clue about who Jesus is or what it means to have a personal walk with Him. This means that we have a tremendous opportunity to share the exclusive claims of Christ with those who need to hear.

The unchurched believe that they are tolerant of different faiths, but many, if not most, think Christians are narrow-minded. They are willing to let Christians worship Jesus, Muslims worship Allah, and Hindus worship their pantheon of gods. But when Christians assert that their way is the only way to heaven, postmodern man calls that bigotry. R.C. Sproul has said, "Though the concept of legal religious toleration says nothing at all about the validity of truth claims, many have drawn the conclusion that equal toleration means equal validity."[23] Hence, we need to be careful in our explanation of the exclusive claims of Christ. We need to help people examine the claims of Christ about Himself, without sounding smug or condescending in our beliefs.

Pluralism is the word of the day when it comes to considering which church to "try out." Strobel goes on to share that the unchurched are no longer loyal to past denominational ties, but they are attracted to places where their needs will be met.[24] Advertising experts have been telling us for years that the day of brand loyalty is largely over. Today, the unchurched are comparison shoppers, even in the spiritual arena. Foremost on their mind are issues of quality, creativity and relevance to felt needs. If they find these items elsewhere, that's where they will probably go. They will even jump from one congregation to another from Sunday to Sunday if there is a special program which will meet their needs. Strobel notes that today up to one in four may be so dividing their loyalty.[25]

Today, the unchurched are comparison shoppers.

This distrust of denominationalism is a great asset to those interested in nondenominational, New Testament Christianity. The values that attract the unchurched are excellence, creativity, authenticity, relevance, meaningful participation by the laity, and servant leadership. The congregation which models these will gain their attention.

Deconstructionism

We need to remember that the deconstructionist does not believe that there is an objective reality "out there" in the "real" world. Reality is only that which we create in our minds through language. In the previous chapter, we have already noted the great skepticism and uncertainty which such a belief produces within culture.

Therefore, it comes as no surprise for us to recognize that the unchurched don't understand even the most basic elements of Christianity. As noted in an earlier chapter, a recent survey showed that, when asked, "Why do Christians celebrate Easter?" 46% couldn't give an accurate answer. The postmodern American view of Christianity is a hodgepodge of New Age thinking grafted into old Sunday School lessons. They may not know the difference between the Old Testament and the New Testament, may not recognize the Lord's Prayer or a literary allusion to the prodigal son. Indeed, many secular people are misinformed about the essence of Christianity. Once they have been exposed to a distorted, diluted form of Christianity, they are resistant to the genuine article! Over a generation ago Alan Walker recognized this when he wrote:

> So today there is almost a complete ignorance of what the Christian gospel really is. You see, Christian knowledge and awareness are now the echo of an echo of an echo too faint to be heard. This means, for example, a feeling of awkwardness, even embarrassment, at entering a sacred building. There is ignorance in the ways of Christian worship. Therefore such people no longer desire to enter churches. It means an almost complete ignorance of Christian stories, biblical references, the traditional language of the pulpit.[26]

Once people have been exposed to a diluted form of Christianity, they are resistant to the genuine article.

Not only are the unchurched biblically illiterate, they don't even know what they do believe. One study showed that 51% of Americans have no thought-out philosophy of life.[27] Gary Zustiak has written concerning what our high school graduates "do not know" when they come out of secondary school:

31.9% do not know that Columbus discovered the New World before 1750.

40% are ignorant of the fact that the Japanese attack on Pearl Harbor occurred between 1939 and 1943.

75% could not place Lincoln's presidency within the correct twenty-year time span.

66% could not place the American Civil War in the fifty-year span between 1850 and 1900.

43% did not know that World War I occurred during the first half of the twentieth century.

50% could not place Franklin Roosevelt's presidency in the years between 1929 and 1946.[28]

The Christian interested in preaching the gospel and teaching those we win "everything" Jesus commanded us may seem to face a daunting task. But this is no more intimidating than the task which faced the first-century church. They too faced a totally pagan, biblically illiterate, pluralistic population, and were able to see tremendous evangelistic growth. They had, indeed, been taught "everything" Jesus had commanded them. We would do well to follow their example.

Nihilistic Fatalism

The pervasive attitude of our generation is PESSIMISM. Nihilistic Fatalism is the belief that there is no ultimate meaning or significance in anything and there's nothing we can do about it. If there was ever a generation that needed the optimistic hope that is found in the Christian gospel, it is our current, growing postmodern population.

There are numerous reasons for the defeatist view of our contemporary culture. Hunter observes that secular people have multiple alienations.[29] Many sense being alienated from nature, as evidenced by the mounting ecological crisis around the world. Secular people experience the world around them as "out of control."

From the assassinations of John and Robert Kennedy and Martin Luther King, Jr., from the Vietnam war to the cold war to the sudden dismantling of the Soviet Union to the sudden Persian Gulf crisis, from volatile stock markets and oil prices to threats of recessions, unemployment, urban violence, the onslaught of drugs and the AIDS epidemic. Many people feel that "no one is in charge.[30]

The philosopher Unamuno contended that "those who deny God deny Him because of their despair at not finding Him."

Others are alienated from their fellow man on a personal level, as evidenced by the anonymity of urban dwellers and people's abuse of each other in the business world. Most feel extreme alienation from their fellow man corporately as represented by political and economic systems.

Perhaps the most telling alienation is the estrangement people feel from their own lives. Many feel trapped by meaningless jobs and jump from one leisure pursuit to another in search of the momentary illusion of well-being. Robert Schuller has made much of the fact that secular people are afflicted with a loss of dignity, or low self-esteem. Schuller believes that our natural inability to trust God's love or to trust Christ's offer of salvation and forgiveness stems from our deep lack of self-worth.

> We simply do not value ourselves enough to believe that we can truly be loved unconditionally and nonjudgementally. So we resist at a profoundly deep level the divine invitation to salvation "by grace." Our innate sense of shame and unworthiness compels us to believe that we have to "earn love" and "do something."[31]

However, it seems that Schuller has missed the point. It is not that postmodern man does not value himself. Our modern culture has combined narcissism with nihilism — every energy is spent trying to satisfy the self, and yet nothing seems to accomplish the task. Postmodern man seems to value the self above all else. However, his worldview has no adequate basis, other than "a flight into the experience of the moment," to sustain the self. Such a baseless view of man leads most people into pessimism.

Alienation from the world, others, and self are outlined in Scripture as the result of sin and alienation from God.

These three alienations — alienation from the world, others, and self — are precisely those outlined in Scripture as the result of sin (see chapter 3). Each one of these three are based upon one ultimate alienation: man's estrangement from God because of his sin. Those interested in carrying out the Great Commission can take heart in the fact that we alone hold the key which will unlock the doorway of true life for each and every person trapped in the meaninglessness of postmodern culture.

Fraternalism — Search for Community

Fraternalism is the search for a community where an individual can find identity and significance. As we saw in the last chapter, the postmodern outlook on life does not provide the typical individual with the ability to create for himself meaning, purpose or a place in society. These traits are sought today within social community.

Jimmy Long has observed this search for community when he writes:

> *Friends* has endured for years as one of the top five most-watched TV shows. It is easily the most emulated show, with close to ten new shows trying to use the same concept — a group of friends trying together to make sense of life. The show's popularity is due to the fact that these six friends (Chandler, Joey, Monica, Phoebe, Rachel and Ross) have become a community of people who care for each other. They have become the family that they all lacked growing up.
>
> In the 1950s and 1960s most popular TV shows were built around the traditional family, such as *Ozzie and Harriet* and *Father Knows Best.* Why has the emerging generation become so caught up with friends and community rather than the traditional family? The traditional family is not meeting the needs for belonging that are such a part of this generation.
>
> Their longing is for a place to belong, a place to call home. As we have already seen, Generation X is suffering from the effects of the dysfunctional family, which are causing them to search for new places to belong. The traditional family, because of its dysfunctionality, has become a place many Xers feel they no longer belong.[32]

Single-parent families, once a rarity on the American scene, are now nearly as numerous as traditional nuclear families. According to the March 1988 report of the Census Bureau, a third of single-parent families were headed by a divorced mother, 28 percent by a never-married mother, 22 percent by a separated mother, and 6 percent by a widow. Divorced fathers, meanwhile, headed 6 percent of single-parent homes: separated fathers, 3 percent; never-married fathers, 2 percent; and widowers, 1 percent.[33]

Each year more than one million teens will become pregnant. Four out of five will be unmarried, and 30,000 under the age of fifteen. When we consider minorities, the statistics become even more alarming. Ninety percent of the babies born to blacks between the ages of fifteen and nineteen are born out of wedlock. As teen mothers of all races are less and less inclined to marry or put their children up for adoption, most of their infants will be reared in fatherless homes.[34]

By 2001, more than half of all American adults will be single. Older single women, either divorced or widowed, are the fastest growing household group in the nation.[35] This creates an unprecedented opportunity for those who long to share the good news of Christ with our current generation.

Lee Strobel has noted that the unchurched don't want to be some-body's project, but they would like to be somebody's friend.[36] They are hungering for close friendships. The average American moves 14 times in his lifetime. About every decade half the average town's population moves. People today desperately want confidants who care about them.

Because of the displaced nature of our culture, Strobel writes that there are two persuasive evangelistic steps we can take with those we seek to win. First, we must demonstrate the unconditional love of Christ in our relationship with the unchurched. We cannot simply view them as "evangelism projects."[37] We must make friends with those we seek to win.

In trying to convince my students of this, I ask them how they feel when contacted by a telephone solicitor. I am usually surprised by the amount of hostility the topic arouses in a classroom filled with Christians. One young lady told me that she keeps a referee's whistle by her phone and blows it vigorously before hanging up. I then asked, "Why do you feel such animosity toward the solicitor?" She responded, "Because they have invaded my home without an invitation. They care nothing about me. All they are interested in is "closing the deal." If we are to be serious about bearing fruit in our evangelistic efforts, we will have to be sure that we utilize a methodology that does not leave the above impression with the people we seek to win.

Secondly, Strobel notes that we must let our non-Christian friend know about the kind of rich, deep relationship that can exist when people have God in common. We run the risk of repelling the unchurched unless they see in our churches the kind of authentic community, honest accountabil-ity, freely offered forgiveness, and mutual care that Scripture calls for.[38]

The need for community is a relentless pursuit in our current culture. This community will either be expressed in its intended form within the redeemed community of the church, or it will be expressed in unredeemed forms. These may take the shape of anything from a country club to an inner city gang.

Many Christians are succumbing to the postmodern temptation to fragment or tribalize into smaller unredemptive units within their own local churches.

Many Christians are succumbing to the postmodern temptation to fragment or tribalize into smaller unredemptive units within their own local churches. Jimmy Long observed this in his own church. He writes:

God does want us to be involved in smaller communities. However, when those smaller communities become tribal groups, we are in danger of fragmenting. Tribal groups are groups through which we gain identity and to which we give loyalty, even to the exclusion of the larger group. This past summer I gave a sermon at our church entitled "Postmodern Tribalism or Biblical Community?" In this sermon I named the groups in our church that seemed to be in tension with each other: contemporary versus traditional worship, public versus home school, spiritual versus cognitive, and programmatic versus relational. I challenged the groups to try to understand each other and to try to unite in biblical community rather than confront each other in their tribal groups.[39]

The constant challenge for the church of Jesus Christ is to be genuine and consistent as we live in harmony with one another. The people of a postmodern, fragmented culture will hardly believe our theology about the power of Christ to change and renew lives if they are unable to witness such changed and renewed lives within our local congregations.

From the perspective of our unsaved friends, we must recognize that the typical postmodern American isn't quick to join an organization, but he is hungry for a cause he can connect with. There are millions in our society who want to change the world. They want to leave their mark. They want to make a difference.

Gary Zustiak again notes the statistics for Generation X which support this claim.

❖ More young people volunteer than at any time in the past 30 years.

❖ When asked whether each of us has an obligation to make a contribution to our community, over 70% of 16- to 29-year-olds said "yes," the highest percentage of any generation.

❖ Almost 45% of all college students surveyed said that influencing social values was an essential or very important goal in life. This represents an all-time high in the past 25 years.

❖ One in three consider becoming a community leader a very important or essential goal — more than double the number who thought so when the question was first asked in 1972.

❖ Almost half of all 18- to 24-year-olds volunteer at least one day a year, and about 25% of all college undergrads volunteer an average of five hours a week for a community service program.

❖ 40% of all first-year college students participated in some form of organized demonstration during 1992 — more than double the number that did so in 1966 and 1967, during the Vietnam War and civil rights uprisings.[40]

When asked, "What would attract you to a church?" outside of better preaching (the #1 answer — which makes this preacher happy), the second most common answer was for the church to become more involved in its "community."[41]

Because the postmodern crowd is reluctant to make firm commitments until they have examined every option, churches need to expect a long, slow courtship of the unchurched. Churches can adjust to this by making as many opportunities as possible for participation by people who haven't yet made a decision for Christ.

Spirituality

Our final trait of Postmodernism is found in its deep search for spirituality. However, this search for spirituality is not exactly a source of unbridled optimism for Christians. Generation X is spiritual — just not very Christian in the orthodox sense. In America, nine out of ten teens would still identify themselves as "Christian"; however, when they use the term "Christian" they are only using it in a generic sense. They would equate all Americans as Christians by default. After all, what else would you be? Since this is our nation's heritage, as opposed to Buddhist or Muslim, they would say that they were Christians by national heritage, but not Christians in the biblical sense.[42]

Generation X is spiritual — just not very Christian in the orthodox sense.

Strobel notes the positive and negative sides of our current popular spirituality. Negatively, he observes that the unchurched have legitimate questions about spiritual matters, but they don't expect answers from Christians.[43] Many non-Christians look at churches and imagine a sign out front that says, "No questions allowed." The problem is, that a Christian worship service would probably fill a typical unchurched visitor with a hundred questions.

"Why did they pass out crackers and grape juice?"

"What is an 'invitation hymn'?"

"Should I kneel during the prayer time?"

"How much was I expected to put in the offering plate?"

All of these questions would be followed by numerous other questions which the typical sermon would evoke. Common Christian words are unintelligible to the average nonbeliever. Words or phrases like:

- faith
- redeemed
- lost
- Lamb of God

- justification
- saved
- sin
- accept Jesus

might as well be Pig Latin when it comes to the biblically illiterate seeker. We no longer enjoy the luxury of simply "proclaiming" the biblical message. We must also "explain" biblical terminology, or the message will likely fall upon deaf ears.

Positively, the church should be a place where questions are welcomed, even encouraged. Churches need to develop an avenue in which the unsaved not only have an opportunity to have their questions answered, but are ENCOURAGED to ask those questions. When interacting with the unchurched, the manner in which we respond to their questions is extremely important. Those outside of Christ want to see if we will take them seriously. Hebrews 11:6 says God will reward those who "earnestly seek him." In the church, we need to discover ways which will allow the lost to do just that.

Aspirations for Their Children

One final aspect of our current cultural spirituality requires our consideration. Postmodern Americans may have turned their backs on organized religion, but statistics show that they want their children to get quality moral training. Strobel writes that 55% of unchurched boomer men said they had no plans to join a church in the next five years, but 73% of them said they wanted their children to get religious training. Forty-eight percent of unchurched parents currently have their children enrolled in some sort of religious instruction.[44]

Several years ago I took a group of college students to a suburb of Washington, D.C., to help do survey work in the hopes of helping a new church form in that community. We stood on the sidewalk of a shopping mall all day long for several days, surveying anyone who would give us their time. One of our questions was, "What sort of programs should a new church adopt that would best serve this community?" Well over half the people I spoke to commented that they would love to see a church in their community with a strong program for the youth!

If the unchurched see a youth program that's relevant, dynamic, and staffed by people who have an authentic faith, they're going to be more likely to explore what adult programs the church provides. The challenge is to provide the type of quality children's program that today's parents expect.

Reaching Out to Our Postmodern Culture

The consideration of our cultural setting is not simply an exercise in philosophical speculation. It is a commitment to see, REALLY SEE, the lost who are all around us. So often, when confronted by the traits of our lost generation, many Christians simply shake their heads in fits of disgust. While many would not say it, some deep down inside may even long for their demise on the Day of Judgment. Yet the Lord Jesus has commanded that we not only tolerate these people, but that we also associate with them so closely that they will see Him living through us and find life through His witness in our lives. Such associations will initially make us uncomfortable. This is the inescapable price of taking the Great Commission seriously.

When confronted by the traits of this generation, many Christians simply shake their heads in disgust.

I grew up on a farm in northern Missouri. One of my least favorite jobs was taking care of the hogs. They were dirty, smelly, and always getting into trouble. Yet, they needed me. They couldn't feed and water themselves. I learned something about working with hogs. You don't need to get down into the mud and roll around with them. That would be pointless. But if you work with them, no matter how clean you attempt to stay, you can't avoid the smell. If we are serious about reaching lost people, we are going to have to stretch our comfort zones by getting close enough to them to show them Jesus.

On one occasion, Jesus sat down by a well outside a city filled with "lost people" (John 4:1-42). He sent His disciples into that city to purchase bread. While they were gone, the Lord had an amazing encounter with a sinful woman. In the end, her life was changed as she came to believe in Jesus. John paints an interesting picture. The disciples arrived back at the scene just as the woman was leaving. They were perplexed that Jesus had been talking to a woman (and a Samaritan woman, at that!). They ended up in an extended discussion with the Lord. In the meantime, the woman returned to the village and gave evidence that Jesus had changed her life. In response to the obvious change which had occurred, the Bible states that many in the community came streaming out over the fields to see Jesus for themselves. I believe that as they were coming, Jesus instructed the disciples, "I tell you, open your eyes and look at the fields! They are ripe for harvest" (John 4:35b).

The disciples had spent much of the afternoon in a city filled with lost people and all they came back with was lunch. The only thing they had seen was the strangeness of the Samaritans. The only thing they had felt was contempt at having to spend an afternoon in a sinful Samaritan village. Jesus commanded them, and he commands us: "Open your eyes." The fields around us are indeed white unto the harvest.

1. Peterson and Kim, *The Day America Told the Truth*, pp. 199-200.

2. Hunter, *How to Reach Secular People*, pp. 35-36.

3. This information is contained in two chapters of Strobel's work, "Understanding Your Unchurched Friends, Parts 1 & 2." *Unchurched Harry and Mary* (Grand Rapids: Zondervan, 1993), pp. 44-81.

4. Hunter describes these characteristics in his chapter, "Profiling the Secular Population," *How to Reach Secular People*, pp. 41-54.

5. A wide number of books are available identifying how these traits work themselves out in the different generations of our culture. For a good example of this, see Gary McIntosh, *Three Generations* (Grand Rapids: Revell, 1995).

6. Strobel, *Unchurched Harry and Mary*, pp. 47-49.

7. Zustiak, *The Next Generation*, p. 76.

8. Quoted in Hunter, *How to Reach Secular People*, p. 46.

9. Strobel, *Unchurched Harry and Mary*, p. 49.

10. Ibid.

11. Ibid., pp. 49-51.

12. Ibid., pp. 56-59.

13. Zustiak, *The Next Generation*, p. 76.

14. Strobel, *Unchurched Harry and Mary*, pp. 59-60.

15. Hunter, *How to Reach Secular People*, pp. 45-46.

16. Augustine, *The Confessions*, Book 1, ch. 1. Found in *Great Books of the Western World*, vol. 18: *Augustine* (Chicago: Encyclopaedia Britannica, 1952), p. 1.

17. Strobel, *Unchurched Harry and Mary*, p. 60.

18. Hunter, *How to Reach Secular People*, pp. 47-49.

19. Ibid., p. 49.

20. Strobel, *Unchurched Harry and Mary*, pp. 45-47.

21. Ibid., pp. 46-47.

22. Ibid., p. 47.

23. Ibid., p. 78.

24. Ibid., pp. 66-69.

25. Ibid., p . 76.

26. Alan Walker quoted in Hunter, *How to Reach Secular People*, p. 45.

27. Strobel, *Unchurched Harry and Mary*, p. 52.

28. Zustiak, *The Next Generation*, p. 61.

29. Hunter, *How to Reach Secular People*, pp. 49-50.

30. Ibid., p. 52.

31. Robert H. Schuller, *Self Esteem: The New Reformation* (Waco: Word Books, 1982), p. 156.

32. Jimmy Long, *Generating Hope: A Strategy for Reaching the Postmodern Generation* (Downers Grove, IL: InterVarsity Press, 1997), p. 83.

33. Russell Chandler, *Racing Toward 2001* (Grand Rapids: Zondervan, 1992), p. 95.

34. Ibid., p. 96.

35. Ibid., p. 96.

36. Strobel, *Unchurched Harry and Mary*, pp. 60-63.

37. Chandler, *Racing Toward 2001*, p. 61.

38. Ibid., p. 62.

39. Long, *Generating Hope*, p. 96.

40. Zustiak, *The Next Generation*, p. 73.

41. Strobel, *Unchurched Harry and Mary*, p. 70.

42. Zustiak, *The Next Generation*, p. 78.

43. Strobel, *Unchurched Harry and Mary*, pp. 54-56.

44. Ibid., pp. 72-73.

Chapter 8
UNDERSTANDING THE PROCESS
OF LEADING PEOPLE TO CHRIST

Said Alice to the Cheshire Cat, "Would you tell me please, which way I ought to go from here?"

Said the Cat, "That depends a good deal on where you want to go."

"I don't much care," said Alice.

"Then," said the Cat, "it doesn't matter which way you go."

Lewis Carroll, *Through the Looking Glass*

The greatest barriers to evangelism are not theological, they are cultural.

Joe Aldrich, *Life-Style Evangelism*

Though I am free and belong to no man, I make myself a slave to everyone, to win as many as possible. To the Jews I became like a Jew, to win the Jews. To those under the law I became like one under the law (though I myself am not under the law), so as to win those under the law. To those not having the law I became like one not having the law (though I am not free from God's law but am under Christ's law), so as to win those not having the law. To the weak I became weak, to win the weak. I have become all things to all men so that by all possible means I might save some. I do all this for the sake of the gospel, that I may share in its blessings.

1 Cor. 9:19-23

The first five chapters of this book attempt to give a general overview of the biblical concept of carrying out the Great Commission. The last two chapters seek to give a basic overview of the current condition of the world to which we would take this gospel, realizing that it is a postmodern world. If we have done our work in theology, coming to grips with the basic message of the Lord Jesus, and if we have done our work in sociology and philosophy, coming to grips with the society we wish to challenge and win to the Lord Jesus, then the next real issue to be addressed is methodology. What method of sharing the good news will produce the most fruit in our current cultural setting?

Many Christians wish to ignore this question, being locked into one single method. However, if we wish to bring in the crop, understanding the nature of the grain is absolutely necessary to determine the right "machinery" to use to ensure the greatest harvest. My father raised two cash crops on the farm where I grew up. One was corn and the other was soy beans. Not even the dumbest farmer would think about pulling the corn picker into a soy bean field come harvest time. Real farmers interested in bringing in the harvest spend hundreds of thousands of dollars and hundreds of man-hours ensuring that just the right equipment is ready to "man the fields" come harvest time.

If farmers understand the simplest rules of harvesting grain, it would stand to reason that Christians, interested in an infinitely more valuable harvest, would seek to employ the methods which would ensure the greatest results. The eternal destiny of those around us will be determined by how we reach out to them with the gospel of Christ. I can pick corn like my great-grandfather, by hand, and see results. But how much greater the results if I could use a modern corn picker.

Some consider methodology in the realm of faithfulness. This method of evangelism is more "faithful" to the Lord than that method. I am forced to agree with Rick Warren, when he concludes that the definition of fruitfulness for a local church must include growth by conversion of unbelievers.[1] Simply seeing people make decisions is no justification for being unfaithful to the gospel message contained in Scripture, but neither can faithfulness to the message be used as an excuse for being ineffective in the methods we use. Any church that is not obeying the Great Commission is failing its purpose, no matter what else it does. Warren defines a church as being "successful" only when it carries out the Great Commission. "Faithfulness," on the other hand, is accomplishing as much as possible with the resources and talents God has given us. It is bearing as much fruit as possible given our gifts, opportunities and potential. Warren asks a sobering question when he writes:

> How do you define faithfulness? Are you being faithful to God's Word if you insist on communicating it in an outdated style? Are you being faithful if you insist on doing ministry in a way that is comfortable for you, even though it doesn't produce any fruit? Are you being faithful to Christ if you value man-made traditions more than reaching people for Him? I contend that when a church continues to use methods that no longer work, it is being unfaithful to Christ![2]

As difficult as the above observations are, I believe that it is imperative that we come to grips with the gravity of the task before us. Again, we need to ask: What method of sharing the good news will produce the greatest harvest when we realize that the harvest field is filled with people who are products of a postmodern culture?

Three Basic Forms of Evangelism

When Christians begin to think about sharing their faith in Christ, we often develop sweaty palms and cotton-mouth. Usually we associate evangelism with high-powered sales techniques or with the powerful preaching of a man like Billy Graham. Since most of us are not gifted to follow either of these models, we errantly believe that we simply aren't cut out to be evangelists.

Since most of us are not gifted to follow the stereotyped models of "evangelism," we believe that we simply aren't cut out to be evangelists.

I believe the above misunderstanding comes from a failure to recognize the most effective model for evangelism which the Bible displays for us. It is also a model which proves very sensitive to the needs of postmodern man. Let's examine several models of evangelism and see where we can best fit in. There are three main forms of evangelism utilized today.

Proclamational Evangelism

The first is "proclamational evangelism." This is the formal preaching of the gospel. All of us are appreciative of men who give their lives in learning how to proclaim the gospel message in a formal setting. This is the activity of preaching which the New Testament so often speaks about (Rom. 10:8-15; 1 Cor. 1:23; 2 Tim. 4:2).

As powerful as evangelistic preaching is in the New Testament witness, we need to make two observations: (1) most people are not gifted to be great preachers, and (2) most people today are not brought into a right relationship with Christ (evangelized) only through preaching. Most who read this book were not won to Christ by "spontaneously" attending a revival meeting or evangelistic crusade. Some perhaps, but not many.

This should come as no surprise, considering what we know about our growing postmodern culture. The typical American (especially Generation X) does not believe that truth is conveyed in the rational form provided by most sermons. And since they distrust all authority except the authority of their own experience, many would not attend a preaching service or evangelistic crusade on their own. Most non-Christians I know would rather have a root canal than attend a weekend evangelistic meeting at a local congregation.

This is not to say that proclamational evangelism does not produce fruit. Most of us can think of at least a few people we know who came to Christ the very first time they heard the preaching of the gospel. I can remember a particular Sunday morning in Norfolk, Nebraska, when I was preparing to preach to our late morning worship service. I noticed a young woman and her six-year-old daughter sitting in one of the front pews. They were visiting for the first time. At the time of invitation, she came down the aisle to accept Christ as her Savior. It turned out that she had been into the occult, drugs, the new age movement, and was struggling with her third marriage. She told me that she had come to church that morning simply because her little daughter had been asking her for months if they could go to church. She went on to become a powerful witness for the Lord, leading most of her family to make decisions for Christ. On her silent roll call card that morning she had written the following: "Thank you, thank you, thank you. I've finally found what I've been looking for!"

Proclamational evangelism will produce fruit. In fact, it is an essential part of most people's decision to follow Christ. But it is not the "initial or sole emphasis" in the journey most people make on their way to the cross.

Proclamational evangelism is an essential part of most people's decision to follow Christ, but it is not the first or only stage in the journey to the cross.

Confrontational/Intrusional Evangelism

This is the practice of walking up to a total stranger and initiating a presentation of the gospel which will result in that individual being asked to give his life to Christ. It is practiced by many of the cults (e.g., Mormons and Jehovah's Witnesses) in their door-to-door calling campaigns. Some churches use this approach as well. While this method also bears fruit, most individuals are not won to Christ by a total stranger confronting them.

Joe Aldrich has noted two positive aspects of this type of evangelistic method.[3] First, it is a legitimate form of sharing Christ. Some will accept

Christ as their Lord and Savior through this approach. It also allows more of the body of Christ an opportunity to do evangelism than the "proclamational" approach. More people could see themselves using this approach than those who would seek to "ascend to the pulpit."

However, this approach is extremely limited. It is naive to assume that the majority of people in our current culture will trust Christ as the result of a stranger witnessing to them during a one-time spiritual transaction. Just cornering a stranger, witnessing to him, and pressing for a decision will turn more people "off" instead of "on" to the gospel. A man once asked me why I no longer taught my church people how to do this type of evangelism. My response was simple. I asked, "How do you feel when you respond to a knock at the door and open it to find a Jehovah's Witness standing there with his *Watchtower*, waiting to argue with you? Does that create a positive response in your life?" When he replied, "No," I said, "I don't want the majority of people I meet to have that same first negative impression of the gospel of Christ."

Most individuals are not won to Christ by a total stranger confronting them.

We live in a day and age in which people value and guard their private lives. While one of the traits of postmodernity is fraternalism, we must remember that people will not be ready to open their innermost lives to total strangers. Relationships must be cultivated and established before individuals will feel comfortable talking about their deepest inner needs. This is the heart of the concept of fraternalism. Relationships take time and energy in order for trust and intimacy to occur. This is precisely what our generation is seeking, and it will seldom be found by a stranger invading the privacy of someone's living room.

All of this is so unfortunate, considering the fact that most evangelical Christians identify the concept of "evangelism" with this intrusional/confrontational method. The reason the typical Christian today so seldom takes evangelism seriously is partly due to the fact that they consider themselves unable to take part in this particular evangelistic methodology. Many say to themselves, "I could never just walk up to a total stranger and start talking about anything serious, let alone my faith in Christ." This is a normal feeling in our culture because in relationships, we must begin with the trivial and then move to the true issues of life. Our culture has programmed us to be this way. I don't mind standing in line at the supermarket and having a total stranger ask me about the weather. But I would find it extremely odd and uncomfortable if that stranger immediately wanted to know about my personal financial retirement plan, and pressed me to consider investing in his particular firm. I would probably make some excuse about my ice cream melting and attempt a speedy getaway.

If discussing personal finance with a random stranger makes us feel so awkward, is it any wonder why so many feel awkward in sharing the ultimately more personal issues of our inner need for God? And even if we could start the conversation, many in our relativistic, postmodern culture are not ready to be swayed by the claims of the Bible.

If discussing personal finance with a random stranger makes us feel awkward, is it any wonder why so many feel awkward in sharing the ultimately more personal issues of our inner need for God?

Church growth expert, George Barna, has noted that none of the fastest growing churches in America use the intrusional/confrontational method of evangelism as their main methodology. He writes:

> Falling into the familiar patterns and routines that have worked in the past is a trademark of stagnant churches. Cold-call evangelism is one such pattern that appeals to many such churches.
>
> During the first three-quarters of this century, it was not uncommon for churches to develop evangelistic teams that would get together one or two nights a week and go knocking on people's doors, attempting to share the gospel on people's front door steps, or in their living rooms.
>
> Times have changed, however, and successful churches grow because they have generally understood the change. They may have an evangelism team, but the efforts of that team are directed either to "response evangelism" — visiting those people who request such a visit, or "event evangelism" — providing public interest events that include some type of evangelistic thrust. They know that the chances of meeting a responsive individual who gets a cold call at their front door are minimal. They know that their good-hearted attempt at service may close the person's mind to the gospel. Given the range of other, proven means of affecting change in the person's heart, they simply do not believe that the methodology warrants the high risk of failure.[4]

Again, we must note that this sort of evangelism does bear fruit. I can remember doing door-to-door evangelism in Omaha, Nebraska, when I was a college student. It had been a long morning of rejections ranging from polite to hostile. We decided to try one more block of houses. About halfway down the block, an older lady responded to our knock. When we introduced ourselves and told her the purpose of our visit, her face lit up and she invited us in. As we sat sharing the good news of Jesus, she related the great difficulties in her life. She then told us that last night she had prayed that if God were real that He would send somebody to her. And there we were! It was the only positive response we received in an entire weekend of calling, but for that one precious lady, it was all worthwhile.

Anyone who has done this form of evangelism can relate many such victory stories. However, can we expect the majority of our church people to be trained to do this sort of evangelism? Are there more fruitful methods which would allow for the mobilization of the vast majority of those who follow Christ, who do not feel they have been gifted with the qualities necessary to carry out either proclamational or confrontational evangelism?

Relational/Incarnational Evangelism

This model of evangelism occurs when a Christian (let's call him "Joe Christian") becomes acquainted with, and eventually becomes friends with, a non-Christian (let's call him "Bob Pagan"). Gradually Bob Pagan becomes introduced to many other Christians within Joe Christian's circle of friends. Through the Holy Spirit working in this personal relationship, Bob Pagan becomes open to examining the claims of Christ as he sees them lived out in the life of Joe Christian and his Christian friends. Eventually, Bob Pagan becomes open to examining the claims of Christ found in the Bible. He may become open to attending the church's worship services. Through Bible study and preaching (proclamational evangelism has its place!) Bob Pagan realizes that he needs Jesus as his Savior. Perhaps Joe Christian sees that his friend has reached the point where he needs to make a decision. By this time Joe Christian has earned the right to confront his friend Bob with the fact that he really needs to make a decision for the Lord. Confrontational evangelism comes into play, only with a friend, not a stranger. Bob Pagan weighs the evidence he has seen, both in his buddy Joe and in the Christian Scriptures, and finally yields his life in faith to Christ.

After making friends with Bob Pagan, Joe Christian has earned the right to confront him with his need.

Joe Aldrich notes that the incarnational/relational model of evangelism is one that a majority of Christians can use very effectively for many reasons.[5] First, it does not depend on immense Bible knowledge. The goal is not to win an argument, but rather to win a person. Because of its very nature, this method deals with persons and not strangers. We do not expect our church people to confront strangers argumentatively, but rather to share with friends in a real and living way. Because each Christian will count on utilizing his circle of Christian friends, the effectiveness of this method employs all the spiritual gifts of the church body, not simply those gifted in evangelism.

Because the relational method teaches that evangelism is a process, this frees the Christian from unnecessary (and often unbiblical) pressure and guilt. No longer does the contemporary Christian have to believe that evangelism is only "closing the deal." It is a process. We need to realize what Jesus taught concerning evangelism:

> Even now the reaper draws his wages, even now he harvests the crop for eternal life, so that the sower and the reaper may be glad together. Thus the saying "One sows and another reaps" is true. I sent you to reap what you have not worked for. Others have done the hard work, and you have reaped the benefits of their labor (John 4:36-38).

Paul taught the same thing when he said, "I planted the seed, Apollos watered it, but God made it grow" (1 Cor. 3:6). When people realize that their job in carrying out the Great Commission is helping others move just one step closer to Jesus, guilt is removed and excitement begins.

The relational method also allows us to build a follow-up network before our nonbelieving friend even makes his decision for Christ. Church is not a scary place for the new believer. Instead, the church is a family filled with many who have already become close to the new convert. Growth and a sense of belonging are readily produced because the individual already feels like he belongs.

When I share these three main methods in my evangelism class, I always take a poll. I average 50 students in each class. First, I ask, "How many of you made your initial decision for Christ, *primarily* by attending a preaching service, where you knew almost no one and were there confronted by the living Christ, through the Word, so powerfully, that you yielded your life in faith?" Usually a hand or two go up. Then I ask, "How many of you made your initial decision for Christ, *primarily* because a stranger came to your door or confronted you in a public place with the truth of Christ?" I almost never have anyone raise their hand for that option. Finally I ask, "How many of you made your initial decision for

Christ, *primarily* through the influence of your Christian friends or family? You saw the truth of the gospel lived out in their lives and became convinced of the truth of Christ through study and preaching. You could no longer hold out under the pressure of the Holy Spirit working through each of these avenues and you yielded your life in faith to Christ?" Every time I ask that question, nearly every hand in the class goes up.

Win and Charles Arn observed a survey of over 14,000 Christians nationwide. They were asked, "What or who was responsible for your coming to Christ and your church?" The results of the survey speak for themselves.

Special need	1-2%
Walk-In	2-3%
Pastor	5-6%
Visitation	1-2%
Sunday School	4-5%
Evangelistic Crusade	0.5%
Church Program	2-3%
Friend/Relative	75-90%[6]

It seems clear that in America today 80-90% of all those won to Christ are evangelized through this relational method!

When we show a friend what it means to have true meaning and purpose in life, the nihilistic fatalism of our society will vanish in the glow of Christian purpose.

Relational evangelism is the method which best takes advantage of the traits of postmodernism in American culture. Because of the relativism and deconstructionism in our society, reliance on an absolute authoritative presentation in argument form is not the best place to begin our work in sharing Christ. For most people today "experience" is the criteria which causes them to believe something is valuable. When they see the genuine Christian life "fleshed out" within the Christian "community," it will prove extremely attractive compared to the shallow and empty relationships the postmodern world has to offer. When we make a friend and show them what it means to have true meaning and purpose in life, the nihilistic fatalism of our society will vanish in the glow of Christian purpose. The pluralism of every idea or group having equal validity will be clearly displayed as the lie it truly is. The deep yearning for spirituality created by our searching culture will be met when people are brought into contact with the true and living God who makes "new creations" and incorporates them into "His body," the church.

All of this allows the New Testament theology of evangelism to be employed on a daily basis. If we remember the outline of evangelism in the life of Jesus (see chapter 4), we see that for the Lord evangelism involved demonstration and proclamation. Proclamational and confrontational evangelism do produce some fruit and are both utilized within the framework of relational evangelism. However, we must recognize that most people in postmodern Western culture are won to Christ through the development of personal relationships with other Christians (friends, parents, spouses, and associates).

Acknowledging this, several things become clear. First, we learn that the most important step in beginning relational evangelism is to MAKE FRIENDS WITH NON-CHRISTIANS. When I do seminars on evangelism, I usually begin by asking, "How many of you believe you have the gift of evangelism?" Very few hands go up. Next I ask, "How many of you believe you can become friends with a non-Christian?" Almost every hand goes up. I reply, "Each one of you already has the first absolutely essential quality to begin the process of evangelism." We will never win people to Christ until we get close enough to befriend them.

Secondly, no special training is necessary to begin this process. Some may believe they lack the ability to make friends. I usually respond by pointing out the traits of the inner life and the shared life taught in the New Testament Epistles. If a person is truly becoming like Jesus on the inside and in his relationship to others, he will have no trouble making friends.

Thirdly, this methodology was one of the main ways the early church grew. Indeed, we do have some tremendous examples of proclamational and confrontational evangelism within the Book of Acts. However, these are usually employed by the apostles. The relational method seems to be at the heart of the common member of the new Christian community.

> All the believers were together and had everything in common. Selling their possessions and goods, they gave to anyone as he had need. Every day they continued to meet together in the temple courts. They broke bread in their homes and ate together with glad and sincere hearts, praising God and enjoying the favor of all the people. And the Lord added to their number daily those who were being saved (Acts 2:44-47).

Finally, when taught properly, every Christian recognizes that they can take part in carrying out the Great Commission using this model. Nothing is as motivational as a believer coming to understand their place in the one great work which God has placed us in the world to do. He never commands us to do something for which He has not equipped us. Every Christian can have a part in the process of leading a lost world to Christ.

When we learn to understand our place in that process, the harvest will indeed be plentiful.

Coming to Christ Is a Process

Most Christians mistakenly view evangelism only as the final event of conversion, when an individual decides to follow Jesus. However, that is just the culminating aspect of evangelism. In the Parable of the Soils (Matt. 13:3-23; Mark 4:3-20; Luke 8:5-15), Jesus likens the evangelism process to growing grain. Let's look at Luke's account of this parable:

> A farmer went out to sow his seed. As he was scattering the seed, some fell along the path; it was trampled on, and the birds of the air ate it up. Some fell on rock, and when it came up, the plants withered because they had no moisture. Other seed fell among thorns, which grew up with it and choked the plants. Still other seed fell on good soil. It came up and yielded a crop, a hundred times more than was sown. . . .
>
> This is the meaning of the parable: The seed is the word of God. Those along the path are the ones who hear, and then the devil comes and takes away the word from their hearts, so that they may not believe and be saved. Those on the rock are the ones who receive the word with joy when they hear it, but they have no root. They believe for a while, but in the time of testing they fall away. The seed that fell among thorns stands for those who hear, but as they go on their way they are choked by life's worries, riches and pleasures, and they do not mature. But the seed on good soil stands for those with a noble and good heart, who hear the word, retain it, and by persevering produce a crop (Luke 8:5-8a,11-15).

This is one of only two parables which Jesus directly interprets (the other is the Parable of the Tares in Matt. 13:24-30,36-43). Jesus' own explanation makes several things obvious. The soil is the human heart and the seed is the Word of God. This is where the battle will take place as the Word of God challenges the sinful man for control over life. The mature plant is the life of an individual truly converted to Jesus Christ. The crop is the power of the Word of God reproducing itself in the true convert a hundred times over. Part of this power will be evidenced in righteous living and some of the power will be seen in others being brought to Christ.[7]

This parable shows that evangelism is a process that can be divided into four basic areas. The chart on the next page outlines these areas. I am indebted to Jim Peterson and K.C. Hinkley for their thinking on these four areas of evangelism.[8]

1 CULTIVATION	2 SOWING	3 HARVESTING	4 MULTIPLYING
(the soil)	(the seed)	(the healthy plant)	(the crop)
Speaks to the HEART through RELATIONSHIP	Speaks to the MIND through COMMUNICATION	Speaks to the WILL through CONVERSION	Speaks to the WHOLE MAN through MATURITY
the emphasis is on the PRESENCE OF THE BELIEVER	the emphasis is on the PRESENTATION OF THE GOSPEL MESSAGE	the emphasis is on PERSUASION IN ENCOURAGING A DECISION	the emphasis is on PARTICIPATION IN THE BODY OF CHRIST
Friendship	Bible Study & Preaching	Invitation & Commitment	Active in a Local Congregation

Understanding Your Place in the Evangelism Process

Cultivating Relationships

Evangelism really is a process. Chances are good that you are already involved in the evangelization process in the life of someone outside of Christ, because most of us have several non-Christian friends! Our goal is to understand the process and see what steps we need to take.

THE VERY FIRST STEP IN EVANGELISM is to develop a meaningful FRIENDSHIP with someone outside of Christ. Here we CULTIVATE the EMOTIONAL SIDE of our new friend with an amazing reality. We Christians are simply normal human beings whose lives have truly been changed because of our relationship with Jesus Christ. This will help the non-Christian observe what Christ has done in our life firsthand.

We Christians are simply normal human beings whose lives have truly been changed because of our relationship with Jesus Christ.

This might come as quite a shock to many people. My personal hobby is weight-lifting. I work out at a local gym. I'm not very big, but I can lift my share of the barbells. It came as quite a shock when some of the lifters discovered that I was a Christian minister. Some responded, "We just thought you were one of the guys." That was the biggest compliment I had received in a long time. Now many of them have opened up to me and allowed me to share my faith in practical ways.

Bill Hybels writes about how we can develop the elements of authenticity within our lives. He states that before we can become highly contagious Christians, we must live in a way that convinces the people around us that we have the disease. These elements are indispensable in building a relationship with our non-Christian friends which will convince them that Christianity is a viable option.[9]

The first element, Hybels calls "authentic identity." It takes all kinds of people to make up the Body of Christ. We all have differing gifts. Not everyone can be a Billy Graham or a Paul Cho. But God can use each one of us if we will just open our eyes to the opportunities around us. Billy Graham probably cannot win the guys at my gym to Christ. But I can! God merely expects us to use what He has given us where we are.

Billy Graham probably cannot win the guys at my gym to Christ, but I can.

Next, Hybels talks about developing an "authentic emotional life." This means having an emotional life that is recognizable and to which the typical non-Christian can relate. Some believe that feelings of anger and grief must always be suppressed. But in relational evangelism, this has two negative impacts. First, if we repress feelings too long, we may lose the ability to "feel" altogether and hence deny our true emotions. This is nothing more than dishonesty. Secondly, seekers are generally repelled by emotional inauthenticity. The Christian who simply smiles at every tragedy of life, or who never shows the hint of a struggle with the issues other mere mortals wrestle with, will generally not be able to develop meaningful friendships with non-Christians. Unbelievers will only open up to those they feel are "real."

Next Hybels discusses what he calls "authentic confession." Many of us are taught that we should hide our failures at all costs. This is unfortunately true in many evangelical congregations. It is very difficult to bear one another's burdens while we spend most of our time pretending that we don't have any. People who are investigating Christianity don't expect perfection from Christians. They want to see someone with the courage to confess their blunders and wish to make them right.

It is very difficult to bear one another's burdens while pretending that we don't have any.

Hybels also outlines what he calls "authentic conviction." Seekers are not impressed by spinelessness. Most of the time seekers, whether they will admit it or not, truly respect Christians who live out their convictions with consistency and grace. Seekers have little respect for weak Christians. Deep down they're looking for somebody — anybody — to step up and proclaim the truth and then live it boldly. If they cannot discover this in the local church, then there is something desperately wrong with the Christians in that church.

This first step, cultivating relationships, is a crucial part of evangelism in our postmodern culture. Most people will generally not respond favorably to detailed argument or high pressure techniques. Nor is this what Jesus desires from us. He calls us to win *people*, not arguments. He wishes people to be convinced of the reality of His Lordship, not simply be convinced of the unanswerable nature of our explanations.

Our friendship will be a giant billboard for what the Christian life is all about. Therefore, it is imperative that we have a faithful and meaningful walk with the Lord. No one has PERFECTED their walk with the Lord, but we do need to be PRACTICING our daily walk with Jesus. He will shine through us (Matt. 5:16).

Sowing the Seed

THE SECOND STEP IN EVANGELISM is to learn how to SOW THE SEED OF THE WORD OF GOD into the lives of our non-Christian friends. Remember, that we have been CULTIVATING A FRIENDSHIP with them, preparing the soil of their hearts with the love of Christ which we show in our daily lives. There comes a time, however, when we need to speak the words of God to them. It is here that we address their MINDS with the good news of Jesus. In our next chapter we will learn how to begin to sow God's word into the lives of our new friends. Our ultimate goal is to involve our friends in a meaningful Bible study where they will begin to see Jesus as He reveals Himself in all His beauty within the Scriptures (Luke 24:27).

Harvesting the Grain

THE THIRD STEP IN EVANGELISM is to recognize when our friend is ready to MAKE A DECISION FOR CHRIST. We do not want to rush the harvest. Many people are not REAPABLE after just one or two encounters. However, everyone is REACHABLE if time is taken to cultivate the soil and carefully plant the seed. As a farmer's son, I know that if you attempt to pick the corn in July, you will not only fail to receive a harvest today, but you will also spoil the chances of any harvest. If you try to bring in a crop before it is ripe, you run the risk of ruining the harvest.

If you try to bring in a crop before it is ripe, you run the risk of ruining the harvest.

However, if we have developed a true relationship with our non-Christian friend, and if we have come to the point of sharing the gospel message with them through Bible study and our own personal witness, then we will become sensitive enough to recognize when we need to help our friend realize he needs to make a decision for Christ. In this harvesting stage our goal is to address the WILL, to help our new friend understand (based on his new knowledge of God obtained in Bible study) that a decision needs to be made. It is here that we need to know a basic method of presenting the simple gospel message. Chapter 10 will address this area. The ultimate goal of this step is to see our friend decide to accept Jesus as his Lord and Savior. I am so glad that at the right time in my life, someone urged me to consider making a decision for Christ (Rom. 15:17-19).

Multiplication — A Hundredfold Crop

THE FOURTH STEP IN EVANGELISM is the process of MULTIPLICATION. In this step, we need to help our newly converted friend become an active part of the local church family. Here they will grow in Christian maturity and also be taught to reach out to their own non-Christian friends. In doing so the evangelism process will begin all over again. Only they will usually be able to move along faster in the process. They do not have to begin from scratch and build relationships with non-Christians. Most of their friends will be non-Christian. When, these friends begin to notice the change which Jesus has made in their lives, the new convert can begin to sow the Word of God gently, as he grows in his Christian maturity. It is not unusual for the best evangelists in the church to be newly converted Christians (Acts 2:44-47).

Contagious Christianity

Bill Hybels has written his view of relational evangelism in the book *Becoming a Contagious Christian*. It parallels what we have presented in our understanding of the Parable of the Soils. Hybels's concept of Evangelism can be boiled down into the following equation:

$$HP + CP + CC = MI^{10}$$

In the above equation "HP": stands for High Potency. This is genuine, dynamic Christianity. Every Christian needs to model a close walk with the Lord God. Jesus set the ultimate example for us. It's impossible to ignore a life invaded by the power of God.

"CP" stands for Close Proximity. This is placing ourselves meaningfully in the lives of those without Christ. Again, Jesus set the ultimate example. One time Jesus' disciples were asked, "Why does your master eat with . . . sinners?" (Matt. 9:11). The obvious answers could have been, "Because He doesn't like to eat alone!" Jesus became known as the friend of prostitutes and tax collectors for one single reason — He *was* the friend of prostitutes and tax collectors! (Matt. 11:19).

"CC" stands for Clear Communication. This is telling the message with word and deed so clearly that a decision is called for. Jesus had a way with this! When confronting the crowd, he sought to help them understand that they were hungry for more than bread (John 6). With the woman at the well, he wanted her to realize that she was thirsty for more than water (John 4). Jesus always found a way to deliver the message of God in a way that was relevant to the individual He was addressing.

Jesus always found a way to deliver the message in a way that was relevant to the individual.

"MI" stands for Maximum Impact. This is using our full potential at the disposal of the Holy Spirit to impact as many lives for Christ as possible. Jesus did this in his own ministry through the training of the Twelve.

Making Mini-decisions for Christ

The old question asks, "How do you climb a tall mountain?" The answer is, "One step at a time."

Why then do we so often believe that when it comes to evangelism, we must transform ourselves into spiritual supermen and bridge the gap between the unbeliever and Christ in a single bound? Evangelism is a process. We can boil the process down into the four major components of cultivation, sowing, harvest and multiplication, and each of these can be broken down into a series of smaller "mini-decisions."

Jim Peterson was one of the first to summarize this concept in his book *Living Proof*.[11] He writes:

> Usually what people are looking for is a one-step launch question — something that will carry them gracefully from a dead stop into an effective discussion about Christ in a single motion. In situations where God has already prepared the way, it's hard to go wrong at this point. Almost anything you say will do. Philip simply asked the Ethiopian man if he understood what he was reading. Peter asked Cornelius why he had sent for him. But most of the people we meet are neither reading the book of Isaiah nor have they had any recent visions. . . . Rather than looking for a single step, it is better to think in terms of mini-decisions. If evangelism is a process, then our function is to accompany our acquaintances on the road to Christ, showing them the way. We must walk the road with them, a step at a time. So we think in terms of steps, or mini-decisions.[12]

K.C. Hinckley has expanded on Peterson's work by giving a working model of the mini-decisions most people need to make in their journey to Christ.[13] We can divide these mini-decisions between the first three main steps of the evangelism process.

In *the cultivation stage*, where we primarily address our new friend's emotions, there are four mini-decisions that the unbeliever will make. If we assume that he is outside of Christ and without any Christian influence in his life, the mini-decisions are as follows:

(1) *Coming into contact with a genuine Christian:* This may be as simple as meeting a new neighbor or a new coworker.

(2) *Developing a positive attitude toward the Christian:* Through interacting in a social setting, the non-Christian recognizes you to be a nice person. Any Christian who displays the fruit of the Spirit (Gal. 5:22-25) will generally be well received by those outside of Christ.

(3) *Becoming aware that the Christian is different:* This is not a "weird" sort of difference. But when the truth of Christ's life is lived out on a daily basis, the non-Christian cannot help but notice that there is just something different about us. He probably will not understand what makes us different, but it is a difference he will not be able to deny. This will intrigue him.

(4) *Becoming aware of the Bible's relevance for life:* As the relationship grows, we will naturally discuss how following the teachings of Jesus, recorded in the Bible, has made a dramatic impact in our life. This will usually come as a true revelation to the unbeliever. He might not be ready to accept the Bible, but he will not be able to deny that it has indeed made a positive difference in our day-to-day routine.

When the truth of Christ's life is lived out on a daily basis, the non-Christian cannot help but notice.

In *the sowing stage,* the emphasis begins to shift from establishing ourselves as a presence in the life of the unbeliever to seeking ways to present the good news of Jesus to them. We will discuss this stage of the process more completely in chapter 9. The following mini-decisions are generally made in this stage of the evangelism process:

(1) *Developing a positive attitude toward the Bible:* As we learn to share our faith with our new friend, he will examine our life to see if it is genuine. When he is satisfied that we are genuine and are truly concerned about him as an individual, he will begin to develop a positive attitude toward the Bible. He will want to study it to see what it says.

(2) *Becoming aware of the basics of the gospel:* Our friend may begin looking at the Bible to help him discover how to approach some practical aspect of his life, like raising his children or interacting with his spouse. Our goal will be to get him involved in a Bible study which will begin to point out the person and work of Jesus. Our goal will be to help our friend see who Jesus is and what He has done for them.

(3) *Understanding the meaning and implications of the gospel:* Jesus said that if He were lifted up, He would draw all men to Himself (John 12:32). When we study the story of Jesus in the Bible, through the power of the Holy Spirit Jesus will make Himself known to our unbelieving friend, and he will begin to realize the true love of God for him displayed in the cross.

(4) *Having a positive attitude toward the gospel:* Once Christ begins to work in the life of our non-Christian friend, he will begin to recognize that all the teachings of the Bible about Christ are "good news indeed." He will begin to understand that this is the greatest message he has ever heard.

The final stage of the evangelism process leading up to conversion is *the harvesting stage.* Here, our non-Christian friend will go through a series of mini-decisions that will center around his "will." His emotions have been addressed through our unreserved love and acceptance of him as a friend. His intellect has been satisfied as he has worked through the message of Christ found in Scripture. The time has come for him to make a decision. We will deal with addressing the will as we learn to share simple gospel presentations in chapter 10. The mini-decisions for this final stage of the evangelism process can be summarized as follows:

(1) *Recognizing personal need:* By now the Holy Spirit will be doing His mighty work in the life of our friend. Christ will be tugging at his heart as he realizes that he is going to have to decide whether or not he will follow Christ.

(2) *Deciding to act:* Finally, our friend will make his decision. If it is a positive decision, he will yield up his will to Christ. He will say in his heart, "I will obey Christ." It will be extremely helpful if we are available to guide our friend into how he is to display his faith and trust in Christ. The use of a simple gospel presentation and our own personal testimony are invaluable at this point.

(3) *Accepting Christ by faith:* The decision of the will is accompanied by a response to the gospel by faith, and our friend will display his faith and trust in Christ as outlined in the Scriptures (see chapter 11).

(4) *Becoming a new creation in Christ:* God is faithful to reward the faith of those who turn to Him through Christ. Our friend will now become a coworker with us, as together, we follow Jesus.

Our job in the evangelism process is to discover where people are in their journey toward Christ. Some of the people in our lives are only in the earliest stages of the cultivation process. They do not need us to share a full-blown gospel presentation. They need us to become their friend, showing them the authentic love of Christ as we develop a meaningful relationship with them. Others need to have the Word of God sown into their lives. We may have been friends with them for quite some time. We need to be open for the Lord to use us in planting God's Word into their hearts. Some of the people we know may be ready for the harvesting stage. We have become their friend and they have been studying the Bible with us. What they really need is a simple gospel presentation and for us to be brave enough and concerned enough to ask them, "Is there anything keeping you from accepting the love of God through Jesus Christ?"

Evangelism is a process. Our task is to be sensitive to the lives we touch each day and to determine where each person is in their journey toward Christ. Once we determine this, we will know the proper tools to use to help move them "one step closer to Christ." When this begins to happen, every day can become an exciting adventure as we see ourselves tools in God's hands. It's time to bring in the harvest.

Evangelism is a process.

Taking Our First Steps into the Harvest Field

Many churches in America today are like farms run by crazy people. We build vast and huge barns to house the stockpile of planting seed. In those huge barns we also house the harvesting equipment. We hire the best trained farmers money can buy to help us understand every minute detail about the seed. We seek to know its germination period, its yield and a thousand other technical horticultural questions. We also spend long hours fixing the corn pickers to ensure that they are in top-notch working order. In fact, life in the barn is so interesting and wonderful, that most of us never want to leave it. We spend all of our time studying the seed and oiling the machines! BUT THE HARVEST IS NOT IN THE BARNS! IT IS OUT IN THE HARVEST FIELDS! It's time to take the seed and the equipment out of the barns and get them out into the harvest fields where they belong.

Life in the barn is so interesting and wonderful, that most of us never want to leave it.

Whether we use the model of the Parable of the Soils, or Hybels's formula, the main issue seems clear: Evangelism is a process! And the very first step is for each one of us to begin to develop meaningful relationships with those who are outside of Christ.

When we do this, it is imperative that we do not approach unbelievers as if they were simply "evangelism projects." People can usually tell if they are meant to be a notch on somebody's evangelism pistol. Remember how warmly you usually react to all those telephone solicitors! We must seek out real, meaningful relationships. Why? Because as followers of Christ, we will always be compelled to share the gospel with those to whom we are closest. And non-Christians will be compelled to listen to the gospel when lovingly guided by one of their best and nearest friends.

Remember Jesus' words: "Ask the Lord of the harvest, therefore, to send out workers into his harvest field" (Matt. 9:38). Building relationships with those outside of Christ is how we take our first steps out into the harvest field.

> Evangelism for us isn't relegated to a time slot, nor to one or two types of activities. In short, evangelism is practiced as a way of life. It's not surprising, then, that barriers come down, and that people hear and believe the good news of the gospel. As Jesus said, "By this shall all men know that ye are my disciples, if ye have love one to another" (John 13:35, KJV).
>
> Myron Augsburger[14]

---

1. Rick Warren, *The Purpose Driven Church* (Grand Rapids: Zondervan, 1995), p. 64.

2. Ibid., p. 65.

3. Joe Aldrich, *Life-Style Evangelism* (Portland: Multnomah Press, 1981), p. 79.

4. George Barna, *User-Friendly Churches* (Ventura, CA: Regal Books, 1991), p. 180.

5. Aldrich, *Life-Style Evangelism*, pp. 84-85.

6. Win Arn and Charles Arn, *The Master's Plan for Making Disciples* (Monrovia, CA: Church Growth Press, 1991), p. 44.

7. Fruitfulness is a major theme of the New Testament. We are called by Christ to bear fruit (John 15:16). Being fruitful is the way we glorify God (John 15:8). Being fruitful pleases God (Col. 1:10). Jesus reserves his severest judgment for the unfruitful tree (Matt. 21:19). The nation of Israel lost its privilege because of unfruitfulness (Matt. 21:43). The word "fruit" (or its variations) is used 55 times in the New Testament. Fruit may be: repentance (Matt. 3:8), practicing the truth (Matt. 7:16-21), answered prayer (John 15:7-8), an offering of money given by believers to Christ (Rom. 15:28), and winning unbelievers to Christ (Rom. 1:13). In considering the Great Commission, the definition of fruitfulness for a local church must include growth by conversion of unbelievers. Paul referred to the first converts in Achaia as the "first fruits of Achaia" (1 Cor. 16:15). Paul connected bearing fruit with church growth (Col. 1:6). See Warren, *The Purpose-Driven Church*, p. 63.

8. The basic structure of this chart is an application of the material found in K.C. Hinckley, *Living Proof: A Small Group Discussion Guide* (Colorado Springs: NavPress, 1993), pp. 24-31.

9. Bill Hybels, *Becoming a Contagious Christian* (Grand Rapids: Zondervan, 1994), pp. 53-65.

10. Hybels, *Contagious Christian*, pp. 39-50.

11. Jim Peterson, *Living Proof* (Colorado Springs: NavPress, 1992), pp. 147-152.

12. Ibid., p. 150.

13. Hinckley, *Living Proof*, pp. 25-27.

14. Calvin Ratz, Frank Tillapaugh, and Myron Augsburger, *Mastering Outreach and Evangelism* (Portland: Multnomah Press, 1990), p. 24.

Chapter 9
DEVELOPING STRATEGIES FOR SOWING THE WORD

The Scriptures declare that God himself is the chief evangelist. For the Spirit of God is the Spirit of truth, love, holiness, and power, and evangelism is impossible without him. It is he who anoints the messenger, confirms the Word, prepares the hearer, convicts the sinful, enlightens the blind, gives life to the dead, enables us to repent and believe, unites us to the body of Christ, assures us that we are God's children, leads us into Christlike character and service, and sends us out in our turn to be Christ's witnesses. In all this the Holy Spirit's main preoccupation is to glorify Jesus Christ by showing him to us and forming him in us . . . .

Our first responsibility is to witness to those who are already our friends, relatives, neighbors, and colleagues. Home evangelism is also natural, both for married and for single people. Not only should a Christian home commend God's standards of marriage, sex, family, and provide a haven of love and peace to people who are hurting, but neighbors who would not enter a church usually feel comfortable in a home, even when the gospel is discussed.

The Manila Manifesto[1]

And beginning with Moses and all the Prophets, he explained to them what was said in all the Scriptures concerning himself. . . . Then he opened their minds so they could understand the Scriptures.

Luke 24:27,45

In thinking about sharing Christ with a non-Christian friend, I am reminded of the story a rural preacher. It seems that a snowstorm had descended on the farming community one Saturday evening, and when the preacher arrived at the church house on Sunday morning, only one member of his congregation had braved the weather to attend services — one old farmer. When the preacher asked if the farmer wanted him to go ahead with the Sunday service, the old farmer replied, "If I only have one cow come up to the feed lot at night, I still feed her."

Encouraged, the preacher proceeded with the service, and delivered a stirring forty-five minute sermon. At the conclusion, he went to the back of the sanctuary and was greeted by the old farmer who had sat patiently through the entire proceedings.

"You know," said the farmer, "I know I said that if only one cow came up to the feed lot that I would feed her, but I wouldn't give her the whole load of feed!"

In learning how to share our faith with a new friend, we may want to avoid giving them "the whole load" the very first time we mention our relationship with Christ. It may be overwhelming to them. We want to learn to share our faith in such a way that we will create in their lives a growing spiritual hunger. As time goes by, we will be able to share more and more until they are ready to be confronted with a gospel presentation (which we will discuss in chapter 10).

The Evangelism Process

We would do well to remember that evangelism is a process that generally proceeds through three stages leading up to a decision to trust Christ as Lord and Savior.

> **STAGE 1 — THE CULTIVATION STAGE** in which we address the *emotions* by building a relationship with a non-Christian.

> **STAGE 2 — THE SOWING STAGE** in which we address the *mind* by sharing the Word of God with our new friend.

> **STAGE 3 — THE HARVESTING STAGE** in which we address the *will* in seeking a decision from our friend to accept Christ.

The Cultivation Stage

While in the cultivation stage of the evangelism process, our new friend probably isn't ready to hear an entire gospel presentation. However, they need to hear how Christ is real to us, so that our faith and trust in Jesus will create a spiritual hunger in their lives as they desire more and more knowledge of God's love. Therefore we are going to suggest a four-fold strategy which will help us to sow the word of God in our new friend's life in a way that it will foster their trust and develop their spiritual hunger. These sowing strategies are developed by Jim Peterson and K.C. Hinkley in the *Living Proof* book and video series.[2] I have found them extremely helpful in teaching Christians the nature of "sowing the seed of the Word" in the lives of their non-Christian friends. As we consider sharing the Word of God in the life of our non-Christian friend, we need to become familiar with the following four sowing strategies: (1) Learning to Raise Our Flag, (2) Utilizing Faith Stories, (3) The Necessity of Bible Study, and (4) The Importance of Sharing Our Personal Testimony.

Let's examine each of these sowing strategies and see where they fit into the evangelism process.

Learning to Raise Our Flag

When I was a youth, we learned a little song in Bible School entitled, "Joy Is the Flag Flown High from the Castle of My Heart." As our personal witness for Christ moves from our loving actions toward loving proclamation of the message of Jesus, we need to find a way to identify ourselves as followers of Jesus in a nonthreatening manner. In ancient times travelers approaching a castle would know if the people were friendly or not by the flag which was flying above the castle walls. While still a long way off, the flag let the traveler know who was lord of the castle.

Early in the cultivation stage of developing our new friendship with a non-Christian, we need to learn how to **raise our flag** — to identify ourselves as followers of Jesus Christ in a way that will create an interest in what we possess through Christ.

There are several principles we need to learn about raising our flag.[3] First, raising the flag should happen as a natural part of a conversation. Remember that our postmodern friend initially judges truth by the feeling that it creates. Anything that appears to be contrived or rehearsed will appear inauthentic and phony to our friend. This could give the negative impression that we are insincere and hence destroy the effectiveness of this early sowing method.

Raising the flag should happen as a natural part of a conversation.

Second, raising the flag should highlight a positive aspect of our faith. It should be a statement that shows something that a Christian does which makes a positive influence on his life. For instance, if our friend is sharing with us how their boss at work is driving them crazy, we might respond by showing concern and then saying, "Tomorrow morning, during my devotional time, I'll pray that God will help you deal with your boss and that the situation will improve." At this early stage in our relationship, we don't need to say any more than this and we don't need to go into a long explanation of our morning devotion routine. We just want to identify ourselves as followers of God by describing in a positive manner, something that Christians do. We just "pitch it out there" for our friend to hear.

At all costs we should avoid raising our flag in a negative or argumentative manner. If, for instance, our new friend should offer us an alcoholic beverage in their home (and we have concluded that, for us, drinking alcohol is wrong), a negative response might be, "Are you kidding!? There's no way I'm going to put that stuff in my body. The body is the temple of the Holy Spirit and there are some things you don't put in the temple!" That might get our point across and identify us as a Christian, but it will do little to create in our "former" friend an interest in the life that Jesus has to offer. The negative approach should be avoided for a number of reasons. It reinforces a gloomy cultural stereotype of Christianity. Most non-Christians already think that the Christian faith is a giant set of rules that limit or destroy our ability to have fun. We don't need to do anything that reinforces this stereotype. We also want to avoid such a response because it is bad witnessing theology. Christianity is not a list of dos and don'ts. Rather, it is a *personal* relationship with Jesus Christ. The Apostle Paul wrote,

> Since you died with Christ to the basic principles of this world, why, as though you still belonged to it, do you submit to its rules: "Do not handle! Do not taste! Do not touch!"? These are all destined to perish with use, because they are based on human commands and teachings. Such regulations indeed have an appearance of wisdom, with their self-imposed worship, their false humility and their harsh treatment of the body, but they lack any value in restraining sensual indulgence (Col. 2:20-23).

It is true that because of our relationship to Christ, we will choose to avoid certain activities. However, we want to be recognized not by the things that we avoid, but by the things we embrace!

At all costs we should avoid raising our flag in a negative or argumentative manner.

Third, when we raise the flag, it may create an opportunity for us to immediately launch into our personal testimony and ask our friend for a decision about Christ. At this early stage in building our friendship, we should usually avoid "giving them the whole load" unless they clearly ask us to do so. Too much information before a friendship reaches a certain depth can short-circuit the whole process.

I remember going to a banquet with my wife. We sat across the table from a nice older woman who immediately struck up a conversation with us. At first, we thought it was nice that she would share her life with us. However, the polite conversation turned into an avalanche of her whole life story. It went on and on. Soon my wife and I were both wishing we could crawl under the table to escape.

Too much information before a friendship reaches a certain depth can short-circuit the whole process.

Early in a friendship we do not want to bury our friend with more information than they are ready to process. When we first begin to raise the flag, we should avoid the temptation of saying too much. If it takes more than thirty seconds, we're probably giving them more than they are ready to handle. Remember, the purpose of raising the flag is simply to begin to whet our friend's spiritual appetite. The time will come when they will be ready for more.

Finally, we need to remember that raising the flag is simply meant to establish our identity as a member of God's family. Early in the cultivation stage, we are not trying to share a gospel presentation or even specific information about Jesus. We are simply declaring ourselves to be a follower of Jesus Christ in a simple, nonthreatening and positive manner.

As our relationship begins to develop with our non-Christian friend, we need to use these simple "flag raising" statements to help them see that our life is different because of our relationship to Jesus. Statements like: "I will keep you in my prayers this week," or "I don't know how I would have gotten through this difficult time without God's help," or "What I read in the Bible this morning really helped me through the day"; anything like this will help our new friend see the reality of our personal walk with Christ.

If we live a consistent Christian life, and our new friend begins to realize that we really do care for them, a spiritual hunger will begin to grow in their lives as we continually raise our flag.

Utilizing Faith Stories

Near the end of the cultivation stage of the evangelism process, our friendship should be on solid ground. Our new friend will be ready to hear more from us than merely "flag raising statements." It's time to utilize a "faith story." The faith story is an actual time when a biblical truth really made a difference in our lives. This is more than merely a "flag raising" statement, but less than "the whole load." It is explaining how a biblical principle made a positive influence in our daily life. There are several principles to remember when developing a faith story.

The faith story is more than merely a flag raising statement, but less than the whole load.

First, we try to think of a real time in our life when a biblical truth made an impact on us. It might be as recently as today in our daily devotional time, or maybe we made a decision years ago, based upon biblical teaching, that led to success in our business life or in the life of our family. Remember, our generation judges truth by experience, and they primarily want to know if "Christianity works." If we experience Christ daily and let that be known in positive practical ways, we will become walking billboards pointing our friends to Christ.

Second, we need to remember that we are not writing our personal testimony of the time when we came to Christ as Savior. Our friend probably isn't close enough to understanding the gospel for that to be very intelligible to him. Rather a faith story needs to be a time when we realized that we needed to change our actions or our thinking based on God's message in Scripture. The purpose of our story is to demonstrate to our friend that the message of the Bible is relevant to everyday life!

Each semester, I ask students in my personal evangelism class to write out such a faith story. Many find it difficult and want to launch into how they came to accept Christ. We need to remember that at this stage of the cultivation process, our friend probably isn't yet interested in "accepting Christ." He may not even understand what that means. What he does need to see is that our relationship to Christ has made a difference in the "real world" that he must function in each day. When he recognizes that the Christian faith actually "works" at the job or at home, he will be intrigued and want to look into these things more closely.

Lee Strobel's conversion story closely follows this model.[4] He was a successful journalist and the legal affairs editor of *The Chicago Tribune*. His wife Leslie became acquainted with a Christian who attended the dynamic Willow Creek Church in Chicago. Ultimately, Leslie gave her life to Jesus Christ. Strobel wrote that he was outwardly supportive but inwardly skeptical. Yet, there was something about her life that had changed. In pondering this change, Strobel writes,

> . . . over the next couple of months, I started to sense subtle changes in Leslie's character as the Holy Spirit began to change her. I'm not saying that she turned into Mother Teresa overnight, but there was a definite blossoming of her personality.
>
> I detected it in the way she related to the children. I saw it in

her more loving demeanor toward men and others. I watched her develop more self-confidence and patience.[5]

It was this living faith story which helped launch Strobel upon his journey toward Christ. When our faith makes a difference in our daily routine, it provides irrefutable evidence that Jesus does indeed have something to offer. A faith story helps make this real in the life of our friend, who may not have a chance to see us as closely as a husband would watch his wife.

Third, the faith story should only take a minute or two to tell. Don't preach a sermon. Just share in a concise manner what God has done for you when you followed His teaching. The faith story should be open ended. In other words, it should not call for a decision, but rather leave room for more information in the future. Its purpose is to bear witness to the power of Christ and to increase the spiritual hunger in the life of our friend. Tell it in a way that will make him want to hear more.

I remember sharing a faith story in the locker room of the gym where I work out. One of the fellows I lift weights with was getting dressed and sharing with me the anxiety he felt in trying to raise two rambunctious boys as a single father. I had the opportunity to relate some of the struggles my wife and I faced in raising our oldest daughter while she was going through a particularly rebellious stage. My daughter eventually made a dramatic recommitment of her life to Christ and has married a young man studying for the ministry. She has become a powerful witness for Christ. I shared with my friend that during the struggle my wife and I had to rely on God's power through prayer. We learned to center our energies into transforming ourselves into better parents rather than simply attempting to change our daughter's behavior. At the end of sharing my experience, I said, "Most of what we learned came right out of the Bible. Sometime, if you are interested, I could share it with you." This faith story related a real life situation and how biblical principles helped us to see positive results. It did not ask my friend to make any type of outward commitment, but it left the door open for him to respond.

Finally, when it comes to sharing a "faith story," many people find it hard to think of something God has done or taught them. But planning a faith story is a great chance to remember that God really is at work within our lives, even if we are just a beginner in the faith. I challenge my evangelism students to prepare to share two or three faith stories. In fact, I make them a guarantee. I say, "If you will prepare to share two or three different faith stories, if you will write them out or even practice them on a Christian friend so that you can communicate them in a clear and sincere manner, I guarantee that in the next three weeks, while you are talking with a non-Christian friend, the PERFECT time will arise in the conversation for you to tell that story. In fact, the situation will be so right for you to share your story that you will have to directly disobey the Holy Spirit's prompting within your life if you fail to share that story." I offer ten dollars to anyone who does not find this to be the case. I've never had a student come close to collecting the money.

When we prepare to bear testimony concerning the work of Christ within our lives, God will always open the door to allow such testimony in the normal affairs of life. This is the work of the Holy Spirit in our lives. Jesus said, "When the Counselor comes, whom I will send to you from the Father, the Spirit of truth who goes out from the Father, he will testify about me" (John 15:26). God will not open the opportunity to share about Christ's power if we have not prepared to do so. But if we are prepared, God will begin to open such doorways on an ever increasing basis. My guarantee to my students really isn't mine at all. It is God's.

God will not open the opportunity to share about Christ's power if we have not prepared to do so.

A faith story might be something like this. Picture yourself talking to your new friend about raising children. You begin to talk about how important consistency is in your life as a parent to instill values in the life of your children. You recognize that you and your spouse are by no means perfect at parenting, but the lessons you have learned from the Bible have proven invaluable in helping to guide your children (Eph. 6:1-4). Then you leave the conversation open by concluding, ". . . and sometime, if you are interested, I could share some of these things from the Bible." Make sure such stories are "real," and that you can turn immediately in your Bible to the passages of Scripture to which you have referred.

The Sowing Stage

As we grow in our relationship with our new friend and begin to create a hunger in his/her life for spiritual things by continually raising our flag and utilizing faith stories, there will come a time when our friend will be very open to being invited to a Bible study.

The Necessity of Bible Study

Nothing can take the place of sharing the Word of God with someone who needs Jesus. Early in the cultivation stage of evangelism, many non-Christians will not be open to becoming involved in an organized Bible study. However, after we have developed a true caring friendship, in which we have raised our flag and told faith stories, a spiritual hunger will begin growing in our friend's heart. If we live out our faith in a consistent and loving manner, our new friend will usually respond favorably to being invited to a Bible study. Once he becomes open to being involved in a Bible study, he enters the "Sowing Stage" of evangelism.

A Bible study can be on Sunday morning at the Bible school hour, or at a home group meeting, or even in a private one-on-one study between us and our friend. Remember that the more Christians we can introduce to our new friend, the more resources the Holy Spirit will have at His disposal in exerting His influence.

Many people today struggle with the problem of loneliness. They feel isolated or cut off from deep relationships with other people. Our postmodern culture has witnessed a breakdown in the networks of "natural" community which give its members a sense of identity and of personal worth and dignity. Getting our friend involved in studying the Bible with others is a tremendous tool in preparing the soil of his heart to respond to the message of the gospel. A small group setting with others is the perfect place for this to happen.

Small groups expert, Roberta Hestenes, has observed that while people remember approximately 10% of what they hear, they remember up to 90% of what they say. Therefore, to increase the amount of learning that occurs, we need to increase the amount of talking about the Bible which each member does during a Bible study. A group discussion provides more opportunity to examine the biblical material, which increases the likelihood of our friend remembering what is being examined.[6] Hestenes writes,

> Another significant benefit of using the Bible in groups is the possibility of increasing personal application of the biblical material. It can be relatively easy in much of our society to ignore the necessity of considering the relationship of biblical truth to our own lives. In a group setting where people look at the Scriptures together, it often happens almost automatically that members discuss whether the passage is relevant today and how they can apply it to their own lives. Although groups can function at a fairly high level of abstraction, usually the group setting encourages a more concrete discussion with the possibility of personal and group response to the passage being discussed. People are often helped to see how the biblical material can be related to their own lives as they hear other group members sharing how they have applied this material to themselves as appropriate circumstances have arisen. This helps members to be "doers of the word, and not hearers only" (Jas. 1:22, RSV).[7]

There are a number of other positive aspects about leading your friend into studying the Bible in a small group. Small groups often provide the affirmation of unconditional love that can be modeled in a recognizable form. The truth of Scripture can be experienced through the interpersonal dynamics of the group, as well as be understood by the mind. Small groups also offer the advantage of availability. As the leader of the group, when we convey that our time, energy, insight, possessions are at our friends' disposal, we again allow them to see doctrine "fleshed out" in a way that they can feel.

Small groups also allow for openness. Remember that most formal church settings do not allow the unchurched to ask honest questions about our faith. But in the open interaction of a small group of friends, where questions are welcomed, appreciated, and taken seriously, true learning takes place. Honesty and sensitivity are also absolutely essential in a small group study. We attempt to be honest with the content of Scripture and sensitive to each other's feelings. If this means risking pain for either of us, we will trust our relationship enough to take that risk, realizing it is in speaking the truth in a spirit of love that we grow up in every way into Christ who is the head (Eph. 4:15).

A small group of friends also allows for confidentiality and accountability. We begin to trust each other with some of the deeper issues of life. When confronted with Jesus within the Word, we begin to move past the more surface elements of friendship down into the nitty-gritty of what life is all about. And when Jesus makes a certain claim upon our lives in the study of Scripture, we need to be open enough to ask each other if we are ready to take that claim seriously.

A small group of friends allows for confidentiality and accountability.

All of these aspects will begin to meet the need of fraternalism in the lives of our postmodern friends. Within a small group Bible study, God will be able to bring into play three powerful tools in His conversion arsenal: (1) our own personal witness and the witness of our Christian friends in the group, (2) the witness of the Word of God, and (3) the Holy Spirit's own divine power as He works through our lives and Scripture within the heart of our friend. In all of this, our friend will begin to experience the true family nature of the Christian community. Our postmodern culture has created this vacuum within his life, and studying the Bible in such a setting will allow for that emptiness to begin to be filled.

Principles for Leading an Evangelistic Bible Study

There are several principles to remember in leading an evangelistic Bible study. First, we need to remember our primary purpose. The Bible study should center on Jesus' character and personality, Jesus' message, Jesus' mission, and Jesus' identity. The purpose of the Bible study is to bring our friend face-to-face with Jesus.

I recently read of an individual who listened to hundreds of taped sermons and held discussions with scores of Christians.[8] He concluded that the most common complaint about Sunday morning sermons is that they contain "too many ideas." These people did not want shorter messages. Their complaint was that sermons contained too many separate ideas that were not related to one uniting idea. In sermons, we preachers call this, "the big idea." The same thing is true of many Bible studies. When I finally succeed in involving my unchurched friend in a Bible study, I don't want to look at eschatological theories or predictive prophecy. I don't even want them to center on the ethical demands on the life of a disciple. I want them to come face to face with Jesus.

The most common complaint about Sunday morning sermons is that they contain "too many ideas."

Bob and Betty Jacks have written,

The purpose of the home study group is to present Jesus Christ. You don't talk about denominations, controversial issues or your church. You don't use lofty words or brilliant ideas. You talk about Jesus.

And how do you do this? Just as well as you know how. You don't have to possess all knowledge or have all the skills in the world. No one is that gifted by God. All you can do is your best with the gifts God has given you. Yet, along with God's delegation of the task is Christ's mighty energy available to work within you![9]

Because of this, it is best to study one of the four Gospels. Your non-Christian friend needs to be brought face-to-face with Jesus Christ. This occurs best when we look directly at His life in one of the Gospels. Each Gospel has its own unique qualities. I particularly like the Gospel of John. It declares itself to have an evangelistic purpose. John writes, "But these are written that you may believe that Jesus is the Christ, the Son of God, and that by believing you may have life in his name" (John 20:31).

Second, it is always best to have everyone involved in an evangelistic Bible study to use the same translation of the Bible. This will help us avoid having to spend a considerable amount of time explaining why we have so many translations. If Bibles with the same pagination are available, this is even better.

Third, recognize that the best method of study is to simply read the Scripture together and ask for basic insights about the message of Jesus. We can use the "Socratic Method" of asking questions as our chief tool for opening up the Scriptures. We will share more about this method in the next section of this chapter. However, as a maturing believer, be prepared to only scratch the surface in an evangelistic Bible study. You will probably see much more in the Scripture than your non-Christian friend will be capable of seeing. This type of Bible study is not the place for technical biblical scholarship. We want to see the forest, not examine every tree.

We want our friend to see the big picture. It is possible to examine the Bible and still miss Jesus. This was exactly Jesus' complaint against the religious rulers of His day. He said, "You diligently study the Scriptures because you think that by them you possess eternal life. These are the Scriptures that testify about me, yet you refuse to come to me to have life" (John 5:39-40).

Jettison the jargon!

The fourth principle we need to remember can best be stated with the phrase: Jettison the jargon![10] We need to be ready to talk about the reality of the Christian life in nontechnical terms which might be unfamiliar to our friend. Instead of saying, "Today we will look at the vicarious, substitutionary atonement," perhaps it would be better to simply say, "Let's look and see what Jesus did for us on the cross."

The fifth principle involves being sensitive about the length of the study session. In our current culture, sessions should be no longer than 45 minutes (an hour tops). Plenty of time should be left after the session for fellowship and bonding. Remember, the bonding that takes place through building relationships will be used by the Holy Spirit to help bear testimony to the truthfulness of the text of Scripture as the non-Christian sees the text come alive in the life of the Christian community.

In addition to these basic principles, there are several do's and don'ts involved in preparing for such a study in your home.

The Do's
+ Do make everyone comfortable and make the proper introductions.
+ Do start each session with polite conversations (about sports, jobs, or the weather).
+ Do provide baby-sitting in another part of your home if possible, or at a neighbor's home.
+ Do take the phone off the hook during the lesson time (or have the ringer turned off and the answering machine turned on).
+ Do be sensitive to the folks who are shy. Look for nonthreatening ways to include them in the conversation.
+ Do provide refreshments and plenty of fellowship time for the people after the lesson.
+ Do prepare to love people. The only truly important things for them to learn is that Christ loves them and that His love can be seen in you.

The Don'ts
+ Don't let those who are already Christians form into little cliques, excluding the non-Christians.
+ Don't talk to others in whispers.
+ Don't belittle or ridicule other religious groups.
+ Don't ask people to read aloud unless you have received their permission before the lesson time.
+ Don't invite your minister to the first meeting. Your non-Christian friend might think he has walked into an ambush.
+ Don't make it formal or stuffy. Remember, postmodern people equate formality with insincerity. Informal and fun is the name of the game. I think Jesus would fit right in, don't you?

Several years ago my wife and I led an evangelistic Bible study in our home. We invited several couples who had shown an interest in our church and were new in the community. They all lived within a mile or two of our home. We contacted them all and lined up one of my college students to entertain all their children in the family room of our basement. We also invited one other mature Christian couple to take part in the study with us. We spent the first session getting to know one another better and making sure everyone had the same translation of the Bible. We met twice a month and worked our way through a biblical book, simply reading the text and asking and answering questions about it. Each session ended with the people staying at least an hour afterwards for fellowship and refreshments. By the end of the year, everyone in the group had made a decision for Christ and come into the fellowship of our church family. All real salesmen know that the secret to success is finding a tremendous product that sells itself. This is what we have in the gospel of Christ. The Lord Jesus "sells Himself" to the lives of needy postmorderns. Our only job is to cultivate the soil and provide a setting in which the Word of God can be demonstrated as well as proclaimed.

Using Questions to Lead an Evangelistic Bible Study

Many Christians believe that they do not have the talents or ability necessary to lead an evangelistic Bible study. This is because they make two false assumptions. False assumption #1 is that the study must be in the form of a lecture where the leader does all the talking. False assumption #2 is that the leader must be able to answer (correctly) any and every possible question which might arise during the study.

Both of these assumptions are faulty. In a good evangelistic study, while pointing out some obvious truths, the good leader will mostly be involved in asking engaging questions which will help those present read and discuss the plain truth of the text of Scripture. The questions must not be phrased in such a way that the answer will simply be a fact. We want to ask questions that help each member of the study consider the facts of Scripture and how these facts engage and interact with their lives. Questions that can be answered with a simple "yes" or "no" will do little to encourage our non-Christian friends to ponder the life and claims of the Lord Jesus.

Someone once said that a good question is one that the questioner does not know the answer to. If I already know the answer to a question, and then I ask the question anyway, the conversation is transformed from a "discussion" into a "test." I want to ask questions which will engage the thought processes of the unbelievers who are studying the text.

If we were studying the account of Jesus feeding the multitude in John 6, bad questions might be, "How many people did Jesus feed?" or "Did the disciples think the food would be easy to obtain?" These are bad questions because you as the teacher would already know the answer and they can be answered briefly. They also deal with the bare statistics of the passage instead of the message of the passage.

I want to ask questions which will engage the thought processes of the unbelievers who are studying the text.

A far better question would be, "Why do you think Jesus used His divine power to feed so many people?" Or how about, "If you had been present at this preaching session, how would you have felt if you had witnessed this miracle?" These questions make an expert out of the person who is answering because only he can tell us how he would have felt or what he would have perceived. They also allow for the main message of the text to shine through: Jesus is the divine Son of God who has supernatural power to meet the needs of people.

There are three types of questions which can be employed in working your way through Scripture in an evangelistic Bible study: (1) launch questions, (2) guide questions, and (3) summary questions. In the study, the leader can set the stage by giving some very basic background material on the passage in question. Then the group can simply read through the chapter, paragraph by paragraph, employing these three types of questions.

Launch questions are designed to help the group get into the main thought of the paragraph in question. A launch question has contained within it, the setting of the text in question. In reference to the first two brief paragraphs in John 6, a good launch question might be, "Why do you think Jesus asked the disciples about how to feed all those people?"

After several share their thoughts, guide questions can be used to help ensure that the main emphasis of the passage is perceived and that those in the study ponder that message's significance. Examples of guide questions might include:

☞ Why do you think He said that?
☞ What do you think He was getting at?
☞ What else do you see in this verse?
☞ Why do you say that?
☞ What do you mean?
☞ Why do you think He uses that word here?[11]

Finally, when we think that the basic message of the section of Scripture has been considered, a summary question can be used to tie up any loose ends. This is a question that simply asks the individuals to put in their own words the main point of the passage. Some summary questions might include:

☞ How would you summarize the main idea of this paragraph?
☞ How would you say this in your own words?
☞ How would you summarize the idea we've been discussing?[12]

The great fear of many novice Bible teachers is that someone will ask a question to which they will not know the answer. I tell my students that this should never keep anyone from seeking to teach the Scriptures. If we wait until we know all the answers, we will never get around to sharing the good news. I have five earned theological degrees and have been a Christian minister and teacher for nearly twenty-five years. Hardly a day goes by that a student doesn't ask me a thought-provoking question that I have never considered before.

There are several rules to follow if you are asked a question to which you do not know the answer. First, NEVER act as if you know the correct answer when you don't. I remember as a college student on one occasion, I was leading a group of older adults in a study of the latter section of John 3 (vs. 22) dealing with Jesus and His disciples' baptizing those who came to them. One of the people asked if Jesus actually did the baptizing. At that point in my life, I was usually only a Saturday night's study hour ahead of my class. I did not have a clue. However, "I was the teacher" and thought I was supposed to have the definitive word on the subject. I stated, "Why, yes! That is what the Scripture says at this point." You can imagine my horror the following Saturday night, to discover in John 4:2 that "in fact it was not Jesus who baptized, but his disciples."

Never act as if you know the correct answer when you don't.

If someone asks a question to which we do not know the answer, it is perfectly acceptable to say, "I don't know!" The questioner will appreciate our honesty and probably feel a greater affinity toward us, recognizing that a person doesn't have to know everything before he can follow Jesus. I usually respond, "That's a great question, and to tell you the truth, I haven't the slightest idea, off the top of my head, what the answer would be. But I know that there is an answer. Let me work on that awhile and next time we get together, let's see if we can figure it out." You may ask if anyone in the group has any idea about the answer or challenge them to work with you during the coming week or two to discover the answer. In any event, never argue about an issue to which you have no immediate resolution.

The pattern of setting the stage with brief remarks and then leading the group through launch, guide, and summary questions can be an effective method of helping people "read the Bible for themselves" allowing Jesus to meet them in the pages of Scripture. Our non-Christian friend will come face to face with Jesus as He reveals Himself in the Word. The Holy Spirit will begin to do His mighty work. Our friend will begin to move into the harvesting stage of the evangelism process.

The Harvesting Stage

The Importance of Sharing Your Personal Testimony

Eventually our friend will come to a place in his life when he is ready to move from the Sowing Stage of evangelism to the Harvesting Stage of evangelism. His emotions will have been prepared through Christ at work within your friendship. His mind will have been confronted with the message of Jesus as the word has been sown in his heart. It will now be time to address your friend's will. The last personal aspect of an individual to be yielded up to Christ is the will. Your task in this stage of evangelism is to help your friend understand that a decision needs to be made concerning Christ. This is usually a time of struggle for most people, because the sinful man is often reluctant to turn over the control of his life to Christ.

One great tool which we can use to help our friend understand how to yield in the struggle of this will is to share our own "Personal Testimony" of how we came to accept Christ as our Lord and Savior. Several aspects should be included in our own personal testimony.

First, we need to be sure to relate the struggle which we had in being convinced to turn our life over to the Lordship of Christ. With every person, the story is different, but each of us had to turn from sin to serve Christ. Share your struggle. I remember during Vacation Bible School, in the summer of my sixth grade year, I became convinced of my own need for Christ. I doubt that I had committed many heinous sins (as far as the world counts sinfulness) at that young stage of my life. But I knew that without Christ I was lost. In fact, I would pray each night that Jesus would not return until I got up the courage to accept Him as my Savior and Lord. It was on a Wednesday evening about 9:00 P.M. that I could stand it no longer. I came downstairs from my bedroom, the tears running down my face and I declared to my mother that I HAD TO ACCEPT JESUS INTO MY LIFE. After a discussion with my minister, the following day I made my confession of faith in front of the entire Vacation Bible School and was baptized into Christ. As far as the people at church were concerned, I was a good little boy before my confession of faith and I remained a good little boy after my confession. But I knew that inside of me everything had changed. It was the defining moment of my life for all eternity. I don't remember anything else about that year of my life, but that one struggle and decision has determined every other aspect of the decades which have followed.

With every person, the story is different, but each of us had to turn from sin to serve Christ.

After we describe to our friend our struggle, we need to share how we became convinced to yield our life to Christ. What was it that finally helped us to turn our will over to Christ's control? Share your story. Now is the time to give them the whole load! When we share our testimony, we need to emphasize that we are not perfect but that Christ is continually at work within our life to help us live for Him.

Personal testimonies can be rather nonspectacular (as I consider my own to be), or quite dramatic. Several years ago, Kent Williams spoke at one of the morning chapel sessions of Ozark Christian College. At the time Kent was preaching at Christ's Church of Oronogo, MO. The church is out in the country. You have to get lost to find this place, and yet the attendance had gone from 150 to over 1,000 during Kent's ministry. In his sermon Kent was sharing with us how no one is outside of the reach of God's changing power through Christ. He told the story of witnessing to the local Harley Davidson repair shop owner. His name was "Crazy Frank." At least that's what everyone in the area called him. Kent related that Crazy Frank had lived as far away from Christ as a "bad boy biker" could possibly live. But Kent decided to strike up a friendship with this rough character. Through the process of lifestyle evangelism, Crazy Frank decided to accept Christ as his Lord and Savior.

Then Kent stopped his sermon and said, "Nobody can tell you what a change Christ can make in a life more powerfully than Crazy Frank himself." At that moment Steppenwolf's "Born to Be Wild" began playing over the sound system and Crazy Frank rode his Harley right down the aisle of the chapel and parked it in front of the platform. Then, clad in his leathers and chains, he walked up onto the stage and told our student body that if Christ could change his life, Christ could change anyone. Not many will forget that chapel session.

It doesn't matter if your personal testimony is as unspectacular as mine or as amazing as Crazy Frank's. The only issue is that we use it to help our unbelieving friend recognize that it is normal to have an inner struggle as the time grows near to make a decision for Christ.

After we share our story, we need to ask our friend if he would like to know how to accept Christ as his Lord and Savior. If he responds that he is not ready yet, we should affirm our understanding and let him know that we will be praying for him. If he responds positively, it's time to share with him a simple presentation of the gospel message. We will cover this in the next chapter.

A Summary of the Sowing Strategies

We can summarize our strategy for sowing the Word of God into the life of our friend by examining the chart below.

Cultivation Stage	— Raising the Flag (establishes your identity) — Faith Stories (create a spiritual hunger)
Sowing Stage	— Bible Study (provides information & perspective)
Harvesting Stage	— Personal Testimony (clarifies the final step of faith) — Gospel Presentation (shares the simple gospel message)

God has promised that His Word will always accomplish its intended purpose. He is only waiting for us to take Him at "His Word" and begin to utilize a strategy to sow that Word in the lives of those around us.

Do not be deceived: God cannot be mocked. A man reaps what he sows. The one who sows to please his sinful nature, from that nature will reap destruction; the one who sows to please the Spirit, from the Spirit will reap eternal life.

Galatians 6:7-8

---

1. J.D. Douglas, ed., *Proclaim Christ until He Comes: Calling the Whole Church to Take the Whole Gospel to the Whole World* (Minneapolis: World Wide Publications, 1990), pp. 31-32.

2. Peterson, *Living Proof*, pp. 153-166; Hinkley, *Living Proof*, pp. 55-58.

3. Hinkley, *Living Proof*, p. 56.

4. Strobel, *Unchurched Harry & Mary*, pp. 17-54.

5. Ibid., p. 27.

6. Roberta Hestenes, *Using the Bible in Groups* (Philadelphia: Westminster, 1983), p. 17.

7. Ibid.

8. Bob and Betty Jacks, *Your Home a Lighthouse* (Colorado Springs: NavPress, 1986), p. 50.

9. Ibid., p. 30.

10. Hinkley, *Living Proof*, p. 69.

11. Ibid., p. 79.

12. Ibid.

Chapter 10

PLANNING TO SHARE THE GOOD NEWS OF CHRIST: SIMPLE GOSPEL PRESENTATIONS

To evangelize is to spread the good news that Jesus Christ died for our sins and was raised from the dead according to the Scriptures, and that as the reigning Lord he now offers the forgiveness of sins and the liberating gift of the Spirit to all who repent and believe.[1]

Lausanne II in Manila, 1989

Now I saw in my dream, That the highway up which Christian was to go, was fenced on either side with a wall, and that wall was called Salvation. Up this way therefore did burdened Christian run, but not without great difficulty, because of the Load on his back.

He ran thus till he came at a place somewhat ascending, and upon that place stood a Cross, and a little below, in the bottom, a Sepulchre. So I saw in my dream, That just as Christian came up with the Cross, his Burden loosed from off his shoulders, and fell from off his back, and began to tumble, and so continued to do, till it came to the mouth of the Sepulchre, where it fell in, and I saw it no more.

Then was Christian glad and lightsome, and said with a merry heart, "He hath given me Rest by His Sorrow, and Life by his Death."[2]

John Bunyan, *The Pilgrim's Progess*

In the previous chapters we have examined the evangelism process. We began with the "cultivation stage" in which we saw our primary emphasis as developing a meaningful relationship with someone who is outside of Christ. Our goal in this stage is to help the nonbeliever feel comfortable with us while at the same time revealing to them in a positive way that we are Christians. This is so important, considering what we have learned about our growing postmodern culture. We have also realized that there comes a point when the words of the message of Jesus must be spoken. In the "sowing stage" of the evangelism process, we have seen several strategies which will help us to begin to move our friend into considering what the

Bible has to say about a personal relationship with Jesus Christ. In this stage, we address our friend's intellect with the content of the message of Scripture. Finally, our new friend will know enough about the Christian faith to realize that he must make a decision for or against Christ.

It is this final "harvesting stage" of the evangelism process which causes many Christians anxiety. It is here that we need to speak to our friend's "will." His emotions and intellect will have been addressed and for the most part satisfied. Our job in the harvesting stage is to help our friend understand that a decision needs to be made. We can help him by answering any difficult questions that may remain before he is ready to make his decision. Each of us needs to be ready to share a basic presentation of the gospel and then learn to ask a very simple question: "Is there anything keeping you from accepting Jesus Christ as your Lord and Savior?" This is all we can do. It is then up to the Holy Spirit to do His mighty work in our friend's heart, convicting him of his need for Christ.

I firmly believe that most Christians truly desire to share what Christ has done for them. I believe that most Christians have a true desire to win their lost friends to Christ. They are good at the cultivation and even the sowing stages of the evangelism process, but they have difficulty in the harvesting stage. In life, most Christians never experience the joy of being a "harvester," helping to lead another person to make their final decision for Christ. It is not from the lack of desire that they fail in this area, but rather from the lack of a plan.

Many Christians are like the water boy sitting at the end of the bench throughout the whole football season. He was a part of the team and faithfully attended every game and every practice. Week after week, he would sit and dream about what it would be like to quarterback the team, leading it to victory. One day the coach noticed the water boy was daydreaming and asked, "What are you thinking about?" The boy hesitantly shared his athletic dreams.

Then the coach asked, "Have you ever practiced to be a quarterback?"

"No," came the reply.

"Have you ever studied the play book to learn the things every quarterback must know?"

Again the reply was, "No."

"Do you ever plan to do so?"

Silence.

The coach shook his head and said, "How can you ever expect to achieve your dreams if you don't have a plan of how to accomplish them?"

Many Christians fail to actually present the gospel message because they simply have no plan for how to go about it. We can hardly expect God to open doorways of opportunity for people who have not prepared themselves for the task. But if we prepare ourselves to share the good news of Christ in a simple, systematic presentation, then God has a way of opening many doorways of opportunity. Christians need to learn the old Boy Scout motto: Be Prepared!

How can you ever expect to achieve your dreams if you don't have a plan of how to accomplish them?

In his book *Essentials of Discipleship* Francis Cosgrove shares four reasons why it is imperative that we develop a plan to share the gospel in a simple systematic manner.[3] A plan enables us to be prepared at all times to witness. A plan also enables us to go through a biblical presentation point by point without leaving anything out. We will have covered everything vital to that person's coming to Jesus Christ. It also serves as a set of tracks that provide direction. If the person with whom we are sharing the Lord takes off on a tangent, having a plan enables us to come back to where we ought to be after we have taken care of the diversion. Finally, a plan is a transferable tool by which we can teach others to share Christ as well.

In preparing to learn a gospel presentation it is essential to recognize that these are always most effectively presented when they are shared with a friend in a genuine manner. Win and Charles Arn have written,

> Evangelism methods have become simplistic. There is strong research evidence to indicate that new Christians who accept Christ and continue as responsible church members first perceive the Gospel message in terms of its relevance to their own lives. Evangelism training which relies on "canned" presentations, memorized testimonies, and universal spiritual dictums has difficulty responding to the unique needs of the non-Christian in terms of his/her day-to-day experience and the resources available in Christ.
>
> New Christians who continue as responsible church members have first perceived the Gospel message in terms of its unique application to their own lives, situations, and problems. Dr. Arthur Glasser observes, "People today must see Jesus Christ as the liberator from injustice, transformer of human culture, as well as personal Savior of the human heart."[4]

Remember, for those in a postmodern culture, information that is genuinely shared between friends and that is "real" in the life experience of the presenter will have the greatest chance of being heard and understood.

In this chapter, we will learn several very simple plans to prepare us to share the gospel message. We will also consider several of the most common questions that arise here in the "harvesting stage" of evangelism. We will learn how to deal with them quickly while keeping our focus on Christ.

Simple Gospel Presentations

The "One-Verse Method"

Some people have a fairly limited knowledge of the Bible and don't feel comfortable turning to many different Scriptures as they explain what Christ has done. The "One-Verse Method" is perfect for those who like to stick with a single verse or two. The verse is Romans 6:23, and the presentation is quite simple. You can draw this presentation on a single piece of paper or even on a napkin at a restaurant. The finished product is provided for you as an example of what this should look like when you are through (see figure #1).

First, write the text of Romans 6:23 across the top of the page: "For the wages of sin is death, but the gift of God is eternal life in Christ Jesus our Lord." This is such a simple verse that any Christian can devote it to memory. This will enable the presentation to be shared even if a Bible isn't available. After writing this passage, select the word "wages" and underline it. As you explain what wages are (what we receive for what we do), write the word below your verse on the left side of what will become a gulf or cavern in your illustration to display that which separates us from God.

Next, select the word "sin" and repeat the above, underlining it in the verse and then writing it below the word "wages." We need to explain that sin is missing the mark, as transgression, or falling short. Finally for the left side of the gulf, we will underline as well as write the word "death." Every person needs to think of several illustrations that will help display the truth of our predicament living as sinners before an all holy God. I make it a point to emphasize that everyone is guilty of breaking God's laws and that for God to be true to His perfect nature, He must remove sin from His presence. At this point, draw two parallel lines, running up and down which will separate the words "wages, sin, and death" from the words we are about to write.

Now we proceed to describe what God has done to solve the problem of our sin. At the bottom of the gulf we have created write the word "but" to show that God is not going to sit by and do nothing to help us. Then, in the text at the top of the page, underline the word "gift" and then write it directly across from the word "wages." Contrast how coming into a

Romans 6:23

"For the **wages** of **sin** is **death**,
but the **gift of God** is **eternal life**
in **Christ Jesus** our **Lord**."

Repent		Be Baptized
Wages	Christ Jesus Lord	Gift
Sin		of God
Death		Eternal Life
	But	

Figure 1

relationship with God through Jesus Christ is nothing that we can earn or deserve. It must be received as a gift. Next underline and write the words "of God" and contrast how our sinful actions have created our problem but it is God who will rescue us. Finally, underline and write the words "eternal life" and contrast what God desires to give us with the death we actually deserve.

By now the gulf between our death in sin and God's desire of eternal life should be clear. It is now time to share the good news of what Jesus has done for us on the cross. Underline the words "Christ Jesus" and "Lord" and write them in the middle of the gulf. At this time draw a cross (see figure #1) around these words and describe what Christ has done for us by becoming our substitute. God allowed His own Son to die so that sin could be punished and yet life could be offered to us.

At this point it is always good to have a story or event which can help our friend conceptualize what Christ has done. I particularly like an illustration shared by John Hendee[5] involving the great physician, Louis Pasteur.

Even though the role of germs in disease is now accepted, when Louis Pasteur first advanced what was then called the "Germ Theory," he was met with ridicule and great opposition from the medical community. The Medical Association even exiled him from Paris, forcing him to go into hiding in the woods outside that city with his experiments. His partner in the attempt to show that germs were more than just a theory was a Parisian Jewish doctor named Felix Ruh. Dr. Ruh knew the tragedy of disease at first hand, having lost his granddaughter to the black diphtheria, which was invariably fatal in those days.

On the day when Pasteur and Ruh werre prepared to demonstrate their work, twenty beautiful horses were led out to the improvised lab in the forest. Dr. Ruh brought a pail of carefully cultivated black diphtheria germs out of a steel vault, a pail that contained enough germs to kill everyone in France. The coworkers swabbed the nostrils, tongue and throat of each horse with the contents of the pail, and before long, all of the horses were deadly ill with the disease. Over a period of several days, the horses died one by one, and many of the observers grew tired of the experiment and left. Finally, at two in the morning, an orderly brought the news the scientists were awaiting. The single remaining horse had a half degree drop in its temperature. By nightfall of that day, the fever was gone and the horse showed every sign of having recovered.

Having avoided death from disease, that horse was now killed with a sledgehammer blow to the head. The scientists drew the blood from the dead horse and were then driven into Paris to the Municipal Hospital, where they forced their way into a ward where 300 babies sick with black diphtheria had been segregated and left to die. Using the blood of the horse which had overcome the disease, they inoculated every one of the babies. Of all those infants thought doomed to inevitable death, only three did not recover.

After telling our illustration, we then need to ask our friend if he has any questions about just what it is that Jesus has done. He should be fairly familiar with the message of Christ if he has been a part of an evangelistic Bible study (see chapter 9).

At this point we need to explain how we get from one side of the gulf to the other. In other words, we need to share with our friend how to go about displaying his faith in Christ. We will outline the basic New Testament message of this in our next chapter (chapter 10). For this simple one-verse method, we could simply ask, "Do you believe in what Jesus has done for you on the cross?" If the answer is "yes," then we follow up immediately by asking, "Would you like to accept Him into your life by faith?" If the answer again is "yes," I would quote from memory Acts 2:38 to show what people who have believed the gospel message need to do in order to complete the display of their faith in Jesus. At this point write the words "repent" and "be baptized" at the top of your chart. Inquire if there are any questions. If not, ask if he is ready to turn from his sin and declare Jesus as his Lord. If the answer is yes, arrange for his immediate baptism.

I recognize that many in the evangelical world would wonder why I have made no reference to the "sinner's prayer" at this point. I believe that this could be seen as a part of the expression of repentance and it could be used appropriately at this point. However, as well used as the "sinner's prayer" has become in many churches, it must be noted that we never have a biblical example of any converts to the resurrected Christ being instructed to "pray the sinner's prayer." In chapter 11, I outline what I would call "Model Evangelism" to present a more biblical instruction of what it means to accept Christ by faith. All of the evangelistic presentations offered in this chapter follow the pattern of what we will discuss in the next chapter.

The "One-Verse Method" is simple, requires very little Bible knowledge, and can be used even when no Bible is present. A friend of mine has successfully used this little presentation to win hundreds of people to the Lord. When it comes time to enter the "harvest stage" of carrying out the Great Commission, this is a gospel presentation that will produce fruit.

The "Roman Road Method"

Many would like a gospel presentation which is a little more complete than the "One-Verse Method" but does not have the presenter jumping around the Bible looking up numerous passages in many different books. For those who would like to be able to stay in a single New Testament book to outline the gospel message, "The Roman Road Method" is very appealing.

This method can be delivered in several ways. A chart can be made with the verses in Romans already written out. This will save time and is easy to place on a single sheet of paper (see figure #2). Others will prefer to write these references in their Bibles so that, turning to Romans, the presenter can turn and read each of the Scriptures from the Bible itself. The best way to do this is to write the first reference (Rom. 1:16) at the top of the title page of the Roman Epistle and then highlight that verse in the text. In the margin beside Romans 1:16, write the next reference, that being Romans 3:23, and so on. This way the presenter will not have to memorize the seven different references, but will be able to turn to them easily.

"The Roman Road" examines seven key passages in Paul's great Epistle to the Romans, outlining the basic elements of the gospel message. First, Romans 1:16 describes how the gospel is the "power of God" to bring salvation to everyone who believes. The word in the text for "power" is from the Greek word δύναμις (*dynamis*) from which we get the English word "dynamite!" God's great power to save us is at work in the world through the gospel.

Next, Romans 3:23 discusses the problem of human sin. Romans 6:23 expands upon this problem and also relates God's solution through Christ. Much of the information of the "One-Verse Method" could be employed at this point. Romans 5:8 expands on God's solution by displaying that the motivation for God was His great love for us, while the price of that love meant the death of His own Son on our behalf.

During any communication of the gospel, between each point we should frequently ask our friend if things are clear or make sense. If our friend understands what Jesus has done for him on the cross, we move to Romans 10:9. Here we see Paul discuss how an individual begins to display his faith and trust in Christ. The heart believes in Christ's finished work and the mouth confesses that "Jesus is Lord." We need to remember to point out that in order to come to Christ, we must commit ourselves to follow Christ and learn to obey Him as we continually learn His will in the Bible.

The Roman Road

Rom. 1:16 *I am not ashamed of the gospel, because it is the power of God for the salvation of everyone who believes: first for the Jew, then for the Gentile.*

Rom. 3:23 *for all have sinned and fall short of the glory of God,*

Rom. 6:23 *For the wages of sin is death, but the gift of God is eternal life in Christ Jesus our Lord.*

Rom. 5:8 *But God demonstrates his own love for us in this: While we were still sinners, Christ died for us.*

Rom. 10:9 *That if you confess with your mouth, "Jesus is Lord," and believe in your heart that God raised him from the dead, you will be saved.*

Rom. 6:3-4 *Or don't you know that all of us who were baptized into Christ Jesus were baptized into his death? We were therefore buried with him through baptism into death in order that, just as Christ was raised from the dead through the glory of the Father, we too may live a new life.*

Rom. 12:1-2 *Therefore, I urge you, brothers, in view of God's mercy, to offer your bodies as living sacrifices, holy and pleasing to God — this is your spiritual act of worship. Do not conform any longer to the pattern of this world, but be transformed by the renewing of your mind. Then you will be able to test and approve what God's will is — his good, pleasing and perfect will.*

Figure 2

Five Facts that Concern You

Fact #1

You are a sinner.

Romans 3:9-10

Romans 3:23

Fact #2

Your sins condemn you.

Romans 6:23

Revelation 21:8

1 Corinthians 6:9

Fact #3

God loves you!

John 3:16

Romans 5:6-8

Ephesians 2:4-7

Fact #4

You must respond to God's love.

Acts 2:37 / 16:29-30

Hear the gospel — Romans 10:17

Believe the gospel — Hebrews 11:6 / Acts 16:31

Repent of your sins — Acts 17:30

Be baptized into Christ — Acts 2:38

Fact #5

God responds to your faith!

You are forgiven — 1 John 2:12

You are saved — Titus 3:3-8

You are sealed — Ephesians 1:13-14

You have been added to the church — Acts 2:47

Figure 3

In Romans 6:3-4, we explain how Christians are to display their faith in Jesus through Christian baptism. Baptism allows us to act out, in a visual way, the events of Jesus' death, burial, and resurrection. We display for all to see that we now stand in solidarity with Him. Finally, Romans 12:1-2 relate the complete nature of the life of faith. We are to yield up our bodies to serve God our whole life long. I always spend time contrasting the animal sacrifices of the Old Testament period with the living sacrifice that we can now be in service to the Lord. No longer are we to spend our energy trying to "fit" into the sinful world around us. In Christ, we are continually being transformed through the renewing of our minds as we study and learn of Christ. When this occurs, we will demonstrate to ourselves and everyone we meet that God's way of living is the best way.

At the conclusion of sharing the "Roman Road Method," again, we need to ask our friend if he understands what Christ has done for him. If so, then we need to ask if he is ready to commit himself to Christ in faith as outlined in Romans. This presentation is more detailed than the previous one, but is easy to use. For many who love the Roman Epistle, this is a wonderful method of sharing the "Gospel according to Paul."

The "Five Facts that Concern You Method"

Some people are very "fact" oriented. They want to know the main points of God's message in a very logical, concise package. For them, the "Five Facts that Concern You Method" is very helpful. This presentation is a bit more detailed and less tied to a particular passage or biblical book (see figure #3). Until this method can be memorized, we should keep a copy of the presentation in our Bible for reference.

When sharing this method with a friend, we simply begin by stating that in yielding up our lives to Christ, there are five ultimate facts with which we must contend. Fact #1 states that *we are sinners.* Several Scriptures can be used (Rom 3:9-10,23) to display the universal nature of sin. Fact #2 displays that *our sins condemn us.* Again, we can turn in our Bible to the passages listed (see figure #3) to display the problem of living condemned in sin before a holy and righteous God.

Fact #3 is good news indeed. We can now share that in spite of our unworthiness *God still loves us.* Numerous Bible verses express how God has shown His love for us in the sacrifice of His Son on the cross. Fact #4 discusses how *we must respond in faith to God's love* for us in Christ. The evangelistic response modeled in Acts is presented here on our chart. Finally, Fact #5 concludes this presentation with a discussion of several *great promises for those who accept Christ by faith.*

In giving any gospel presentation, it is always good to remember that we need to place ourselves alongside our friend when describing the sinfulness of man. Even though this method talks about how "you" are a sinner, when making the presentation, we should always say, "*Our* sins condemn us." Our friend needs to know that in and of our own efforts, we are just as sinful and in need of God's grace as the worst sinner who has ever lived.

It is always good to remember to place ourselves alongside our friend when describing man's sinfulness.

Again, at the conclusion, we need to clarify anything that our friend does not understand and then proceed to ask him if he is ready to make such a commitment to Christ. The "Five-Fact Method" is a very orderly approach to sharing the biblical message of what Christ has made available to each one of us.

The "ABC Method"

Another very simple way to describe to our friend the good news of Christ is what we call the "ABC Method." Sometimes a friend may be nearing the point where she needs to make a decision for Christ, and yet she is confused by several peripheral issues. We can help to focus her attention by helping her understand that in the final analysis becoming a Christian is as easy as "ABC." Only a few verses are necessary for this presentation and the acrostic nature of the presentation makes it easy to memorize. It is so easy that it doesn't even need to be written down in order to be remembered. If necessary, a chart of the delivery can be kept in our Bible until we have the appropriate verses memorized (see figure #4).

In this presentation, we begin by telling our friend that while many people would seem to make it difficult, accepting Christ is as easy as "ABC." The "A" stands for "acknowledge." The first step in coming to Christ is to acknowledge that we have a problem and our problem is sin. Quoting or looking up Romans 3:23 can illustrate this from Scripture. We can take as much time as is necessary to discuss how pervasive and devastating our sin is.

The "B" stands for "believe." In order for the problem of our sin to be conquered, we must believe in what Christ has done for us on the cross through His death and resurrection. Numerous passages could be employed to demonstrate this. The one I suggest for this presentation is 1 Peter 3:18. This passage talks about the singular sacrifice of Christ and how His death brings us to God.

The "ABC" Method of Leading a Person to Christ

Becoming a Christian is really not complex. It's as easy as ABC.

Acknowledge your problem (Separation from God).

"For all have sinned and fall short of the glory of God" (Romans 3:23).

Believe in Christ (His death and resurrection).

"For Christ died for sins once for all, the righteous for the unrighteous, to bring you to God. He was put to death in the body but made alive by the Spirit" (1 Peter 3:18).

Commit your life to Christ and receive Him by faith.

"Believe in the Lord Jesus, and you will be saved" (Acts 6:31).

"Repent and be baptized, every one of you, in the name of Jesus Christ for the forgiveness of your sins. And you will receive the gift of the Holy Spirit" (Acts 2:38).

Repentance is turning your life to God. It is giving your whole life in service to the Lord who died for you.

Baptism is being immersed to display your faith in the death, burial, and resurrection of Jesus.

Figure 4

Evangelism Explosion

Q₁ Do you think that you have gotten to the place in your life where you know that if you were to die today that you would go to heaven?

Q₂ If you were to die today and stand before God, and He asked, "Why should I let you into my heaven?" what do you think you would say?

THE GOSPEL

Grace (Romans 6:23)
   1. Heaven — a gift
   2. Can't earn / don't deserve it

Man (Ephesians 2:8-10)
   1. Sinner
   2. Can't save himself

God (1 John 4:8)
   1. Loving — doesn't want to punish
   2. Just — must punish

Jesus (John 1:1,14; Isaiah 53:6)
   1. Who He is — God / man
   2. What He did — paid the penalty for our sins

Faith (James 2:19)
   1. What it is not
      – mere intellectual assent
      – temporal faith
   2. What it is
      – trusting Christ alone (Acts 4:12)
      – displaying faith (Acts 2:38)

COMMITMENT

Qualifying Question: Does that make sense to you?

Commitment Question: Do you want to receive God's gift of life right now?

Figure 5

Finally, the "C" stands for "commit." Once we intellectually believe in the work of Christ on our behalf, we must commit our lives to Him in order to receive Him by faith. Two Scriptures from Acts are suggested to illustrate that this was a part of the preaching of Jesus' apostles. Repentance and baptism display the inner working and the outer assent of faith.

It is always a good idea when sharing a gospel presentation to discuss the difference between intellectual assent and biblical faith. One of my favorite stories which illustrates this involves a tightrope walker named Blondin. When I was visiting Niagara Falls, I saw a monument for this great daredevil. He toured the entire country putting on exhibitions. When he went to Niagara Falls, he put on a three-day show. Blondin stretched the tightrope across the Falls, and for two days walked this rope, drawing a tremendous crowd. On the third day he said he was going to walk the rope blindfolded and pushing a wheelbarrow. Before he tried this feat, he went among the crowd and asked, "Do you believe I can do this?" There wasn't anyone in the crowd who doubted. So he climbed up on the rope and asked, "O.K., who will come up and get in the wheelbarrow?"[6]

The difference between mere intellectual belief and biblical faith can be seen in that story. Most Americans may intellectually believe that Jesus is the Son of God, but far fewer are willing to trust their whole lives uniquely to that belief. Remember, our postmodern generation is very pluralistic in their approach to life. However, Jesus cannot simply be held out as an option to be added to their already busy schedule. He must be Lord, or He must be rejected. Christ has left us no other options (Luke 14:25-35). Joyous servitude is the life to which Christ calls us. We must make this clear when we are encouraging our friends to place their "faith" in Jesus.

Most Americans may intellectually believe but far fewer are willing to trust their whole lives to that belief.

The "ABC Method" of evangelism is a simple presentation. It shines the spotlight of Scripture on our need, Christ's work, and the call to commitment.

The "Evangelism Explosion Method"

Dr. James D. Kennedy has seen tremendous success in the development of his "Evangelism Explosion Method" of sharing the gospel.[7] This particular method was developed to be shared in a more confrontational setting. However, it can be adapted to the lifestyle evangelism approach.

If used in a confrontational evangelistic approach, this presentation utilizes two questions which force the non-Christian to consider his eternal standing before God. The questions are: "Do you think that you have gotten to the place in your life where you know that if you were to die today that you would go to heaven?" and "If you were to die today and stand before God, and He asked, 'Why should I let you into my heaven?' what do you think you would say?" The remainder of the presentation is a fivefold description of the gospel message. If the lifestyle approach to evangelism has been used, we can use this fivefold description in outlining to our friend what God has done through Christ with or without the first two questions (see figure #5). This method can be memorized or carried in written form in our Bible.

We begin by telling our friend that there are five aspects about the gospel which must be accepted. Each of these aspects is supported by accompanying Scriptures (see figure #5). The first aspect is "grace." We need to explain that eternal life with God is a gift which cannot be earned. No one deserves what God wishes to give. To understand the concept of grace is to begin to understand the gospel. The next aspect of the gospel we need to understand is the truth about "man." Man is a sinner who cannot save himself. The third aspect of the gospel deals with "God." Here we emphasize the fact that God is loving and does not desire to punish anyone. However, the Bible also teaches that God is perfectly holy and just. He must punish sin, or He would be untrue to His perfect nature. If God failed to punish sin, He would cease to be God (and this is an impossibility).

The fourth aspect of the gospel centers around "Jesus." Jesus is wholly God and wholly man. He is God come in human flesh. Christ has invaded human history to save His people from their sins. This He did through His substitutionary death on the cross. In this section, we can use any Scripture and illustrations we need to make clear what Christ has done for us on the cross. The final aspect of the gospel is "faith." Here, we make clear the difference between intellectual assent and true biblical faith. We can then move to the apostolic message in the Book of Acts which instructs people how to display their submission to and faith in Christ.

After outlining these five aspects of the gospel, there are two remaining questions: "Does that make sense to you?" and "Do you want to receive God's gift of life right now?" As in the other methods, if there are any questions, we need to do our best to deal with them and attempt to help our friend realize that the only thing keeping him from Christ is the decision of his will.

The "Evangelism Explosion Method" is one more simple tool which enables us to outline the grace of God through Jesus Christ. A unique feature about this particular approach is that it begins with the good news of God's grace instead of the bad news of our sin. For those who like to begin on a positive note, this particular method may prove useful.

Any Biblical Method Is Better than No Method

The five presentations listed above are simply the starting point in describing what Christ has done. There are scores of gospel tracts and outlines which can be employed in telling the good news of Jesus. The point is: If you know a method, God will open the doorway for you to use it when your non-Christian friend is nearing a decision.

There is an old story about the great evangelist, Dwight L. Moody. He was once confronted by a female detractor who said, "Brother Moody, I don't like the way you do evangelism!"

Upon reflection Moody replied, "I don't much care for it either. Tell me, how do you do evangelism?"

The woman was taken aback and mumbled, "I don't."

"Well, then," replied Moody, "I can safely say that I like the way I do evangelism more than the way you don't do it!"

I tell my evangelism students that if they don't like any of the presentations we share in our class then they need to develop one for themselves. The only requirements are that the presentation must be true to the content of the Bible and it must be usable. A third requirement might be added that it should bear fruit. Anyone using an evangelistic method which bears no fruit is not a wise harvester. If, however, we prepare to share the gospel message of our Lord and gently challenge our non-Christian friend with the need to make a decision, God will bless our efforts. Be prepared! For those who study the "play book," God will find a way to get you into the game!

If you don't like any of these presentations, then develop one for yourself.

Answering Common Questions

When an individual comes face to face with Jesus Christ, the Holy Spirit will be busy driving the truth of the gospel home into the human heart. However, the Holy Spirit will not be the only one working overtime. Satan will use all of his resources to attempt to take the focus off of the person and work of Christ. The enemy will strive to fill our non-Christian friend's mind with difficult questions. When sharing a gospel presentation, our job is to handle these questions as honestly and briefly as possible while directing the conversation back to the real issue at hand: What will you do with Jesus?

The Holy Spirit will not be the only one working overtime while you present the gospel.

The best approach in handling a difficult question in the midst of a gospel presentation is to simply avoid the question. For instance, let's imagine that we are describing the need for our friend to commit his life in faith to Christ. Out of the blue, he asks us, "But what about all those people in Mongolia who have never had an opportunity to hear the gospel? What will God do with them?"

I know of several lengthy theological books that fail to give an adequate answer to that difficult question. Chances are, we will be unable to give a complete answer in such an informal setting. The best plan for this type of question is avoidance. Satan is simply trying to move the conversation away from the personal decision of our friend to an abstract theological discussion. Our response might be, "That's a really good question, and to tell you the truth, I don't know if I have a complete answer for it. But our real concern probably isn't so much with what God will do with those who have never heard. I'm much more concerned with what God will do with those of us who have had the opportunity to hear and respond to the good news of Christ." This type of response recognizes the importance of the question but moves the conversation back to the details of the gospel.

If our friend is unsatisfied by our "nonanswer," we should answer the question as briefly as possible (less that 2 minutes) and then move the conversation back to the gospel message. If it becomes obvious that the question will take too long to answer (or if you don't know the answer), simply tell your friend that his question is so important that it would take the rest of your time together. Set up a time in the next week to meet and deal with his question. Then move the conversation back to the good news of the message of Christ.

There are a number of common questions or objections which often arise in sharing the gospel. Let's examine a few of them and see how we might answer them in as brief a manner as possible.

God Would Never Punish Anyone by Sending Them to Hell

This is a common objection to the basic gospel message. In our post-modern world, many have difficulty believing in a standard outside of themselves by which they must be judged. As Christians, we know that all judgment belongs to God. If a person does not believe in God's justice and hell, we may need to show them several of the warnings contained in Scripture concerning the reality of God's judgment of sin and sinners (Isa. 57:21; Ezek. 33:11; 2 Pet. 2:4,6,9; Rom. 2:4,5). One of my favorite ways of handling this is to show my friend the many places that Jesus Himself warned of the coming punishment by His Righteous and Holy Father (Matt. 25:41,46; Mark 16:16; Luke 13:3; John 3:18,36; 5:28-29). He taught that God will assuredly punish sin. In fact, Jesus taught almost as much about hell as he did about heaven.

James Kennedy talks about our aversion to the thought of eternal punishment.

> In dealing with the denial of the reality of hell, sometimes we find it helpful to say "You know, it is a fact of psychology that we deny most passionately those things we fear most desperately. I wonder if the reason you don't believe in hell is that deep in your soul you fear that if there is such a place you may go there?" Often the reply is, "I guess you're right!"
>
> You must go on then and assure our prospect, "I don't want you to believe in hell so that you can live your life in mortal terror of going there. You can know that you're not going to hell. That's what the Gospel is all about. I believe in hell but I know that I'm not going there because of God's promise. This is much better than saying, 'I know I'm not going to hell because I don't think there is such a place.'"[8]

In dealing with this common objection, we need to lovingly allow the Bible to speak for itself. The real blessing is that if the question arises in the midst of a gospel presentation, we can point out that today we have the tremendous opportunity to accept the gift of eternal life through Christ. In Christ, we will never have to worry about the wrath of God, because Christ guarantees forgiveness and heaven.

Isn't There More Than One Way to God?

Our postmodern culture is increasingly pluralistic. It will be very easy for our non-Christian friend to see the gospel as one truth among many. Our task is to help them see that the Jesus they are falling in love with has made very exclusive claims. We did not invent the idea of Jesus' being the only way to God. This is not our claim; it is His. We are merely relating His claim and the claim of the writers of the New Testament. Scripture is filled with the exclusive claims of Christ:

> Jesus answered, "I am the way and the truth and the life. No one comes to the Father except through me" (John 14:6).

> "I told you that you would die in your sins; if you do not believe that I am [the one I claim to be], you will indeed die in your sins" (John 8:24).

> "Salvation is found in no one else, for there is no other name under heaven given to men by which we must be saved" (Acts 4:12).

> For there is one God and one mediator between God and men, the man Christ Jesus (1 Tim. 2:5).

This is very difficult for many in our postmodern world to accept. However, if we have been faithful in displaying Christ's unconditional love and acceptance to our seeking friends, and if we have been faithful in helping them discover Jesus as He reveals Himself through Scripture, then this will go a long way in helping them to move past their cultural conditioning and be open to accepting the exclusive claims of Christ. My witness and the united witness of a loving, faithful group of Christians is hard to ignore.

One good way to illustrate how foolish a pluralistic approach to religious faith can be is to use the illustration of the doctor found in chapter 3. There are numerous creative approaches to show the intellectual bankruptcy of the pluralistic stance of postmodern thinking.

Suppose you are at the intersection of a busy city street and a stranger walks up to you and asks directions to the city hall. What would happen if your response went something like this:

"Friend, there is no one true way to get to city hall. Everyone must find their own way. You see, we stand at the intersection of four possible roadways. Beyond this intersection are countless others. You must choose the path that leads to city hall, because only you can walk that path. No one else may choose it for you. Good luck on your journey."

The stranger would probably think that you had escaped from the mental ward of a local hospital. However, this is the same lunacy that we hear from postmodern thinkers who declare that everyone must find their own way to God. I would suggest that God is more "real" than city hall and that finding our way back to Him requires definite instruction. Thankfully for us, God has taken the initiative by coming into the world through Jesus

Christ, to point out the way back home to Himself. Jesus knew exactly what He was talking about when He said, "I am the way and the truth and the life. No one comes to the Father except through me" (John 14:6).

How Can a Good God Allow Evil and Pain to Exist?

The problem of evil in the world is a tremendously haunting question for the Christian. There are no easy answers. If God is perfectly good and is also almighty, why isn't He alleviating the pain and suffering which we see all around us? If the Bible taught that the world is now the way God intended it to be, we would find ourselves in an intolerable setting. It would make God the author of evil and pain. However, the Bible is emphatic concerning the fact that the world is not presently how God created it to be. It is abnormal, and the abnormality was caused by man, not God.

James Sire writes about this in his book, *The Universe Next Door*:

> Human "history" can be subsumed under four words: creation, Fall, redemption, glorification. We have just seen the essential human characteristics. To these we must add that human beings and all the rest of creation were created good. As Genesis records, "And God saw everything that he had made, and behold, it was very good" (Gen 1:31). Because God by his character set the standards of righteousness, human goodness consisted in being what God wanted people to be — beings made in the image of God and acting out that nature in their daily life. The tragedy is that we did not stay as we were created.
>
> As we have seen, human beings were created with the capacity for self-determination. God gave them the freedom to remain or not to remain in the close relationship of image to original. As Genesis 3 reports, the original pair, Adam and Eve, chose to disobey their Creator at the only point where the Creator put down limitations. This is the essence of the story of the Fall. Adam and Eve chose to eat the fruit God had forbidden them to eat, and hence they violated the personal relationship they had with their Creator.[9]

Because of the fall, the world is now abnormal. Things are not as God intended them to be. Man has separated himself from God through sin. The four areas of alienation which we discussed in chapter 3 (alienation from God, nature, fellowman, and self) have all resulted from man's sin, not from God's design. Any solution to the problem of evil in the world must take into consideration that the world as it stands now is not normal.

Our great hope as Christians is that God is in the process of solving the problem of evil while at the same time providing a way for us to escape its judgment. He does this through the work of Christ on the cross. Josh McDowell writes,

> Although evil is here and it is real, it is also temporary. It eventually will be destroyed. This is the hope the believer has. There is a new world coming in which there will be no more tears or pain because all things will be made new (Revelation 21:5). Paradise lost will be paradise regained. God will right every wrong and put away evil once for all, in His time.[10]

What about All the Hypocrites in the Church?

Whenever I hear this objection seriously raised, I'm always tempted to warn my friend that if he ever finds the perfect church, he shouldn't join it! One of the favorite ploys of Satan is to get people to center on the failures of God's people instead of the victorious work of God's Son. The old saying still rings true that the church isn't filled with perfect people, just forgiven people. However, for our postmodern generation, if the majority within the church fail to give evidence of "experiencing" new life in Christ, the gospel will have a difficult time shining through our darkened lives. It must be admitted that the church in every age and in every location contains people who are hypocritical — proclaiming one thing and living another.

It is important not to confuse hypocrisy with sin.

It is important not to confuse hypocrisy with sin. All Christians are sinners, but not all Christians are hypocrites. Hypocrisy is claiming one thing and living another. All Christians sin (1 John 1:9), and true Christians would never claim to live in sinless perfection. In fact, one of the primary requirements in order to become a Christian is to admit that "I am a sinner." All believers are fallible human beings who are prone to all types of sin. Just because a person is not perfect does not mean he is a phony. The distinction between the two is important. The occasional sin of a believer does not invalidate the truth of the Christian faith. Josh McDowell again comments,

> Christianity does not stand or fall on the way Christians have acted throughout history or are acting today. Christianity stands or falls on the person of Jesus, and Jesus was not a hypocrite. He lived consistently with what He taught, and at the end of His life He challenged those who had lived with Him night and day,

for more than three years, to point out any hypocrisy in Him. His disciples were silent, because there was none.[11]

We should also point out that there are hypocrites in every other institution on planet earth. I happen to be a St. Louis Cardinals baseball fan. When I am in the St. Louis area, I love to attend a ball game. It is true that several in the stands who wear the Cardinals' colors are not true fans. They come to the park late and leave before the game is over. What hypocrites! But I don't let them keep me from enjoying the game.

There is an old poem about perfect churches.

I think that I shall never see
   A church that's all it ought to be,
A church whose members never stray
   From the straight and narrow way,
A church whose deacons always deak,
   And none are proud and all are meek.
Such perfect churches there may be,
   But none of them is known to me.
But still, I'll pray and pay and plan
   To serve my church the best I can.

Won't God Accept Me? I'm a Good Person

This question shows a failure on the part of the questioner to take seriously the momentous nature of their sin and the absolute holiness of God. If our salvation depended upon our good deeds, God would be in debt to us. He would owe us salvation because of our labors in righteousness. However, the Bible is clear that all our righteous deeds are like a filthy garment compared to God's righteous character (Isa. 64:6).

There's a great old story which illustrates how lacking we are in our ability to live up to His absolute and holy standards. One day three men meet on the end of the pier off a Florida beach. One is an alcoholic and homeless. The second is the average fellow. The third is a fine, upstanding, pillar-of-the-community sort of guy. All of a sudden, the alcoholic jumps off the edge of the pier five feet out into the water. The other two yell, "What are you trying to do?"

The man in the water yells back, "I'm trying to jump across the Atlantic Ocean!"

The second man, the average Joe, says, "Watch me. I can do better than that!" He takes a mighty leap and lands ten feet out, twice as far as the alcoholic. The third man, the outstanding person laughs and says, "That's nothing. Watch this." He moves back about fifty yards, takes a running leap and lands twenty feet out, twice as far as Joe Average, and four times as far as the Bum. If we could view such a sight we would think all three men were idiots for attempting to do the impossible. No human being can jump across a small lake, let alone the Atlantic Ocean.

No human being can jump across a small lake, let alone the Atlantic Ocean.

People trying to earn their own salvation are even more foolish. God cannot be approached by man on the basis of his own moral integrity. God's holiness is infinitely greater than any of our righteous deeds. We can only approach God with the empty hands of faith and receive the gift which He offers us through the atoning work of Jesus Christ on the cross. "No, God will not accept me because I'm not a good person!" When an individual realizes this, he is well on his way to recognizing and receiving the "free gift of God through Jesus Christ."

The list of questions that can arise within a gospel presentation are almost endless. Josh McDowell and other apologists have done a good job in their books dealing with the most often asked questions.[12] However, no book is big enough to contain everything which may arise. In my evangelism class, we play a little game called "Sit in the Chair." An individual is called to the front at random and another student is called upon to ask any question they can think of which might arise while sharing a gospel presentation — the harder the better. The student in the chair is responsible for fielding the question and handling it as best they can while guiding the discussion back to the person and work of Christ.

Remember, Satan will do his best to get us and our friend sidetracked. Don't let him succeed. When sharing the gospel, avoid questions if possible. Give brief answers if necessary or schedule another time to address difficult issues. We need to make sure that our friend understands the gospel message. We also want to make clear that they need to make a decision about Christ based upon their understanding of God's great love for them. When we rely on the Holy Spirit to take our witness in word and deed and apply it to our friend's heart and life, we have done our part in carrying out the Great Commission.

When our friend is ready to trust Christ, we need to instruct him on how to place his faith in Christ and enter into a covenant relationship with God.

Have a Plan! Be Prepared!

Long ago the apostle Peter said,

> But in your hearts set apart Christ as Lord. Always be prepared to give an answer to everyone who asks you to give the reason for the hope that you have. But do this with gentleness and respect (1 Pet. 3:15).

There are many, many ways to present the simple message of what Christ has done and how to accept Him by faith. If you don't care for any in this chapter, develop one of your own that is true to the Bible. The issue is: Be Prepared! God will open doorways of opportunity and bless the lives of those who PLAN to share the good news of Christ.

There is a great difference between the dying words of those who are without Christ and those who have come to Christ. Consider these last words of two skeptics:

> If I had the whole world, I would give it to live one day. I shall be glad to find a hole to creep out of the world at. About to take a leap into the dark!
>
> Thomas Hobbs, philosopher and skeptic

> I would give worlds if I had them, that The Age of Reason had never been published. O Lord, help me! Christ, help me! O God, what have I done to suffer so much? But there is no God! But if there should be, what will become of me hereafter? Stay with me, for God's sake! Send even a child to stay with me, for it is hell to be alone. If ever the Devil had an agent, I have been that one.
>
> Thomas Paine, noted American atheist and author

Now consider these dying words of two famous men who had placed their faith and trust in Christ:

> "John Quincy Adams is quite well. But the house where he lives is becoming dilapidated. It is tottering. Time and the seasons have nearly destroyed it, and it is becoming quite uninhabitable. I shall have to move out soon. But John Quincy Adams is quite well, thank you." At death he said: "This is the last of earth. I am content."
>
> John Quincy Adams, American president

> Weep not for me, but for yourselves. I go to the Father of our Lord Jesus Christ, who will, through the mediation of His blessed Son, receive me, though a sinner, where I hope we shall meet to sing the new song, and remain everlastingly happy, world without end.[13]
>
> John Bunyan, author of *Pilgrim's Progress*

We must prepare ourselves to share the good news in a simple, systematic fashion. We must also learn to call our non-Christian friend to consider the gravity of his decision for or against the Lord. Then the Holy Spirit will do His work, so that our friend will face death with the same courage as the great men of faith above, and millions of others like them.

Thank you, Lord Jesus, for the privilege and honor of speaking your name before men!

---

1. J.D. Douglas, *Proclaim Christ until He Comes* (Lausanne II) (Minneapolis: World Wide Publications, 1990), p. 20.

2. John Bunyan, *The Pilgrim's Progress* (Westwood, NJ: The Christian Library, n.d.), pp. 35-36.

3. Francis M. Cosgrove, Jr., *Essentials of Discipleship* (Colorado Springs: NavPress, 1980), pp. 113-114.

4. Win Arn and Charles Arn, *The Master's Plan for Making Disciples* (Monrovia, CA: Church Growth Press, 1991), p. 10.

5. John Hendee, *Ambassadors for Christ: Training for Evangelism* (Cincinnati: Standard, 1984), p. 21.

6. Ibid., p. 25.

7. James D. Kennedy, *Evangelism Explosion* (Wheaton, IL : Tyndale, 1970).

8. Ibid., p. 97.

9. James W. Sire, *The Universe Next Door* (Downers Grove, IL: InterVarsity, 1988), pp. 36-37.

10. Josh McDowell, *A Ready Defense* (San Bernadino, CA: Here's Life, 1991), p. 412.

11. Ibid., p. 415.

12. There are numerous evangelical studies to help in the area of difficult questions concerning the Christian faith. See Clark Pinnock, *Reason Enough: A Case for the Christian Faith* (Downers Grove, IL: InterVarsity, 1980); Frank Morison, *Who Moved the Stone?* (Grand Rapids: Zondervan, 1958); Josh McDowell, *Evidence That Demands a Verdict*; and *More Evidence That Demands a Verdict.* (San Bernadino, CA: Here's Life, 1979 & 1981); Peter Kroft and Ronald K. Tacelli, *Handbook of Christian Apologetics* (Downers Grove, IL: InterVarsity, 1994).

13. John W. Lawrence, *The Seven Laws of the Harvest* (Grand Rapids: Kregel Publications, 1975), pp. 55-59.

Chapter 11

THE BIBLICAL PATTERN FOR ACCEPTING CHRIST BY FAITH

He then brought them out and asked, "Sirs, what must I do to be saved?"

They replied, "Believe in the Lord Jesus, and you will be saved — you and your household." Then they spoke the word of the Lord to him and to all the others in his house. At that hour of the night the jailer took them and washed their wounds; then immediately he and all his family were baptized.

Acts 16:30-33

When the people heard this, they were cut to the heart and said to Peter and the other apostles, "Brothers, what shall we do?"

Peter replied, "Repent and be baptized, every one of you, in the name of Jesus Christ for the forgiveness of your sins. And you will receive the gift of the Holy Spirit.

Acts 2:37-38

There is no greater joy for the Christian than helping an individual place his faith and trust in Christ. To see the barriers of our postmodern culture removed through both the demonstration and proclamation of the gospel is to see the power of God at work within the world. When our friends come to the point of understanding the gospel message and want to appropriate the merits of Christ's finished work on the cross into their own lives, they usually ask (in some way, shape, or form) the most important question in the whole world: "What must I do to be saved?" (Acts 2:37; 16:30).

The universally recognized answer to such an important question is: "Believe in the Lord Jesus Christ and you shall be saved." (Acts 16:31) The problem is that not every Christian or church group agrees as to the precise nature of exactly how an individual goes about placing his faith in the Lord Jesus Christ. For some church groups, faith is a miraculous work infused into the soul of infants at the time of their baptism.[1] For some, faith is displayed through the praying of a simple prayer.[2] For others faith is the work of the Holy Spirit upon the heart which excludes all other things, even repentance.[3] For others, true faith must include repentance.[4]

While we cannot pretend to solve every theological argument on this vastly important issue, we ought to be able to come to some basic conclusions on the matter. Our goal should be to attempt to find a biblical and universally accepted answer to this question. In other words: "What was the apostolic response to the question, 'What must I do to be saved?'" Instead of seeking to find a theological answer which will appease every theological tradition, perhaps a better approach would be to simply study the examples of people accepting the preached message of the crucified and risen Christ.

In order to accomplish this task, our study of the Acts of the Apostles in the New Testament can give us key information on this vital question. Why center our study in the Book of Acts? The answer is simple. The entire Old Testament was God's revelation of His work with the nation of Israel in preparation for the coming of the Messiah — Jesus. Yet, no one in the Old Testament responded in faith to the preaching of the death, burial, and resurrection of Jesus. In the New Testament, the Gospels were a record of the life, death, and resurrection of the Lord Jesus. However, all of the Gospels end before we see an example of the apostles' preaching about Christ's death and resurrection, calling people to faith in the risen Christ. All of the New Testament Epistles, from Romans through the Book of Revelation, were written to churches or individuals who had already accepted Christ as Lord and Savior. Hence, while we can find details of a faith already received, still we see no concrete example of a gospel sermon being preached and sinners being told to respond to that preaching in faith.

Only in the Acts of the Apostles do we see sinners hear the preaching of the crucified and risen Jesus. Only in Acts do we see those outside of Christ ask what steps need to be taken in order to be brought into a right relationship with this Jesus. Only in Acts do we see Christ's apostles answering this question by sinners: "What must I do to be saved?"

Only in the Acts of the Apostles do we see sinners hear the preaching of the crucified and risen Jesus.

We don't want to be insensitive about opinions held by any church group or individual Christian. We simply want to discover the apostolic response to people desiring to accept Christ by faith. Perhaps we can call this approach "Modeled Evangelism." Others have recently also sought out this same approach.[5] What, if any, model do we see in Acts that would give us insight into what it means to accept Christ by faith?

Belief in Jesus

When confronted with individuals who had never heard the good news of the message of Jesus, how did Jesus' apostles instruct them to put their faith and trust in Christ? We have such an example in the book of Acts.

In Acts 16:29-34 we see Paul and Silas in a Roman prison in Philippi (in Northern Greece). They confronted their Roman jailer who had been on the verge of committing suicide, fearing that his prisoners had escaped. All this man knew of the gospel was that Paul and Silas had been singing songs about a God who was able to give life meaning. The Bible records what happened next:

> The jailer called for lights, rushed in and fell trembling before Paul and Silas. He then brought them out and asked, "Sirs, what must I do to be saved?"
> They replied, "Believe in the Lord Jesus, and you will be saved — you and your household." Then they spoke the word of the Lord to him and to all the others in his house. At that hour of the night the jailer took them and washed their wounds; then immediately he and all his family were baptized. The jailer brought them into his house and set a meal before them; he was filled with joy because he had come to believe in God — he and his whole family (Acts 16:29-34).

Here we see a pagan man who knew nothing of the God of the Bible or Jesus Christ confronted with the gospel message. Here we see the inaugural response of what it means to place faith and trust in Christ. The initial answer to the most important question is: "Believe in the Lord Jesus Christ."

What did Paul instruct this man concerning Jesus? It is obvious that Paul told him the story of Jesus. In 1 Corinthians 15:1-4, Paul writes about this message which he always preached:

> Now, brothers, I want to remind you of the gospel I preached to you, which you received and on which you have taken your stand. By this gospel you are saved, if you hold firmly to the word I preached to you. Otherwise, you have believed in vain.
> For what I received I passed on to you as of first importance: that Christ died for our sins according to the Scriptures, that he was buried, that he was raised on the third day according to the Scriptures" (1 Cor. 15:1-4).

Yet, as the story in Acts 16 shows, more is necessary than a mere intellectual assent to the facts of the gospel message.

Repentance to Jesus

Once an individual accepts the reality of the finished work of Christ on the cross — to understand that it was our sinfulness which sent Jesus to His death — God has an additional instruction on what it means to place our faith and trust in Christ. In order to do this, we must turn away from our sin. Fortunately there is an example of this very scenario in the book of Acts.

In Acts 2:36-38, we find quite a different situation than that which confronted Paul at Philippi. Here we see the apostle Peter standing before a Jewish crowd which is quite familiar with the Old Testament Scriptures. They had just finished hearing a sermon on the Lordship of Jesus (His death, burial, and resurrection), showing that Jesus of Nazareth was the promised Messiah of the Old Testament. The crowd had obviously believed the facts of the gospel message because the Bible says, "They were cut to the heart" (Acts 2:37). The crowd had believed in the facts of the gospel, and the people asked Peter our most important question: "Brothers, what shall we do?" (Acts 2:37). The Bible records the event as follows:

> "Therefore let all Israel be assured of this: God has made this Jesus, whom you crucified, both Lord and Christ."
>
> When the people heard this, they were cut to the heart and said to Peter and the other apostles, "Brothers, what shall we do?"
>
> Peter replied, "Repent and be baptized, every one of you, in the name of Jesus Christ for the forgiveness of your sins. And you will receive the gift of the Holy Spirit. The promise is for you and your children and for all who are far off — for all whom the Lord our God will call."
>
> With many other words he warned them; and he pleaded with them, "Save yourselves from this corrupt generation" (Acts 2:36-40).

It is interesting to notice that Peter didn't respond by saying, "Nothing — since you have already believed." Peter understood that for those who believe the gospel message, the next aspect of saving faith is to "Repent!"

In the original language of the New Testament, repentance (μετανοέω, *metanoeo*, vb.; μετάνοια, *metanoia*, n.) means a radical turning point in life. Today, we would liken it to doing a U-turn with our life. Repentance is more than being sorry. Repentance is being so sorry that our mind is converted to change. When we truly believe the gospel of our Savior Jesus, to know our sins sent Christ to the cross, then we shall be driven by the truth of that gospel to repent — to turn away from our sins and embrace the forgiveness of Christ. Jesus Himself said, "Unless you repent, you too will all perish" (Luke 13:3-5). The apostles remembered this when they asked those who wished to accept Christ by faith to repent.

Repentance is being so sorry that your mind is converted to change.

Once an individual has heard the good news of what Christ has done

Confession of Jesus

and has turned his life away from sin and towards Christ in repentance, he has exhibited two inner aspects of faith. Yet biblical faith is never simply an inner aspect of the heart. Biblical faith must find its expression in the outer actions of life (see Jas. 2:19-20). Faith in Jesus must be expressed in order to be complete. Fortunately, in the Book of Acts we see how this was to be displayed by the preaching of early Christians.

In Acts 8:26-39, we find the most detailed picture of one individual becoming a Christian that exists in the New Testament. A high-ranking Ethiopian, who had been to Jerusalem to worship at the temple, was on his way back to Africa when he happened to meet a Christian preacher named Philip. He invited Philip into his chariot and asked the preacher to explain a passage of Scripture from the Old Testament which happened to be a prophecy about the coming Messiah. Philip took advantage of the situation to preach the good news of Jesus to the official. The Bible records what occurred:

> Then Philip began with that very passage of Scripture and told him the good news about Jesus.
> As they traveled along the road, they came to some water and the eunuch said, "Look, here is water. Why shouldn't I be baptized?" [Philip said, "If you believe with all your heart, you may." The eunuch answered, "I believe that Jesus Christ is the Son of God."] And he gave orders to stop the chariot. Then both Philip and the eunuch went down into the water and Philip baptized him (Acts 8:35-38).

Obviously the Ethiopian believed the message and had repented because he wished to know what was necessary in order to be baptized. Philip asked him for a simple confession of his faith. The Ethiopian responded: "I believe that Jesus Christ is the Son of God."[6] The open confession of faith in Christ is supported silently in every conversion account in the book of Acts. How would the gospel preacher have known whom to baptize and receive into the fellowship of the church if there had been no outward confession of allegiance to Christ? Paul discusses this very topic in Romans 10:9-10: "That if you confess with your mouth, 'Jesus is Lord,' and believe in your heart that God raised him from the dead, you will be saved. For it is with your heart that you believe and are justified, and it is with your mouth that you confess and are saved." Jesus also spoke quite clearly about this in Matthew 10:32-33: "Whoever acknowledges me before men, I will also acknowledge him before my Father in heaven. But whoever disowns me before men, I will disown him before my Father in heaven."

Confession of faith in Christ is made at the beginning of our walk with the Lord and it continues as our lifelong witness, displaying Christ to all we meet.

Baptism into Jesus

So far we have discovered that in the New Testament, when people wanted to accept Jesus as their Lord and Savior, they were told to first believe in the message of Jesus, then to turn their life away from sin and to Christ in repentance. This faith was also to be displayed outwardly by a confession of Jesus as the Lord of all of life. One more aspect of biblical faith remains in all these conversion accounts from the book of Acts.

Let's look at every example from the New Testament that we have examined so far. In Acts 16:31-33, the Philippian jailer was immediately baptized. Notice that the text does not record that he repented or confessed his faith. But these were obviously present since this is what the early Christians were always taught. The author of Acts assumed that his readers would understand this. In contrast to this, however, notice that baptism is specifically mentioned.

In Acts 2:38, baptism was commanded to the crowd at Pentecost when they asked what they should do. This followed their belief and repentance. Notice that the text does not specifically mention their confession of faith, but it was obviously present, otherwise Peter would not have known whom to baptize. It is important to understand that God gave two tremendous promises to those who displayed their faith in Jesus by being baptized. These promises were: 1) God would forgive all of their sins; and, 2) God would grant to each individual the gift of the Holy Spirit.

In Acts 8:35-39, Philip preached Jesus to the Ethiopian (8:35). This preaching of Jesus obviously included baptism because the next question we hear the Ethiopian ask is, "Look, here is water. Why shouldn't I be baptized?" (8:36). Obviously, part of "preaching Jesus" in the primitive church must have included a call to baptism. Everyone in the New Testament who wished to become a Christian was commanded to be baptized. And no one was considered a complete Christian until after they had been baptized. G.R. Beasley-Murray has done the most complete study of baptism available in the English language. In considering a statement by Eduard Schweitzer, he concludes:

> In which case, writes Schweitzer, [Acts] 2:38 teaches nothing other than that for Luke baptism belongs to the much more important fact of conversion. This judgment is surely true to the theology of Acts. It will cause offense to none who refuse to make conversion small, who see in it no merely human phenomenon but a turning of the sinner to God in Christ enabled by the Spirit, answered by the divine acceptance of the penitent, with all that implies of the gift of grace, hence a participation in the redemption of Christ through the Spirit. To such a conversion baptism 'belongs' as its embodiment, its completion and its seal.[7]

In the Acts of the Apostles, it seems that baptism was the final display of faith which taught the new convert what it meant to truly come to Christ.

In Acts 22:16 (11-16), the apostle Paul made what we have noted above perfectly clear when he retold the story of his conversion. Listen to his words:

> "A man named Ananias came to see me. He was a devout observer of the law and highly respected by all the Jews living there. He stood beside me and said, 'Brother Saul, receive your sight!' And at that very moment I was able to see him.
>
> "Then he said: 'The God of our fathers has chosen you to know his will and to see the Righteous One and to hear words from his mouth. You will be his witness to all men of what you have seen and heard. And now what are you waiting for? Get up, be baptized and wash your sins away, calling on his name'" (Acts 22:12-16).

It seems that the apostle Paul did not even consider his own sins forgiven until after he had displayed faith in the finished work of Christ by being baptized!

Jesus placed this same emphasis on baptism in the Great Commission itself.

> Then Jesus came to them and said, "All authority in heaven and on earth has been given to me. Therefore go and make disciples of all nations, baptizing them in the name of the Father and of the Son and of the Holy Spirit, and teaching them to obey everything I have commanded you. And surely I am with you always, to the very end of the age" (Matt. 28:18-20).

The apostles only taught what Jesus had commanded.

In writing to those who had already accepted Christ, the apostles emphasized the significance of baptism in the life of those who walk with Christ by faith:

> Having been buried with him in baptism and raised with him through your faith in the power of God, who raised him from the dead (Col. 2:12).

> For all of you who were baptized into Christ have clothed your-selves with Christ (Gal. 3:27).

> What shall we say, then? Shall we go on sinning so that grace may increase? By no means! We died to sin; how can we live in it any longer? Or don't you know that all of us who were bap-tized into Christ Jesus were baptized into his death? We were therefore buried with him through baptism into death in order that, just as Christ was raised from the dead through the glory of the Father, we too may live a new life.

> If we have been united with him like this in his death, we will certainly also be united with him in his resurrection. For we know that our old self was crucified with him so that the body of sin might be done away with, that we should no longer be slaves to sin — because anyone who has died has been freed from sin (Rom. 6:1-7).

> And this water symbolizes baptism that now saves you also — not the removal of dirt from the body but the pledge of a good conscience toward God. It saves you by the resurrection of Jesus Christ (1 Pet. 3:21).

When we display our faith in Jesus through baptism, the Bible teaches that several things should be clear to us. First, in baptism we declare to God that we want to "clothe ourselves with Christ." Also, in baptism, we display our faith in the death, burial, and resurrection of Jesus. If we unite ourselves with Jesus "like this" in faith, we can be certain of His power to raise us up from the dead. Finally, baptism is "an appeal to God for a good conscience" through the power of Jesus' resurrection. Baptism is faith asking for God's cleansing through the finished work of Christ.

What we have attempted to do in this brief study is to point out the scriptural answer to the question: "What must I do to be saved?" We do not wish to be exclusivistic. We simply want to see the biblical model of accepting Christ by faith as proclaimed by Jesus' apostles. In review let us state that when people wanted to accept Jesus as their Lord and Savior, they were instructed to place their faith in Christ by: (1) belief in Jesus;

(2) repentance to Jesus; (3) confession of Jesus; and (4) baptism into Jesus. To leave out any aspect of biblical faith would display unfaithfulness to the Bible and to the Jesus of the Bible.

When an individual comes to us and asks: "What must I do to be saved?" it would seem a wise response to share with them the basic pattern of response found in the examples of New Testament conversions. Perhaps if more Christians would simply adopt this "Model Evangelism," much debate could be spared by theologians wishing to argue at what millisecond a person receives salvation. Does salvation come when a person believes the facts of the gospel message, or is it only after repentance? Are the merits of Christ's death on the cross applied to the life of the sinner only after he confesses Christ with his mouth, or are the blessings of heaven reserved for only those who have been baptized? Much of the evangelical world has compartmentalized these aspects of faith instead of seeing them as a unified whole. In many churches, an individual may believe in the gospel message and come forward publicly confessing Christ as Lord, only to be baptized weeks or months later. This sort of practice is totally foreign to the spirit of the New Testament. Baptism was so important that the Ethiopian was baptized immediately in the very first water available, which probably amounted to little more that a slimy watering hole along the Gaza road. The Philippian jailer was baptized in the middle of the night along with his whole believing family. The New Testament knows of no compartmentalizing of these responses of faith. In following the New Testament examples of conversion, perhaps we could avoid much of the theological haggling which goes on between Christians from differing theological traditions.

Much debate could be spared by theologians wishing to argue at what millisecond a person receives salvation.

At my home church, my wife and I teach a five-week Bible School class for people considering Christ and His church. The class studies the basic elements of the gospel message and what it means to be a part of Christ's church. On the first Sunday the class meets, we usually have individuals introduce themselves and share a little information about their life and church background (if any). On one occasion, a nice young couple were present and shared that they had come from a background which practiced infant baptism. Their conversation betrayed the fact that their belief in Christ was nominal at best. The wife was quite forceful when she asked, "All I want to know is, will we have to get dunked in order to join this church?" That was hardly a question I wanted to discuss in this initial class session. I assured her that we would address that issue before our five-week study was finished.

On the Sunday before we were to study the biblical material on accepting Christ by faith, I handed out a worksheet (see Appendix B) listing every conversion account recorded in the Book of Acts. I asked the class to read through each account, use the worksheet to make notes about what was taught, and then to draw their own conclusions. I assured them that we would discuss any questions they had at our next class session.

I spent the whole week wondering what sort of argument may arise with the wife who had asked her question about baptism. On the following Sunday, when the class assembled, I asked if everyone had done their assigned work and if they had learned anything. Immediately, that lady's hand shot up. I thought to myself, "Oh no, here it comes," but I smiled and called on her. She stated, "I did learn something. I learned that I need to be baptized." Then, turning to her husband, she slapped him on the arm and said, "And we would do it together this Sunday, if he wasn't so bullheaded!" The whole class burst into laughter and we were able to enjoy examining the simple New Testament examples of people who trusted Christ by faith. Within a few weeks both the husband and the wife were baptized into Christ and became tremendous workers within the church. I have found that most people have no trouble at all simply reading the examples of people accepting Christ by faith and then understanding what they must do to display their own faith and trust in Jesus.

The Practice of Baptism in the New Testament

Because baptism is a debated issue among Christians today, it would be good for us to consider this aspect of faith a little more closely. Let us suppose that an individual is ready to become a follower of Jesus. He understands that Jesus is the Christ, the Son of the living God. He believes it with all his heart. He has repented of his sins and confessed his allegiance to Christ. Now he is ready to be baptized and inquires as to how he is to go about this.

First he talks to a Catholic friend who instructs him that baptism is the sprinkling of water on the head. He is convinced, and yet that evening he watches a movie on television that shows Jesus baptized by having water poured over his head. The next day he asks a Baptist friend to tell him which is the correct way to baptize: by sprinkling or pouring? His friend replies emphatically that neither are correct. Only immersion is the true form of baptism. Now he is totally confused and later in the day, he meets another friend who is Quaker who instructs him that he does not need to be baptized in water at all!

The water of baptism which God means to display our unity with the Lord Jesus has become the very water that divides millions of Christians. Recognizing this, our question should be: "Is there a universally accepted teaching on Christian baptism as recorded in the Christian Scripture?" Whatever the Bible teaches should be our doctrine if we are serious about being unconditionally committed to the authority of the Bible as the Word of God.

The water which God means to display our unity with the Lord Jesus has become the very water that divides millions of Christians.

Does the Bible give plain teaching on who should be baptized and how? As we proceed in this study you may notice that all of the Bible references come out of the New Testament. As stated earlier in this chapter, the reason is simple. No one ever became a Christian in the Old Testament. The Old Testament is a record of God's dealings with His people from the Creation of the world until approximately 400 years before the birth of Jesus. The Old Testament prophets predicted the coming of Christ, but only in the New Testament do we find people responding to the message of the gospel and seeking baptism into Christ. In our study we will attempt to answer two basic questions: Who should be baptized and how should baptism be administered?

Who Should Be Baptized?

The Bible teaches that faith is necessary in order to become a Christian. When an individual asked, "What must I do to be saved?" he was told to believe the gospel, repent of his sins, and confess his allegiance to Christ. Only then was the individual ready for baptism (Acts 2:36ff; 8:35-39; 16:30-33).

Jesus' exhortation is correct in Mark 16:15-16, "Whoever believes and is baptized will be saved." You can find church groups that rearrange the order of what Jesus said. I play a little game with this passage of Scripture in a class I teach on personal evangelism. I take three pieces of paper and write on them "believe," "baptized" and "saved." Then I ask for three volunteers to each take one of the papers. Then I tell them to stand in front of the class in any order they choose. I tell the class that no matter what the arrangement, we could find some Christian tradition which teaches that particular order. For instance, some groups believe that first an individual is baptized, then they are saved and later on in life they can be taught to believe. Other groups teach that first you believe, then you are saved and later on you can be baptized. There are a variety of possible orders, but the divine order of things is clear in Jesus' command.[8] First comes belief (in who Jesus is and what He has done; this includes repentance and confession). Next comes baptism. And finally salvation is the result. Baptism, without consenting faith, is never seen to be a biblical possibility. Who then shall be baptized? Those who hear the gospel, believe it and respond to it in repentance and confession.

What about Infants?

Many would ask: "What about infants?" There is no example of an infant receiving baptism recorded in the New Testament. It is true that there are several "household" baptisms recorded in Acts. However in every one of the them the entire household was said to have believed, rejoiced, or praised God (Acts 10:33,46; 16:27-34; 18:8). Infants could not have been included, because infants can do none of these things.

Some Bible teachers have pointed to the case of Lydia's household in Acts 16:13-15 as an example of infants receiving baptism in the New Testament. The argument states that Lydia's household was said to have been baptized, yet there is no mention of faith on the part of the members of her household. Some "scholars" claim that this is evidence of infant baptism.[9] However, four great assumptions must be made in order for us to consider this a biblical example of infant baptism. First, we must assume that Lydia was married and the Bible is silent on this issue. If she was married, we must also assume that she had children. Again, the Bible is silent. The third assumption requires that if she had children, then at least one of them must have been an infant. Finally, if these children were infants, they must have accompanied Lydia on this business trip.

The word for household used in the text does not require that we understand these individuals to be members of Lydia's immediate family. It would generally also refer to the servants accompanying her on this journey. In fact the Bible is quite clear that the only people with Lydia that day were women (Acts 16:13). This is the closest account in Scripture to infant baptism. Many have noted that this is hardly the basis for a doctrine that has divided the church for centuries.[10]

For an example of infant baptism we have to leave the Bible and turn to the pages of ancient church history. The earliest mention of the practice of infant baptism is found in the writings of Tertullian (*Treatise on Baptism*, ch. 18). He writes at the beginning of the Third Century (A.D. 200-206):

> And so, according to the circumstances and disposition, and even age, of each individual, the delay of baptism is preferable; principally, however, in the case of little children. . . . The Lord does indeed say, "Forbid them not to come unto me." Let them "come," then, while they are growing up. Let them "come" while they are learning, while they are learning whether to come; let them come become Christians when they have become able to know Christ. Why does the innocent period of life hasten to the "remission of sins?"[11]

Not only does the Bible teach against infant baptism, but as can clearly be seen, the earliest reference in church history also speaks against the practice.[12]

What about Original Sin?

Many believe infant baptism necessary because of the belief that infants are born with the guilt of sin and hence can only receive forgiveness by baptism. What does the Bible teach about infants?

> Jesus said, "Let the little children come to me, and do not hinder them, for the kingdom of heaven belongs to such as these" (Matt. 19:14).

> I tell you the truth, unless you change and become like little children, you will never enter the kingdom of heaven (Matt. 18:3).

If children are guilty of Adam's sin, how can Jesus say that we have to become like them to enter the Kingdom of Heaven? While it must be admitted that it is possible that Jesus is simply referring to the intense, unquestioning faith of small children, it is also possible that the Lord is indeed speaking of their innocence.

If children are guilty, how can Jesus say that we have to become like them to enter the Kingdom of Heaven?

Perhaps the most clear and concise passage on the subject can be found in Ezekiel 18:19-20:

> Yet you ask, "Why does the son not share the guilt of his father?" Since the son has done what is just and right and has been care-

ful to keep all my decrees, he will surely live. The soul who sins is the one who will die. The son will not share the guilt of the father, nor will the father share the guilt of the son. The righteousness of the righteous man will be credited to him, and the wickedness of the wicked will be charged against him.

Here is an Old Testament passage which clearly refutes any notion of the guilt of sin being passed from one individual to another. While the Augustinian doctrine of original sin is quite complex and well reasoned, it is based more upon philosophical deduction than upon the clear teaching of Scripture. There are several good works which examine this topic in a more critical manner.[13]

If children are innocent, then there is no need of baptism. This is universally assumed in the New Testament because only those who could respond to the gospel in faith were candidates for baptism. If the Bible is our only book of authority, then there is no room in the church for infant baptism.

How Is Baptism to Be Administered?

If the argument concerning proper candidates for baptism has been severe among believers, the controversy concerning the proper mode of baptism has been even more intense. It is unfortunate that Christians have treated each other with so little love in the midst of this debate, all in the name of being faithful to the Jesus who commands us to "love one another." We do not wish to be close-minded on this subject. We simply want to see what the basic Bible teaching is.

What is biblically necessary for the administration of baptism within the New Testament witness? First, we see that water is necessary. Christian baptism, like the baptism of John, involves a baptism using the vehicle of water. When Philip was witnessing to the Ethiopian, the question was, "Look, here is water. Why shouldn't I be baptized?" (Acts 8:36). They then proceeded to go "down into the water" and "come up out of the water" (Acts 8:38-39). When Peter witnessed the miraculous outpouring of the Holy Spirit upon the household of Cornelius, the first Gentile convert, he asked, "Can anyone keep these people from being baptized with water?" (Acts 10:47). There are numerous places in the New Testament where water is mentioned or inferred in the discussion of baptism (Eph. 5:26; Heb. 10:22; 1 Pet 3:21; also possibly John 3:5; 1 John 5:6,8). The belief that Christian baptism involves no water is foreign to the authors of the New Testament.

Not only is water required, but it seems that "much water" was necessary. "Now John also was baptizing at Aenon near Salim, because there was plenty of water, and people were constantly coming to be baptized"

(John 3:23). While the purpose and result of John's baptism was different from that of Christian baptism (Luke 3:16; Acts 1:5), its mode seems to have been identical. The close description of Jesus' own baptism by John and the Christian baptism of the Ethiopian are nearly identical (minus the miraculous signs which accompanied Jesus; see Matt. 3:16 and Mark 1:10; compare Acts 8:38-39). Both involved going into and coming out of the water. Add to this the imagery of a burial and resurrection which Paul points out in Romans 6:3-4, and it seems apparent that the most natural reading of even the English text would indicate immersion as the normal mode by which baptism is to be administered.

To this we need to add the evidence of linguistics. The word in our English Bible translated "baptize" is from the Greek βαπτίζω (baptizo). The basic root βάπτω (bapto) means "to dip in or under," the intensive form βαπτίζω (baptizo) means "to immerse."[14] No linguist of any background disputes this.

There are, in fact, two places in the New Testament where the root bapto is used outside of the sacramental sense of Christian baptism. The first is in Luke 16:24, in Jesus' story of the rich man and Lazarus. Here Lazarus asks that Abraham "dip" (bapto) the tip of his finger in water. It would be absurd to think that Abraham could "sprinkle or pour" the tip of his finger in the water. The normal linguistic usage of this word makes any translation other than "dip or immerse" impossible.

The second New Testament occurrence is found in John 13:26 in the account of Jesus' identifying His betrayer. Here Jesus declared that His betrayer would be the disciple to whom He gave a piece of bread which Christ Himself had "dipped" (bapto) in a dish. Jesus did not sprinkle or pour the bread into the "gravy." He dipped it. Again, the concept of immersion is mandatory. We have the evidence of simple English usage, and more significant evidence of the basic meaning of the Greek words in question. All the above makes a very strong case for immersion as the original method of baptism.[15]

The fact that the original form of baptism was immersion is agreed upon by scholars from every major segment of Christianity. The Catholic tradition is quick to recognize the primitive form of baptism. In the *New Catholic Encyclopedia* (1967 ed.) in the article on "Baptism in the Bible," we find the following quote: "It is evident that baptism in the early church was by immersion." The Catholic scholar then proceeds to give scriptural examples from Heb. 10:22; Acts 8:38-39; Rom. 6:3-4 and Col. 2:12. Even as late as the 13th century the great Catholic theologian, Thomas Aquinas wrote (*Summa Theologica*, Part 3, Q66, Art. 7): "It is the safer way to baptize by immersion because that is the most common custom."[16] Again, in fairness, it must be noted that Aquinas did not require immersion, but he did understand the original meaning. It was not until the Council of Revenna in 1322 that sprinkling was officially substituted for immersion in the Roman Catholic Church.

In the Reformed Tradition John Calvin wrote in the *Institutes of the Christian Religion* (Book 4, Ch. 15, Sec. 19): "The word baptize, however, signifies to immerse; and it is certain that immersion was the practice of the ancient Church."[17] Again, in all fairness, it must be admitted that Calvin did not see a need to require immersion, but he did recognize the meaning of the word and that immersion was indeed the method practiced by the apostles and the very first Christians.

Even Karl Barth, the most well known Reformed theologian of the 20th century, agreed. He wrote, "The Greek word (βαπτιζω) and the German word (*taufen*) originally and properly describe the process by which a man or an object is completely immersed in water and then withdrawn from it again."[18] He goes on to say that this was, without doubt, the original form of baptism. The German Reformed theologian, Philip Schaff, writes, "The usual FORM of baptism was immersion. This is inferred from the original meaning of the Greek."[19]

Even in the Lutheran Tradition, we see Martin Luther write, "Baptism . . . is that immersion in water from which it derives its name, for the Greek *Baptizo* means 'I immerse' and *Baptisma* means 'immersion.'"[20] As with many others, Luther did not require immersion. In fact, he spiritualized the concept. However, he did understand the clear evidence for the original meaning of the word.

In my own experience, I have never met a minister or priest from any orthodox Christian group who refused to accept the validity of immersion as a proper form for baptism. However, any other variation from the original practice is bound to evoke an argument. If we know the original form of baptism, and, if every Christian group agrees on the validity of that one universally recognized form, does it not stand to reason that the safest course of action is to follow the early church in immersing those who wish to display their faith in Christ? Any other practice seems deficient by comparison.

A Final Word Concerning Baptism

At this point many in the evangelical world would probably raise an eyebrow and ask, "Are you saying, then, that baptism is necessary for salvation?"[21] I must admit a certain uneasiness every time I am asked that question. The answer to such a question has to be an emphatic NO! Infants are saved in God's eternal plan whether baptized or not.

But aside from infants and small children, other serious questions arise. What of those who have not come to the conclusions we have stated in our study? What of those who have truly turned to Christ in their hearts but have not had the opportunity to display such faith in Christian baptism? I have opinions about their salvation based upon my understanding of the vast grace of God as outlined in the New Testament. Yet they remain, only my opinions.

"Must I be baptized to be saved?" This is a question that I simply cannot answer. To do so would be placing myself in the place of God, and this I will not do. When asked this question, I usually point out to the questioner that, "I am in sales, not management!" It is not my place to sit on God's throne and make divine executive decisions.

When anyone asks me this question: "Do I have to be baptized to be saved?" I respond by saying, "You have asked me a question that I cannot answer. And I suspect it is not the real question you expect me to answer. Let me rephrase your question. I suspect your real question is, "Must I be baptized to *display faith in Christ* as outlined in the preaching of Jesus' apostles as recorded in Holy Scripture inspired by the Holy Spirit?" If this is what the individual wants to know, then I do have an answer to that question. The answer is an emphatic YES! To require less than Christ and His apostles is to be untrue to Scripture and to the Christ of Scripture.

To require less than Christ and His apostles is to be untrue to Scripture and to the Christ of Scripture.

What of those who cannot agree with this position? We must be gracious and honor the inner assent of their hearts to the Jesus who has changed our hearts as well. At the same time we must teach what we see the Bible to teach. We must let God sort out the conclusion of these matters. We must speak the truth in love.

The universally recognized practice of baptism in the New Testament appears to be a baptism of individuals who can believe the gospel, repent of their sins, and confess their faith in Christ. Those who came to be baptized by Christ's apostles were immersed in water under the authority of the Father, Son, and Holy Spirit, to obey the command of the Savior, by which they showed their acceptance of Christ as Savior and Lord.

Model-Based Evangelism Bears Fruit

While, doctrine at times can be confusing, example is generally quite clear. While I was ministering in northern Nebraska, I received a phone call one day asking me to visit an older couple who lived in our community. The call was from a relative in Iowa who had attended a family reunion and shared her faith with her uncle and aunt. She gave me their phone number and I called them and set up an appointment.

The couple were quite polite and open to my visit since it had been initiated by their niece. I asked them about their church background and they shared that they had not been involved in the life of a church since the days of their youth. The husband had grown up in a Christian church and had been baptized at the age of twelve. The wife had grown up in a church which practiced infant baptism and had quit attending services in her late teens.

I asked if they would be interested in studying what the Bible had to say about what it meant to be a Christian. They agreed and over the next several weeks, we met to examine who Jesus was and how we accept Him as Lord and Savior by faith. As I was concluding the study of New Testament conversions, I asked the wife if she had any questions. She asked if she could accept Christ and display her faith in Christian baptism. Since the husband had already been immersed as a youth, I wondered how I might proceed with him. But he solved the problem for me.

"You know," he said, "I never understood what it meant to be a Christian. When I was baptized as a youth, I simply went up with everyone else on Easter Sunday. I didn't understand who Jesus was or what it would mean to give my life to Him. Could I affirm my faith in Christ and be baptized too?" The next day it was my privilege to accept their confession of faith and baptize them into Christ.

Example is usually the best teacher.

I have found that example is usually the best teacher. Teaching the things of Christ involves faithfulness to Jesus in His teaching and example. I believe the apostle Paul understood these things when he wrote to the Romans.

> Therefore I glory in Christ Jesus in my service to God. I will not venture to speak of anything except what Christ has accomplished through me in leading the Gentiles to obey God by what I have said and done — by the power of signs and miracles,

through the power of the Spirit. So from Jerusalem all the way around to Illyricum, I have fully proclaimed the gospel of Christ (Rom. 15:17-19).

---

1. See Reinhold Seeburg, *History of Doctrines* (Grand Rapids: Baker, 1977), vol 1, pp. 328-357; vol. 2, pp. 118-124.

2. For a good example, see Paul Little, *How to Give Away Your Faith* (Downers Grove, IL: InterVarsity, 1966), pp. 58-60.

3. Two popular examples of this are Charles C. Ryrie, *So Great a Salvation: What It Means to Believe in Christ* (Wheaton: Victor Books, 1989); and Zane C. Hodges, *Absolutely Free: A Biblical Reply to Lordship Salvation* (Grand Rapids: Zondervan, 1989).

4. See John F MacArthur, Jr., *The Gospel according to Jesus: What Does Jesus Mean When He Says, "Follow Me?"* (Grand Rapids: Zondervan, 1988).

5. A wonderful example of this can be seen in Robert Stein, "Baptism and Becoming a Christian in the New Testament," *The Southern Baptist Journal of Theology* (2:1, Spring 1998): 6-17.

6. While the earliest manuscripts omit Acts 8:37, it no doubt had to occur in this basic form. The Ethiopian had to respond in some manner, and what would have been more appropriate than the Great Confession (Matt 16:16)? I. Howard Marshall notes that the reply is "perfectly sound theology, but the style is not that of Luke and the manuscript evidence is weak." I. Howard Marshall, *The Acts of the Apostles* (Grand Rapids: Eerdmans, 1980), p. 165.

7. G.R Beasley-Murray, *Baptism in the New Testament* (Grand Rapids: Eerdmans, 1981), pp. 121-122.

8. Many scholars question the manuscript evidence for this particular section of Mark's Gospel. If the text was not a part of Mark's original Gospel, surely the doctrine of the text is taught elsewhere in the Acts of the Apostles. In the New Testament the order seems to be clear: first, an individual believes, then they are baptized, and finally they belong to Christ and His body the church.

9. Older scholars such as Barnes weakly attempt to see infants within Lydia's household, see Albert Barnes, *Notes on the New Testament: Acts of the Apostles* (Grand Rapids: Baker, 1953), p. 105. Other more contemporary authors have argued rigorously in favor of infant baptism, see Oscar Cullmann, *Baptism in the New Testament* (Philadelphia: Westminster, 1950); R.E.O. White, *The Biblical Doctrine of Initiation* (Grand Rapids: Eerdmans, 1960); and Michael Green, *Baptism: Its Purpose, Practice and Power* (Downers Grove, IL: InterVarsity, 1987).

10. See Ben Witherington, III, *The Acts of the Apostles: A Socio-Rhetorical Commentary* (Grand Rapids: Eerdmans, 1998), p. 155.

11. Tertullian, *On Baptism*, in *The Ante-Nicene Fathers*, edited by Alexander Roberts and James Donaldson; vol. 3: *Latin Christianity: Its Founder, Tertullian* (Grand Rapids: Eerdmans, 1978), p. 678.

12. Paul K Jewett has provided an excellent study on the practice of infant baptism. Jewett notes that the closer one gets to the time of the New Testament, the fewer and fewer the references to infant baptism. See his *Infant Baptism and the Covenant of Grace* (Grand Rapids: Eerdmans, 1978), p. 43.

13. In addition to Jewett's work also see David W. Fletcher, ed., *Baptism and the Remission of Sins* (Joplin, MO: College Press, 1990); and an older, but quite thorough work by Alexander Campbell and N.L. Rice, *A Debate between Rev. A. Campbell and Rev. N.L. Rice on the Action, Subject, Design and Administrator of Christian Baptism* (Cincinnati: Standard, 1917).

14. Albrecht Oepke, "Βάπτω," *Theological Dictionary of New Testament Words*; also G.R. Beasley-Murray, "Baptism," *Dictionary of New Testament Theology*.

15. In the LXX, βαπτίζω is used only once and βάπτω is used 16 times. In each of these occasions, the idea of an immersion is mandatory.

16. Thomas Aquinas, *Summa Theologica* (Westminster, MD: Christian Classics, 1948), p. 2380.

17. John Calvin, *Institutes of the Christian Religion*, trans. by Henry Beveridge (Grand Rapids: Eerdmans, 1979), vol. 2, p. 524.

18. Karl Barth, *The Teaching of the Church Regarding Baptism* (London: SCM Press, 1948), p. 9.

19. Philip Schaff, *History of the Christian Church*, vol. 1, *Apostolic Christianity* (Grand Rapids: Eerdmans, 1910), p. 468.

20. Martin Luther, *The Babylonian Captivity of the Church* (1520), contained in *Luther's Works*, ed. by Helmut T. Lehmann, vol. 36, Word and Sacrament II (Philadelphia: Fortress, 1959), p. 64.

21. Some of this final argument also appears in Appendix A: Baptism in Its Historical Perspective.

Section 3
"TEACH"

"God has not called us
to produce mere converts.
He has called us
to make disciples."

Chapter 12
Disciple Making:
The Great Commission's Forgotten Task

> Christian discipleship as Paul describes it is challenging and disturbing. For to be like God is to be like the God who revealed himself in Jesus Christ. This God is neither the contemplative God of Aristotle, nor the incorporeal, intelligible God of Philo and Plutarch, nor the detached God of Epicurus, nor the demanding but forgiving God of Qumran. Rather, the Christian disciple will resemble the involved God revealed in Jesus Christ. Likeness to God for the Christian disciple in Paul's thought world entails continual participation in the death of Jesus Christ. It means being, in an unrighteous world, righteous as God is.[1]
>
> L. Ann Jervis

We noted at the very beginning of this book that the command of the Great Commission is: MAKE DISCIPLES. We need to remember that a disciple is "a learner-follower of Jesus Christ." We make disciples by going and baptizing and teaching. In the first section of our study, we learned that "going" involved understanding both the gospel message and the particular culture which is our harvest field. When going, our job is to attempt to discover the best way to bring these two elements together. We wish to share the gospel with our current culture.

In the second section of our study, we learned that our emphasis rests upon finding the most fruitful methodology for sharing the gospel with our generation. Our goal is to ultimately lead people to understand who Jesus is and accept His offer of forgiveness and His claim of Lordship over every area of life. This culminates when an individual responds in faith to the "good news." The culminating display of such faith is seen in the New Testament understanding of baptism.

Finally, we must "teach" the new convert everything Jesus has commanded us. As we noted earlier, many in the church seem to believe that the task of evangelism is over once an individual is "toweling off" after their baptism. Nothing could be further from the truth. Our job of "making a disciple" is just *beginning* when a person comes to Christ. The task of God's people is to *bring to maturity* those who give their lives to Christ. Win and Charles Arn have noted,

> Evangelism focuses on decision-making rather than disciple-making. Most mass and local church evangelism approaches today have a significant common shortcoming. Attention is centered, and success judged around the goal of getting a "decision." That brief verbal commitment is seen as the ultimate response to the Great Commission. Unfortunately, there is often a great gap between "getting a decision" and "making a disciple." A "disciple" suggests a commitment, incorporation into the Body, then an ongoing, reproductive life-style as a follower of Christ. An analysis of many church training programs and parachurch crusades in America today indicates that the bottom line for evangelism is the number of decisions recorded. This "decision-making" mentality may actually be one of the reasons national church membership continues to decline, in relation to population growth, in spite of so much being said and done in mass evangelism, media evangelism, evangelism training, and evangelism conferences.[2]

This was never the idea in the mind of our Savior. A disciple needs to be continually taught everything Jesus commanded. This is a lifelong process. We have come to realize that evangelism leading up to a decision for Christ is a process. So now, we must also realize that the journey toward a mature walk with Christ involves a long process.

Our job of "making a disciple" is just beginning when a person comes to Christ.

The apostle Paul's vision for those who give their lives to Christ is clear.

> . . . so that the body of Christ may be built up until we all reach unity in the faith and in the knowledge of the Son of God and become mature, attaining to the whole measure of the fullness of Christ.
>
> Then we will no longer be infants, tossed back and forth by the waves, and blown here and there by every wind of teaching and by the cunning and craftiness of men in their deceitful scheming. Instead, speaking the truth in love, we will in all things grow up into him who is the Head, that is, Christ (Eph. 4:12b-15).

Our task is to provide a working plan based on God's revealed mind in the Scriptures to allow for everyone who comes to Christ to have the opportunity to grow into the type of individual we find in the Scripture above. Remember, Jesus never asked us to go into the world and make mere converts. He asked us to make "disciples."

Jesus never asked us to go into the world and make mere converts. He asked us to make "disciples."

Studies have shown that less than one percent of evangelical church members are involved in discipling those who are won to Christ.[3] Unless there is a strong emphasis on discipling those who come to Christ, there will be little lasting fruit to show for our efforts. Gary W. Kuhne defines personal discipling as, "the spiritual work of grounding a new believer in the faith."[4] Discipling others is the process by which a Christian with a life worth emulating, commits himself for an extended period of time to a few individuals who have been won to Christ, for the purpose of guiding their spiritual growth to maturity and equipping them to reproduce themselves in a third spiritual generation.

Postconversion Discipleship Takes Four Basic Forms

Personal Discipleship

In leading the new believer into a mature walk with Christ we need to think back to chapter 5's discussion of evangelism in the early church. The earliest Christians devoted themselves to the apostles' teaching, fellowship, worship, and sacrificial service (Acts 2:42-47). Biblically, fellowship involves two levels. First, because of the work of Christ, our fellowship is reestablished with God the Father. This must be appropriated individually at the time of our conversion and personally throughout the remainder of our lives. Hence, there is an aspect of discipleship that is the responsibility of the new Christian. Those who come to Christ must commit themselves to grow in their inner life. No baby in Christ can be "force fed." We all must long for the pure milk of the word so that we may "grow up" in terms of our salvation (1 Pet. 2:2).

No baby in Christ can be "force fed."

All new Christians need to be taught how to study the Bible for themselves, both devotionally and more critically. The devotional aspect of study should come first, with a more critical approach following when the young Christian has begun to grow in his faith. In addition to this, each new believer needs to be taught the basics of a biblical, systematic approach to prayer (see the New Life Study #2, "Developing a Devotional Life" at the end of this chapter).

While this avenue toward Christian maturity is the responsibility of the individual Christian to develop, the new Christian almost always lacks the tools and wisdom to discern how to go about establishing a personal devotional life. It is through the other three forms of discipling (especially one-on-one discipling) that the new believer learns how to carry on his own "personal discipleship" training.

Small Group Discipling

Only after we have established fellowship with God through Christ, can we properly experience fellowship with one another in the church. As we interact with those of "like precious faith," we will be challenged to grow as we help one another in the faith (see all the "one another" passages in chapter 5). Proverbs 27:17 is as timely today in the church as it was in ancient Israel, "As iron sharpens iron, so one man sharpens another." Hence, another aspect of discipleship must involve interaction with others.

As we see the earliest Christians devoting themselves to worship, in Acts 2:42-47, it becomes obvious that worship is described with both *corporate* and *personal* aspects (see chapter 1). The corporate nature of worship is seen acted out in large groups and small groups within the church.

There is an aspect of spiritual growth which is available only in a group small enough that individual needs can be shared and cared for. The first Christians obviously divided themselves into smaller groups which would allow for the type of fellowship commanded by the Lord and His apostles. Small group discipling allows many of the gifts of the body of Christ to take part in the maturing process of the new Christian as he interacts within a family-size unit. In chapter 13, we will examine the key role small group dynamics can play in the maturing process of the new believer.

Large Group Discipling

We also see that the worship of the first Christians was experienced in large groups. Large groups were seen worshiping in the temple and taking part in joint prayer meetings (Acts 2:42; 4:24-31). There is an aspect of worship that is available only in a larger corporate group. We have already noted earlier in this book that large groups contain a dynamic and excitement that is a prelude to the vastness of the worship to be experienced in heaven (Rev. 5:11-14).

Hence, part of the discipling process in the lives of new believers will involve large corporate worship. This large group aspect of discipleship allows the new believer to recognize that he is a part of a vast group which joins with others around the globe to give praise and adoration to Jesus.

Thus far, we can see that "making a disciple" of the new believer will involve "personal discipling," "small group discipling," and "large group discipling." There is, however, one last aspect of the discipling process which needs to be expanded upon — the aspect of "one-on-one" discipling.

One-on-One Discipling

New Christians need special attention to ensure growth. I remember when my wife and I brought our first child home from the hospital. She was so small and helpless that for the first few months, our lives totally revolved around that little bundle of (noisy) joy. What sort of parents would bring a tiny baby home from the hospital, place him in front of the television, and say, "There are steaks in the fridge and the remote is on the coffee table. Have a great week! We'll see you next Sunday!" Child and Family Services would have that child out of such a home immediately if such an event was reported (assuming the child would even survive that first week).

Yet, this is what vast numbers of churches do to "newborn Christians." We spend months (and sometimes years) helping individuals come to be "born again" only to practically ignore their vulnerable spiritual condition during the days immediately following their conversion. We tell them where the Bible school classes are and when the morning worship services meet. Then we hope that all goes well with them for the other six days of the week. During my years of ministry, I have become convinced that new Christians need an intense time of individualistic attention to help them as they begin their new walk with Christ.

New Christians need special attention to ensure growth.

Gary W. Kuhne has emphasized the need of churches and Christians to provide such attention. Kuhne discusses four key reasons why such "one-on-one" care is required to ensure that our new spiritual babies mature into Christlikeness.[5] First, the new Christian is in a tremendously vulnerable state. A recent convert is more easily deceived by Satan than a mature Christian. In fact, a new believer is more vulnerable in the fight against Satan's temptations than perhaps at any other time of their life. It is common for a new Christian to experience doubt regarding the validity of their decision for Christ. Lack of scriptural knowledge makes a new Christian dangerously open to Satan's attacks. This vulnerability is a strong argument for involvement in intensive early discipling.

A recent convert is more easily deceived by Satan than a mature Christian.

Second, the new Christian has a tremendous potential for positive change in his life. Coming to Christ has been a pivotal point in his life. For the first time, he has the potential through the power of the Holy Spirit for real change in his lifestyle. The direction and guidance offered through one-on-one discipling greatly increase both the chance and speed of this transformation. A mature Christian working in such a close relationship with a new Christian should able to detect the areas in their life that need the most urgent attention.

Third, we need to recognize that disciples are produced very effectively through one-on-one discipling. I remember when I was preparing to do postgraduate work at a seminary in Chicago. I needed to learn German for some of the courses. I enrolled in a German class at a local seminary. The class began with only four students. Our teacher was knowledgeable and concerned. I learned a lot during that first semester. However, at the beginning of the second semester, I realized that the other three students had dropped the class (they went *kaput!*). Yet the professor agreed to continue with the class. For the whole semester I had a private tutor for my study. By the end of that semester, I was reading my daily devotions from the German Bible!

One-on-one discipling is tremendously effective. New Christians stand to benefit the most from such attention. What would you rather see for the first year of your newborn daughter's life — being raised in an orphanage with one nurse for every 15 babies or being taken home and cared for by a loving mother? Talk about a no-brainer. Can we not commit ourselves to such concern for those who have recently come to Christ?

Finally, one-on-one discipling is a very effective way of achieving spiritual multiplication. The degree to which we can encourage a new Christian to be fruit-producing has important implications for the fulfillment of the Great Commission. Not only spiritual productiveness, but also spiritual reproductiveness should be the focus of our discipling efforts.

Can we not commit ourselves to such concern for those who have recently come to Christ?

The Goals of One-on-One Discipling

A newborn baby needs certain specific items to guarantee its growth and maturity. Milk is an essential and so is constant attention. As the baby grows, other foods are added and the need for constant attention decreases. There will come a point when milk is no longer a basic need and our grown-up child will be able to stand and walk alone. If all proceeds in a normal fashion, they will get married and become the care givers to children of their own.

The same can be said for a newborn Christian. Early in his walk with Christ, he needs to be taught the absolute basic aspects of the Christian life. Constant attention will have to be given to make sure he doesn't "hurt himself." However, as the maturing process continues, the new Christian will grow to the point of feeding on the meat of the Word and will learn how to feed himself. He may even become a gourmet chef who feeds others. We also hope that our new Christian will grow up to the point of reproducing himself by leading others to find Christ as Lord and Savior.

There are a number of key issues which should be at the top of our priority list in sharing with the new believer. Gary Kuhne has observed at least five.[6] First, *we need to make sure that the new believer receives assurance of his salvation.* One of the enemy's chief tools is to get the new believer to begin to doubt his salvation. This is especially true in our post-modern culture. The new Christian will probably still be operating on the assumption that "feeling" is the highest source of authority. All mature believers know that feelings are often deceiving. There are many days when we simply don't feel ourselves to be on a spiritual "high." The new believer needs to be taught that his salvation depends upon the "fact" of what Christ has accomplished on the cross, not upon how a Christian may "feel" on any particular day.

Second, *each young Christian needs to be taught how to develop their own personal devotional life.* This will allow them to begin the process of personal discipling. I hate to admit it, but in all my theological training, I was never required to take a class on developing a devotional life. Nor did the church where I was converted emphasize this. I stumbled through my teenage years and the early years of my ministry with a "hit and miss" devotional life.

While in my second ministry, I was visited by a young lady I had never met before. She told me she was visiting her parents who had always lived down the street from our church building. We exchanged small talk for a few minutes and then, out of the blue, she asked, "How is your devotional life?" I was taken aback by such a question from a stranger, but in honesty I replied, "It stinks!" She related to me that she received a similar response from many ministers. Then she told me of her association with the British scholar evangelist, Michael Green. He had taught her a simple, systematic method of prayer and devotional study. That afternoon, after she left, I went to the office supply store to purchase a notebook which would become my prayer journal. My devotional life has never been the same since. I teach the techniques she shared with me to all my students. That was over fifteen years ago and I have never seen her since. I don't even remember her name, but when I get to heaven, I plan to look her up and thank her for helping me fill a great deficiency in my spiritual life.

We need to take steps to see that no new believer is left to grope in the dark for a proper method of personal devotion and prayer. It is imperative that a new convert be taught these things within the first few weeks of their coming to Christ.

No new believer should be left to grope in the dark for a proper method of personal devotion and prayer.

Third, *we want to help the new Christian come to a working understanding of the basics of abundant Christian living.* This will involve everything from learning about basic biblical doctrines to understanding the corporate aspects of worship within the local congregation. One of the first things we should share with our friend is an overview of the Bible and some basic principles of hermeneutics (biblical interpretation). The new believer should not have to wonder about such things as the Lord's Supper or the concept of Christian stewardship. He should also be taught lessons on some of the most basic doctrines of the Christian faith.

It is true that the new Christian could probably learn all of these things if he stays active in a vibrant congregation for many years. However, he shouldn't have to learn these important issues in such a hit-or-miss manner. We need to develop a systematic method of teaching them one-on-one to the new believer.

Fourth, *we want to help the new believer become integrated into the body life of the local church family.* We assume that both the large group and especially the small group forms of discipling will aid in this. However, we must also help our friend understand how important it is to take part in the work of Christ within the local congregation. This will help meet the need of fraternalism which the fragmented world of our postmodern culture has created within most people today.

Finally, *our one-on-one discipling needs to help our newly converted friend learn the basic principles of evangelism* which will help him to share his faith with others. If our friend has come to Christ through the lifestyle method of evangelism, his training in evangelism should be relatively easy. He has seen the model of relational evangelism worked out within his own life. He now simply needs to be taught to begin "raising his flag" with the network of non-Christian friends and family which already exists within his life. In one-on-one discipling, the new believer needs to be guided and encouraged to take part in the Great Commission.

The Possibilities of Spiritual Multiplication

One of the largest plagues in the American church is the problem of nominal Christianity (an oxymoron if there ever was one). Eddie Gibbs has done an exhaustive study of this problem within the contemporary church.[7] He defines a "nominal Christian" in the following manner.

> A nominal Protestant Christian is one who, within the Protestant tradition, would call himself a Christian, or be so regarded by others, but who has no authentic commitment to Christ based on personal faith. Such commitment involves a transforming personal relationship with Christ, characterized by such qualities as love, joy, peace, a desire to study the Bible, prayer, fellowship with other Christians, a determination to witness faithfully, a deep concern for God's will to be done on earth, and a living hope of heaven to come.[8]

God will never bless a church filled with the type of people described in the above definition.

One-on-one discipling, if consistently carried out, can prove a solution to much of the nominal Christianity which plagues many churches. If properly discipled, at the conclusion of the first year of a new Christian's walk with the Lord, he will be grounded in the basics of the faith, experiencing the joys of a daily devotional life with Christ, sharing his faith, and the knowledge of how to pass on what he has received to those he wins to Christ.

In the class I teach on evangelism, I ask my students how many of them currently attend a church which has twenty members who can do the things just described. Seldom do I have over five or six hands go up in a class of fifty. What a tragedy! As we have said, one-on-one discipling can provide the solution and promise that within a decade every church can be filled with vibrant, maturing disciples of Jesus.

Gary Kuhne has provided some amazing statistics to verify this claim. Suppose that a single Christian makes it his goal to make one evangelistic contact a week. This may involve anything from making a new friend, raising the flag, or sharing a gospel presentation. At the end of the first year, his goal is to have won a single individual to Christ and lead that individual through a one-on-one discipling program. At the end of the first year, the result will be approximately fifty evangelistic contacts made and now there are two disciples: you and your discipled convert. The following year, each of you repeat the process. Now after two years you have four disciples and over 100 evangelistic contact made. If this model could be continued the results are staggering.

Year One
1. Begin year: 1 disciple (you)
2. End year: 2 disciples (you, plus 1)
3. Evangelistic contacts: 50 approximately

Year Two
1. Begin year: 2 disciples
2. End year: 4 disciples
3. Evangelistic contacts: 100

Year Three
1. Begin year: 4 disciples
2. End year: 8 disciples
3. Evangelistic contacts: 200 approximately

Year Four
1. Begin year: 8 disciples
2. End year: 16 disciples
3. Evangelistic contacts: 400 approximately

Year Five
1. Begin year: 16 disciples
2. End year: 32 disciples
3. Evangelistic contacts: 800 approximately

Year Six
1. Begin year: 32 disciples
2. End year: 64 disciples
3. Evangelistic contacts: 1,600 approximately[9]

Kuhne goes on to write that, if you continue the process, in just ten years, one decade, you will have personally discipled 10 people and witnessed to 50 a year, but you will have caused the development of 1,024 disciples and the annual confrontation of approximately 25,000 people with the gospel!![10] This isn't just mathematical juggling but the logical outgrowth of faithful service to the Lord. We have it within our influence to allow the possibility for every local congregation to find itself teeming with "on fire Christians" within ten short years!

Formulating a Plan for "One-on One" Discipling

Don Hawkins has noted that the process of discipling is a lot like constructing a building.[11] First, you must begin with a plan. No successful building project was ever completed without the careful, detailed work of an architect. A successful disciplemaking program also needs to be carefully planned. Second, it is essential to count the cost. This was Jesus' main point when He told the story of someone constructing a tower without the necessary finances for the project (Luke 14). Discipleship costs both the "discipler" and the "disciplee" time, energy, and emotional involvement. Third, the actual building must take place in an orderly process. It would be ludicrous to consider starting on the roof before finishing the foundation, and the same is true with building up the body of believers. In discussing the life of the church, Paul pointed out that things must be done decently and in order (1 Cor. 14:40).

The Plan: Prepare the Lessons

In order to begin this form of discipling, it is absolutely imperative to prepare the lessons you intend to share during your discipling time with the new believer. These lessons should cover the five elements listed earlier in the chapter:

1. Helping the new believer receive assurance of salvation and acceptance with God
2. Helping the new believer develop a consistent devotional life
3. Helping the new believer understand the basics of abundant Christian living
4. Helping the new believer become integrated into the life of the local church
5. Helping the new believer learn to share his faith with others.

Ideally, the lessons should be shared on a weekly basis covering six to nine months. There are several good examples of what such discipling lessons should resemble. Gary Kuhne's older work *The Dynamics of Personal Followup* (Zondervan, 1976) contains a good initial series of lessons. I have incorporated several of them in my own initial discipling lessons at the end of this chapter. Recently Greg Ogdon has published a fine series of initial discipling lessons in his book *Discipling Essentials* (InterVarsity, 1998). A list of topics for consideration might include:

Making Disciples	Being a Disciple
Quiet Time	Bible Study
Prayer	Worship
The Three-Person God	Made in God's Image
Sin	Grace
Redemption	Justification
Adoption	Filled with the Holy Spirit
Fruit of the Holy Spirit	Trust
Love	Justice
Witness	The Church
Ministry Gifts	Spiritual Warfare
Walking in Obedience	Sharing the Wealth[12]

The Cost: Prepare Yourself

We need to understand that taking part in a one-on-one discipling relationship will take time and energy on our part. Just as Jesus poured Himself into the lives of His disciples, so we must be prepared to pour ourselves into the life of the individual we seek to disciple. The model which Jesus used as His "Master Plan" (see chapter 4) can now become our method in the life of the new Christian.

It is important that we be genuine in our interaction with the new Christian in a discipling relationship. We should not pretend to be a spiritual giant. In fact, we should not pretend to be anything. A false front prevents honesty in the discipling relationship. If we are afraid to admit that we are still growing in our relationship with Christ, we will not be very effective as a spiritual mentor.

We should not pretend to be a spiritual giant; in fact, we should not pretend to be anything.

In spite of our above mentioned honesty, it is imperative that our daily walk display a general spiritual consistency of lifestyle. Nowhere else in life is the need for consistency more critical than in the work of discipling. A phony can fool a stranger, but in a discipling relationship, a genuine Christian life is imperative. There is an old saying, "The pew seldom rises higher than the pulpit." In a discipling relationship the same is true. It will be hard to lead a new convert down spiritual paths we have never trod.

Discipling is a job for those who are serious about their walk with Christ. We must ever be growing in Christ. It is extremely important that in the midst of a discipling relationship, we continue to grow in our own relationship to Christ. We must never assume we have arrived.

The Process: Prepare the New Convert

The process is simple. We schedule a time each week to meet with the new believer to share the discipling material we have prepared in our lessons. Each discipling lesson should contain several elements. It is always good to catch up with what is going on in the new Christian's life. Keep track of the important issues he is dealing with. Ask him if he has been consistent in his daily devotional time. Also inquire about his interaction with the body life of the church in corporate worship and small groups, such as a Bible class or a home fellowship group. This will ensure that the other three areas of discipleship training are being utilized in his process of growth. This should take about ten minutes.

Next the lesson material should be shared. It is good to provide the lessons in the form of a booklet or a packet so that our student can have them to take home and study. Time should be allowed to look up passages in the Bible, as well as discussion time on how the subject material of the lesson can make an impact on the new Christian's life in the coming week. Remember, theology that is not practical is not biblical.

After the lesson material has been shared and discussed, time should be taken to pray together. Ask the new believer to bring his prayer journal to each session and we as teachers also need to bring our own. This will allow each of us to write down the prayer requests of the other, so that every day we can be praying for one another.

Whole books have been written on the details of sharing in a one-on-one discipling relationship. The important things to remember are: prepare the plan; prepare yourself; and, prepare your new friend as we complete the work of the Great Commission by teaching them everything Jesus has commanded us.

An Example of a Series of Discipling Lessons

The remainder of this chapter will contain an example of ten discipling lessons which are meant to be used in the very first weeks after an individual places their faith and trust in Christ. Most of these are single-page outlines which will allow for minimal attention to the lesson sheet. Instead the discipling pair should spend the bulk of the lesson time looking up Scripture and discussing its meaning and application. Lessons 1, 2, 4 and

258   Disciple Making: The Forgotten Task

10 are close adaptations from Gary Kuhne's *The Dynamics of Personal Follow-up*.[13] The exception to the brief format is found in Lesson #5. This is an extended overview of the content of the Bible. I was aided in the development of this lesson by a close friend, Chuck McCoy. This particular lesson will take a bit longer to present. It may be a good idea to simply hit the "high points" and to allow the new Christian to look over the lesson material in-depth on his own. These lessons are not meant to be the final word on what initial discipling lessons should look like. They are only meant to provide an example of at least one possible starting point for a one-on-one series of lessons.

1. L. Ann Jervis, "Becoming Like God through Christ: Discipling in Romans," in *Patterns of Discipleship in the New Testament*, Richard Longenecker, ed. (Grand Rapids: Eerdmans, 1996), p. 161.

2. Win Arn and Charles Arn, *The Master's Plan for Making Disciples* (Monrovia, CA: Church Growth Press, 1991), pp. 9-10.

3. Gary W. Kuhne, *The Dynamics of Personal Follow-up* (Grand Rapids: Zondervan, 1981), p. 13.

4. Ibid., p. 16.

5. Ibid., pp. 19-29.

6. Kuhne, *The Dynamics of Personal Follow-up*, p. 17.

7. Eddie Gibbs, *In Name Only: Tackling the Problem of Nominal Christianity* (Wheaton: Victor Books [BridgePoint], 1994).

8. Gibbs quotes the definition given by the Lausanne Congress held in Thailand in 1980. Ibid., p. 21.

9. Kuhne, *The Dynamics of Personal Follow-up*, p. 28.

10. Ibid.

11. Don Hawkins, *Master Discipleship* (Grand Rapids: Kregel, 1996), pp. 19-20.

12. The items in this list are the lessons shared in Greg Ogden, *Discipleship Essentials: A Guide to Building your Life in Christ* (Downers Grove, IL: InterVarsity, 1998).

13. Kuhne, *The Dynamics of Personal Follow-up*, pp. 153, 159, 170, 193.

New Life Study #1
Assurance of Salvation

Now that you have received Christ as your Lord and Savior by placing your faith in Him as the Bible teaches . . .

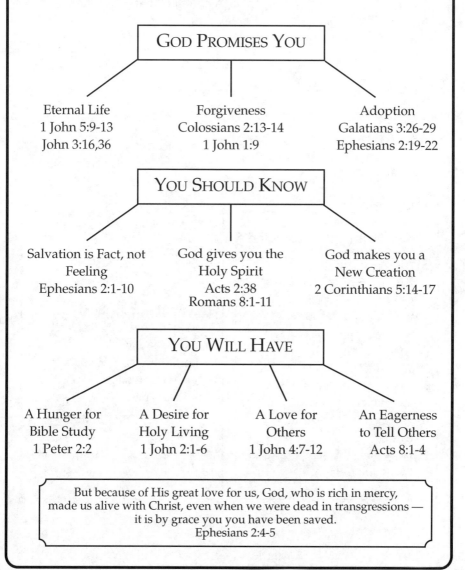

GOD PROMISES YOU

Eternal Life
1 John 5:9-13
John 3:16,36

Forgiveness
Colossians 2:13-14
1 John 1:9

Adoption
Galatians 3:26-29
Ephesians 2:19-22

YOU SHOULD KNOW

Salvation is Fact, not
Feeling
Ephesians 2:1-10

God gives you the
Holy Spirit
Acts 2:38
Romans 8:1-11

God makes you a
New Creation
2 Corinthians 5:14-17

YOU WILL HAVE

A Hunger for
Bible Study
1 Peter 2:2

A Desire for
Holy Living
1 John 2:1-6

A Love for
Others
1 John 4:7-12

An Eagerness
to Tell Others
Acts 8:1-4

But because of His great love for us, God, who is rich in mercy, made us alive with Christ, even when we were dead in transgressions — it is by grace you you have been saved.
Ephesians 2:4-5

New Life Study #2
Developing a Devotional Life

> The Bible makes it clear that
> every Christian must
> develop a devotional life.
> 1 Peter 2:2
> Psalm 1:1-2
> 2 Timothy 2:15
> 2 Timothy 3:16-17

Procedure

1. Read a chapter or a paragraph.
2. Be systematic: Go through a whole book.

Plan for It

1. Set a specific time each day to get into the Word.
2. Set a specific place for devotions.

Ask Questions as You Read

1. Are there any sins to forsake?
2. Are there any promises to claim?
3. Are there any examples to follow?
4. Are there any warnings to consider?
5. Are there any teachings about God to learn?
6. Are there any other important truths?
7. How does this passage apply to my life today?

Devote Time to Prayer

1. Develop a systematic approach to daily prayer.

2. A notebook should be used to jot down daily prayer requests, as well as to record both the time and ways in which God has answered your requests.

The prayer of a righteous man is powerful and effective. James 5:16

Be sure to keep a notebook!

This lesson has been adapted from *Dynamics of Personal Follow-Up* by Gary W. Kuhne.
Copyright © 1976 by the Zondervan Corporation. Used by permission of Zondervan Publishing House (www.zondervan.com).
Available at your local bookstore or by calling 800-727-3480.

New Life Study #3
Getting to Know God's Word

The Bible Is God's Message to Man
2 Timothy 3:16 & 2 Peter 1:20-21

Old Testament: Preparing for the Coming of Christ

Law	History		Wisdom	Prophets	
Genesis	Joshua	Ezra	Job	Isaiah	Obadiah
Exodus	Judges	Nehemiah	Psalms	Jeremiah	Jonah
Leviticus	Ruth	Esther	Proverbs	Lamentations	Micah
Numbers	1 Samuel		Ecclesiastes	Ezekiel	Nahum
Deuteronomy	2 Samuel		Song of Solomon	Daniel	Habakkuk
	1 Kings				Zephaniah
	2 Kings			Hosea	Haggai
	1 Chronicles			Joel	Zechariah
	2 Chronicles			Amos	Malachi

New Testament: Christ and the Kingdom

Gospels	History	Epistles		Prophecy
Matthew	Acts of the Apostles	Romans	Titus	Revelation
Mark		1 Corinthians	Philemon	
Luke		2 Corinthians		
John		Galatians	Hebrews	
		Ephesians	James	
		Philippians	1 Peter	
		Colossians	2 Peter	
		1 Thessalonians	1 John	
		2 Thessalonians	2 John	
		1 Timothy	3 John	
		2 Timothy	Jude	

Five Questions to Ask

1. Who is speaking?
2. Who is being spoken to?
3. When was it spoken?
4. Where was it spoken?
5. Why was it spoken?

Five Rules for Understanding

1. There is one intended meaning for each passage.
2. Seek the original meaning.
3. A passage must be understood in its context.
4. Compare all related passages.
5. A passage should harmonize with other passages.

New Life Study #4
Power for Living

Power for
Living Comes
from . . .

Being filled with God's Spirit
Ephesians 5:18

	What Does This Mean?	What Are God's Promises?	
1. Christ in You Galatians 2:20			1. God Promises Abundant Life John 10:10
2. Controlled by God's Spirit Ephesians 5:18			2. God Promises His Holy Spirit Acts 2:38
3. Filled with the Word of God 2 Timothy 3:14-17			3. God Promises the Fruit of His Spirit Galatians 5:22-23

CONDITIONS

DESIRE	SURRENDER	OBEDIENCE	CONFESSION
Matthew 5:6	Romans 12:1-2	1 John 2:3	1 John 1:9

Continuous Power for Living

Ask God for It

Meet the Conditions

Trust God for It

This lesson has been adapted from *Dynamics of Personal Follow-Up* by Gary W. Kuhne.
Copyright © 1976 by the Zondervan Corporation. Used by permission of Zondervan Publishing House (www.zondervan.com).
Available at your local bookstore or by calling 800-727-3480.

New Life Study #5
A Journey through the Bible

One of the nagging problems which keeps people from understanding the Bible is that many have heard a few episodes of biblical history, but they have no understanding of the general course of the story by which to orient each of the pieces. This study will help you get the big picture of what's going on in the Bible

The Central Plot

The basic plot of the biblical story is established by the end of the third chapter of Genesis. God created the universe (Gen. 1:1–2:4), placed the first man and woman in a garden-like setting with only one restriction (Gen. 2:5-25), and responded to their disobedience (Gen. 3:1-13) with declarations of what he was going to do.

To Satan, God promised humiliation and defeat through the "seed of the woman" who would crush his head, although this coming Savior would be wounded in the encounter (Gen. 3:14-15). Adam and Eve were promised new struggles in their mortal lives (Gen. 3:16-19) and were evicted from the garden (Gen. 3:20-24). They were told that their hope lay in a descendant coming through the woman.

From this point on, the Old Testament continued to prepare for the Messiah's coming. This point is made in the Old Testament genealogies: The Messiah would come through Eve (Gen 3:20), through Seth's lineage to Noah (Gen. 5), through Noah's son Shem's lineage to Abraham (Gen. 9:26; 11:10-26; 12:1-3), through Abraham's son Isaac (Gen. 17:19; 26:1-4), Isaac's son Jacob (Gen. 28:10-14), Jacob's son Judah (Gen. 49:10). This lineage continued and would be culminated in the family of David (2 Sam. 7:8-17). These genealogies aren't intended to be enjoyable reading, but they are one of the essential credentials which God's appointed Savior must possess. The Old Testament Scripture tells us that "Someone is coming" to deal with our separation from God. The Gospels tell us that the "Someone" has arrived. The New Testament letters tell us that the "Someone" is coming again and how we can be prepared to meet our God.

God's Method of Dealing with Mankind

Without being familiar with the Bible, many have guessed at how God relates to humans. Some believe that God remains at a mysterious distance and some people are just more "tuned in" to God's wavelength, or that He selectively zaps some people and they "get religion" all of a sudden. For many, their religious faith is based simply upon subjective experience and they bounce through life from one emotional high to another, hoping to stumble into God's will. Fortunately, we are not left in the world with these inadequate options.

The Bible came to us through the Hebrew people and, although their history is one of general disobedience to God's purposes, they were selected to be the avenue through which God revealed and worked out the final stages of his salvation for all humanity (Rom. 3:1-2; 9:1-5). The Hebrews were not trying to interpret omens or their own experiences to determine the will of God. Instead, they received objective revelation at Mt. Sinai when Moses received the Law (Exod. 19:1–20:21). In response, the Hebrew viewpoint was not based on trying to decipher mysterious or secret things, but in obeying divinely revealed information (Deut. 29:29).

Along with the revelation of objective truth, the relationship of God and man was based on "covenant keeping." A covenant in the ancient world was a solemn relationship between two parties which was inaugurated by passing between two halves of a slain animal and speaking an oath to keep the terms of the agreement and to seek the welfare of the other. The God of the Bible does not deal with mankind whimsically, but through established covenants with Abraham and his descendants (Gen. 12:1-3; 15), the Israelites at Sinai (Exod. 24:3-8), and with all who will swear allegiance to Jesus (Matt. 26:28; Heb. 8:6; 9:15; 12:24). God's will is not a cosmic secret, but is clearly revealed to us in the terms of the covenant as revealed in the Bible (Eph. 1:9; 5:17).

A Brief Journey through the Bible

There is a discernible flow of biblical history as the events unfold
which lead up to the coming of the promised Savior.

The Pre-Flood Period
Creation to the Flood; Gen. 1–8

God created the universe and assigned mankind the responsibility of being stewards of this creation (1:1–2:4). Mankind lost its initial relationship with God through disobedience (2:5–3:24) and sin divided the original family as the line of Cain left God's presence and began to build for this life only (4:16-24) while Seth's line sought the Lord (4:25–5:32). The general course of man on his own is toward evil (6:1-6) and God determined to bring judgment and start over with Noah's family (6:7–8:22).

The Post-Flood Period
After the Flood to Abraham; Gen. 9–11

Following the flood, God gave instructions concerning: repopulating the earth; meat for food; not eating blood; capital punishment as the best way of emphasizing the seriousness of murder; and a promise to never destroy the world through a flood again (9). The linguistic/ national divisions of Noah's descendants are given (10), followed by a brief explanation of how the divisions came about through God's judgment on mankind's attempt to find greatness through worldly development at the Tower of Babel (11:1-9).

The Wandering of the Patriarchs
The Travels of Abraham, Isaac, Jacob and His 12 Sons; Gen. 12–50;
ca. 2100–1800 BC

God called a Shemite named Abram to leave his old life in Chaldea and set out on a journey to an unknown land. He made the journey and found the land already full of people, but God promised him that he would have many descendants and that they would eventually become a great nation and inhabit the land of Canaan. Although only owning a small burial plot in Canaan during his lifetime, this man believed that God would fulfill His promises and thus he became the "father of the faithful." The promises of a nation of descendants and an international blessing (the coming Savior) were passed on from Abraham through Isaac and Jacob. Jacob's 12 sons were destined to be the heads of the 12 tribes of Israel (since Jacob's name was changed to Israel, Gen. 32:28; 35:10). All of these patriarchs were nomadic herdsmen and it was not yet time for them to take possession of Canaan. Jacob, his sons and their families, 70 people in all, moved to Egypt because of famine, and their descendants remained there about 400 years.

Israel's Bondage in Egypt
From Israel's Oppression in Egypt to the First Passover; Exod. 1–12; ca. 1800–1446 BC

After some political changes took place, the Israelites in Egypt had become slaves and were put to hard labor. They cried out for deliverance and, when the time arrived, God protected and raised up a deliverer in Moses. Moses grew up in Pharaoh's household, but was expelled from Egypt and worked as a shepherd in the Sinai peninsula in preparation for his job of delivering the Israelites and leading them in the Sinai wilderness. Although he balked at the first call (Exod. 3–4), Moses and Aaron were used by God to bring plagues on Egypt until Pharaoh released them from their bondage.

The Exodus, the Law and the Wanderings
From the Exodus to the End of the 40 Years of Wandering; Exod. 13—Deut.; ca. 1445–1405 BC

Humbled by the plagues, Pharaoh allowed Moses to lead Israel out of Egypt. They went to Mt. Sinai and camped there about a year. During this year, Israel received the Law, built the tabernacle and showed their unwillingness to obey the covenant. They refused to enter Canaan at first (Num. 13–14) and were punished by 40 years of wandering in the wilderness and Trans-Jordan region. During this time, the generation of Israelites above the age of 20 when they left Egypt, died outside the promised land (cf. 1 Cor. 10:1-13). In his farewell address, Moses reminded the new generation of Israelites of what God had done for them (Deut. 1–3), warned them about disobedience (Deut. 4–7) and the dangers of becoming complacent after they have settled down in Canaan (Deut. 8), and instructed them that they didn't deserve God's favor but were being given Canaan because of God's faithfulness in His promises to the patriarchs (Deut. 9:1-6).

The Conquest of Canaan
Israel Takes Possession of the Land of Canaan; Joshua; ca. 1405–1397 BC

After the death of Moses, Joshua led the Israelites across the Jordan River and began the conquest of Canaan (Josh. 1–5). He destroyed Jericho and Ai and then proceeded up to Mt. Ebal and Mt. Gerizim where the covenant was reconfirmed (Josh. 6–8). Then they made peace with the Gibeonites (Josh. 9) and proceeded to secure their territory with a campaign into southern Canaan (Josh. 10) and then a northern campaign (Josh. 11). Lastly, the land of Canaan was divided amongst the tribes (Josh. 13–22) and Joshua gave them a farewell warning (Josh. 23–24).

The Period of the Judges
From Joshua's Death to Israel's Request for a King; Judges 1—1 Samuel 7; ca. 1397–1050 BC

After the death of Joshua, the tribes began to go their separate ways (Judg. 1:27-36). The key problem which allowed the next generation to turn aside from following the Lord was ignorance (Judg. 2:10). The cycle of apostasy and rescue, which characterized the period, is summarized in Judges 2:10–3:4. The many rescues which follow during the period began as God's Spirit stirred some person to do God's will (Judg. 3:10; 6:34; 11:29; 15:14). The final judge, Samuel, was raised by the Priest Eli and trained in the tabernacle ministry, which he performed along with being a circuit judge (1 Sam. 1–7). As the period of the Judges continued, it was recognized that Israel had no central authority to provide order (Judg. 17:6; 21:25) and the desire grew among the Israelites for an earthly king (Judg. 8:22-23). The book of Ruth not only connects David's lineage with the patriarchal era (Ruth 4:17-22), but also shows us that during the lawless era of the Judges, there were still some Israelites who tried to live by the Law, showing kindness to one another.

The United Israelite Kingdom
The Israelite Kingdom under Saul, David and Solomon; 1 Samuel 8—1 Kings 11; ca. 1050–930 BC

Because his sons were unfit to follow him, the elders of Israel approached Samuel with the request to establish an earthly monarchy (1 Sam. 8). Both God (1 Sam. 8:7-8; 10:18-19) and Samuel (1 Sam. 12:12-20) made it plain that this was an evil request and a rejection of God as King, but the desire persisted. A Benjamite named Saul (1050–1010 BC) was chosen for his outward characteristics (1 Sam. 9:1-2), but he rebelled in two major ways as he offered sacrifice (1 Sam. 13) and did not follow orders in destroying the Amalekites (1 Sam. 15). Because of this disobedience, God announced plans to replace him. Samuel was sent to Bethlehem, where he anointed David (1 Sam. 16). David rose in prominence until Saul's jealousy and anger forced David to flee. David avoided Saul until the king was killed in battle against the Philistines.

David (1010–970 BC) reigned in Judah for seven years while civil war raged with the northern tribes (2 Sam. 2–4). Finally, David was able to unite the tribes again and over all he reigned for 33 years. Although a man of faith, David was unable to control his commander Joab (2 Sam. 3), his lust (2 Sam. 11), or his children (2 Sam. 13–14). Eventually, he lost his throne temporarily to his son Absalom which brought on a civil war (2 Sam. 15–20). While David was on his death bed, his son Adonijah tried to improperly grab the throne (1 Kgs. 1).

Building on David's military success, Solomon (970–930 BC) built Israel into a great political and economic empire (1 Kgs. 1–10). He eventually disobeyed all of the major restrictions on Israelite kings (Deut. 17:16-17; 1 Kgs. 11) and introduced the idolatry which brought on both the initial division of the Israelite kingdom (ca. 930 BC) and the eventual destruction of both kingdoms.

The Divided Israelite Kingdom
From the Division of the Kingdom under Rehoboam to the Babylonian Exile; 1 Kings 12—2 Chronicles 36; Joel, Jonah, Amos, Hosea, Micah, Isaiah, Zephaniah, Nahum, Jeremiah, Habakkuk and Obadiah; ca. 930–586 BC

Because of Solomon's sin, God had determined to divide the kingdom (1 Kgs. 11:9-13) and this happened under Solomon's son, Rehoboam (1 Kgs. 12:1-24). The northern ten tribes were given to Jeroboam, but he decided to consolidate his power through false religion (1 Kgs. 12:25-33). This initiated a spiritual problem which remained with the northern kingdom until its fall to Assyria in 721 BC. The southern kingdom, comprising the tribes of Judah and Benjamin, lasted another century, but lack of faith in the Lord and attempts to preserve power through political alliances brought Judah's destruction at the hands of Babylon in 586 BC.

In this period of Israelite and Jewish history the following prophets warned of God's coming judgment upon His disobedient people before the fall of the northern kingdom: Joel, Jonah, Amos, Hosea, Micah and Isaiah. After the fall of Israel, Zephaniah, Nahum, Jeremiah, Habakkuk and Obadiah warned of the imminent destruction of the southern kingdom.

The Babylonian Exile
Judah's 70-year Exile in Babylon; 2 Kings 25, 2 Chronicles 36, Daniel, Ezekiel, Jeremiah/ Lamentations; ca. 606–536 BC

God's promises to the patriarchs caused him to delay Judah's fall (2 Kgs. 13:23) However, the "final straw" came (2 Kgs. 23:26-27) and the Neo-Babylonian empire was used as Judah's disciplinarian (2 Kgs. 25). They destroyed Jerusalem and Solomon's Temple in 586 BC. The captivity of Judah continued until the Persian conquest of Babylon. The Persian King Cyrus decreed that displaced people could return to their homelands. While the time in Babylon was a period of great sorrow for the Jews (Ps. 137), Jeremiah advised those who would "hear," to go ahead and settle down in Babylon and wait it out (Jer. 29:1-11). During the early part of this exile (606-573 BC), God had the prophets Jeremiah, Daniel and Ezekiel strategically placed in Jerusalem, Nebuchadnezzar's court, and with the exiles in Babylon to coordinate His purposes for each area.

Restoration from Babylon
The Return of the Jews to Judah and the Restoration of the Jewish Commonwealth in Canaan; Ezra, Nehemiah, Esther, Haggai, Zechariah, Malachi; ca. 536–400 BC

Cyrus the Great allowed all displaced people to return to their homelands and this opened the way for the Jews in Babylon to return to Judea. Approximately 42,000 Jews returned in 536 BC under Zerubbabel and the Temple was rebuilt by 516 BC. Another group of about 7,000 Jews returned under Ezra in 457 BC. The seeds of further apostasy are seen in the books of Ezra, Nehemiah and Malachi.

Israel's Intertestamental Period
Judah under the Domination of Persia, Greece and Rome; Daniel 2:39-40; 7:5-7; 11; ca. 400–5 BC

For about 400 years, Israel was without any prophetic voice aside from the books of the Old Testament. During this time, Israel enjoyed peace under Persian rule (400–332 BC). After this came a period of increasing hostilities as the Syrian and Egyptian remnants of Alexander the Great's Greek empire fought over Palestine (332–142 BC). This was followed by a period of self-rule under the Hasmonean priest-governors (142–63 BC). Finally Rome conquered the region as Pompey entered Jerusalem in 63 BC. During this period, the Pharisees, Sadducees, Essenes, Herodians and synagogues developed, along with the emergence of a great deal of apocryphal and pseudepigraphic Jewish literature.

The Coming of the Messiah
The Life and Ministry of Jesus of Nazareth — the Long-Awaited Messiah; Matthew, Mark, Luke & John; ca. 5 BC–AD 30

In the year AD 26, John the baptizer announced the coming of the Messiah and pointed to Jesus of Nazareth as the long-awaited deliverer. In spite of a sinless life, wise teachings true to the spirit of the Mosaic Law, and countless miracles to authenticate His claims, Jesus was crucified at the insistence of Jewish leaders who were threatened by Jesus' popularity and the fear of Roman intervention. Jesus' apostles had been filled with Jewish hopes of an earthly kingdom, but these ended at Jesus' crucifixion and the apostles were in despair. This despair turned to joy as Jesus proved His claims to be the Messiah by rising from the dead. The Gospel accounts tell us that the resurrected Christ appeared repeatedly to the eleven apostles and He taught them further about the New Covenant (Matt. 28; Luke 24; Acts 1:1-8). Forty days after His resurrection, Jesus ascended to heaven (Acts 1:6-11).

The Church Age
The Period between Jesus First and Second Comings; Acts through Revelation; ca. Pentecost, AD 30–until Jesus Comes; the New Testament was completed by AD 95

The New Covenant Church began under the direction of the apostles on the first feast of Pentecost after Jesus' resurrection. It spread throughout Judea, Samaria, Syria,

Asia Minor, Greece and at least as far as Rome during the lifetime of the apostles. The Book of Acts describes the expansion of Christianity from being a small sect within Judaism to spreading throughout the Roman Empire embracing Jews and Gentiles alike. Acts ends with the Apostle Paul preaching the gospel in the capital of the Empire, Rome itself. The Epistles were written during and immediately after the historical period related in the book of Acts.

The Church was persecuted by Judaism (AD 30–65) and then periodically by the Roman empire (AD 65–313). Yet it spread in one generation to every major metropolitan center in the Roman Empire.

The true church of Jesus Christ is not to be found in any one denomination, but rather is made up of all those throughout the world who have accepted Jesus as their Lord and Savior and are living a life of obedient faith, awaiting His return. Today there are well over one billion people throughout every continent of the globe who claim Christ as their Lord and Savior. As a Christian, you have become a part of this great panorama of history as God carries forth His mighty work in the world through His church.

Fourteen Periods of Biblical History

I.	II.	III.	IV.
Preflood Period	Postflood Period	Wanderings of the Patriarchs	Israel in Bondage
Creation to the Flood	Flood to Abraham	2100–1800 B.C.	1800–1446 B.C.
God creates the universe and assigns man as the caretaker. Man sins and his relationship with God is broken. A Savior is promised. The general course of man is toward evil and God determines to bring judgments on the earth and start over with Noah's family.	After the Flood, God gives instructions concerning repopulating the earth. Capital punishment is given to man, and God promises never again to destroy the earth with water. The linguistic divisions of Noah's descendants are created when God confuses the languages at the Tower of Babel as a judgment on man's attempt to elevate himself to God's level.	God calls Abram to leave Chaldea and journey to Canaan. He makes the journey and finds the land already inhabited. God promises that Abraham will have many descendants and they will inhabit the land of Canaan. God also promises to bless the whole world though Abraham. The promise is repeated to Isaac, Jacob and Joseph. Abraham's descendants move to Egypt and live there for 400 years.	The descendants of Abraham become slaves during their 400 years in Egypt. God hears their cries for deliverance and raises up Moses. Moses grows up in Pharaoh's household, but is expelled from Egypt at age 40. For the next 40 years he works as a shepherd in the Sinai desert. At the burning bush God sends Moses (and brother Aaron) to Egypt to convince Pharaoh to let His people go.
Genesis 1–8	Genesis 9–11	Genesis 12–50	Exodus 1–12

Fourteen Periods

V.	VI.	VII.	VIII.
Exodus, Law & Wanderings	Conquest of Canaan	Period of the Judges	United Israel
1445–1405 B.C.	1405–1397 B.C.	1397–1050 B.C.	1050–930 B.C.
Humbled by the plagues, Pharaoh allows Moses to lead Israel out of Egypt. They travel to Mt. Sinai and camp for a year. During this time, they receive the law, build the tabernacle, and show an unwillingness to obey the covenant. After initially refusing to enter Canaan, they wander in the desert for 40 years, until the disobedient generation has died. Moses is not allowed to enter the Promised Land.	After the death of Moses, Joshua leads the Israelites across the Jordan and begins the conquest of Canaan. At Mt. Ebal and Mt. Gerizim the covenant is renewed. The Israelites make peace with the Gibeonites and then proceed to secure southern and then northern Canaan. Finally, the land is divided between the tribes and Joshua makes his farewell address and warning.	After the death of Joshua, the tribes begin to go their separate ways. They continually forget the ways of the Lord. A cycle develops of apostasy followed by God raising up a judge (Gideon, Samson, etc.) to deliver Israel. The final judge is Samuel. Samuel judges well but the people of his day desire an earthly king.	The elders of Israel request Samuel to anoint a king. God is displeased but allows this request, and Saul is anointed Israel's first king. Saul begins well but eventually disobeys the Lord. Samuel is instructed to anoint David to replace Saul. David rules as a man of faith, but has many faults. Solomon succeeds his father and builds the first temple.
Exodus 13–40 Leviticus Numbers Deuteronomy	Joshua	Judges 1 Samuel 1–7	1 Samuel 8–31 2 Samuel 1 Kings 1–11 1 Chronicles 2 Chronicles 1–9

# of Biblical History

IX.	X.	XI.	XII.	
The Divided Kingdom	Babylonian Exile	Return from Babylon	Intertestamental Period	
930–606 (586) B.C.	606–536 B.C.	536–400 B.C.	400–5 B.C.	
Because of Solomon's sin, God determines to divide the Kingdom. Rehoboam (Solomon's son) leads the Southern Kingdom (Judah), and Jeroboam leads the 10 tribes of the Northern Kingdom (Israel). Israel is destroyed by the Assyrians in 721 B.C. and Judah falls to the Babylonians in 606 B.C. and finally in 586 B.C. Many prophets give their messages to both kingdoms during this tumultuous time.	The Babylonians destroy Jerusalem and Solomon's temple in 586 B.C. The captivity of Judah lasts until the Persians conquer Babylon. The time in Babylon is a period of great sorrow for the Jews. During the period of the exile God's prophets continue to give His word: Daniel from Nebuchadnezzar's court, Jeremiah from Jerusalem, and Ezekiel with the exiles.	Persian king, Cyrus the Great, decrees that displaced people can return to their homelands. Approximately 42,000 Jews return to Palestine in 536 B.C. under Zerubbabel and the temple is rebuilt by 516 B.C. Another group of about 7,000 Jews returns under Ezra in 457 B.C. The seeds of further apostasy are seen in Ezra, Nehemiah, and Malachi.	No prophetic voice comes to Israel (Jewish nation) during this period. Israel is under Persian rule (400–332 B.C.) and then under Syrian and Egyptian rule (332–142 B.C.). After this the Jews gain self-rule under the Hasmoneans (142–63 B.C.). Finally Rome conquers the region when Pompey enters Jerusalem in 63 B.C. During this period Pharisees, Sadducees, Essenes, Herodians, and the synagogues arise.	
1 Kings 12–22 2 Kings 2 Chronicles 10–36 (Prophets to Israel) Jonah Amos Hosea (Prophets toJudah) Joel Micah Isaiah Zephaniah Nahum Jeremiah Habakkuk Obadiah	2 Chronicles 36 Daniel Jeremiah Lamentations Ezekiel	Ezra Nehemiah Esther Haggai Zechariah Malachi	Daniel 2:39-40; 7:5-7; 11:1-45	

Fourteen Periods of
Biblical History (concluded)

XIII.	XIV.
Coming of the Messiah	The Church Age
5 B.C.–A.D. 30	A.D. 30–96 to the present
John the Baptist announces the coming of the Messiah and points to Jesus as the long-awaited Messiah. In spite of a sinless life, wise teaching and countless miracles, Jesus is crucified at the insistence of Jewish leaders. His disciples were in despair but their despair turns to joy as Jesus proves his Messiahship by rising from the dead. After his resurrection, Jesus teaches his disciples for 40 days and ascends to heaven.	The church begins under the direction of the apostles on the feast of Pentecost, 10 days after Jesus' ascension. It spreads throughout Jerusalem, Judea, Samaria and the Roman world. The book of Acts begins with Christianity as a small sect of Judaism in Jerusalem and concludes with the faith spread among Jews and Gentiles throughout the Empire, and Paul is preaching in the capital city of Rome, itself.
Matthew Mark Luke John	Acts of the Apostles (Paul's Epistles) Romans 1 & 2 Corinthians Galatians Ephesians Philippians Colossians 1 & 2 Thessalonians 1 & 2 Timothy Titus Philemon (General Epistles) Hebrews James 1 & 2 Peter 1, 2 & 3 John Jude (Prophetic Epistle) Revelation

New Life Study #6
Saved for Service

Two Eternal Truths

Accepting Jesus as our Lord and Savior results in two life-changing realities.

1. We are "Redeemed"
   On the cross, Christ redeemed us (i.e., He purchased us) so that now we belong to Him. 1 Cor. 6:20
2. We Are God's Stewards
   A "steward" is a manager who is in charge of the affairs of a master. Since all we have is God's, we are to be responsible stewards of all the things in our lives for His sake. Matthew 25:14-30

Stewards of Abilities

God expects us to use what he has given. Matthew 25:15 Not every Christian has the same abilities. However, every Christian has something he can use for the Lord. 1 Corinthians 12:17-18

Stewards of Opportunities

We take opportunity to study God's Word. 2 Timothy 2:15 We take opportunity to encourage fellow Christians. Galatians 6:10

Stewards of Time

Our time is one of God's most valuable gifts. Ps. 90:12; Eph. 5:16 We will use our time for prayer, devotion, worship, witnessing, and study. Every moment is lived to bring God glory and honor.

A Steward of Our Possessions

We guard against making things more important than God. Luke 12:13-21 Greed is idolatry. Colossians 3:5 God's people are expected to provide the finances for the work of His Church. 1 Corinthians 16:1-4 gives a guideline for financial giving to the church:
1. Regular (Sunday)
2. Planned (Set aside)
3. Proportional (in keeping with his income)

Giving is an honor. Acts 20:35 If the Jews gave 10% under the Law, what should we give out of love for Jesus? Matthew 6:28-33 2 Cor. 9:7

Stewards of Service to Others

God has left the care of others to us. James 1:27; 1 John 3:16 We will show God's love to all we meet. Matthew 5:13-16

New Life Study #7
Celebrating the Lord's Supper

Jesus gave his disciples a special way to remember Him
through the celebration of the Lord's Supper.
Matthew 26:19, 26-29

The Jewish Passover

1. This was to celebrate God's delivering Israel from their bondage in Egypt.

2. A lamb was slain and the blood was placed on the door frame of every Hebrew home, so the death angel would pass over the house. Exodus 13:3-7, 13

3. The Hebrews were to eat the lamb's flesh. This meal would give them strength for their journey. Exodus 12:8-10

4. The annual passover for the Jews was a continual reminder that God judges sin and mercifully delivers those who seek Him in obedient faith. Exodus 12:14

The Lord's Supper

1. This is to celebrate our deliverance from sin through Christ.

2. Jesus was the Lamb of God, whose blood (death) pays the penalty for our sin. John 1:29; 1 Peter 1:18-21

3. Christians are to eat the bread of communion, recognizing the body of Jesus and the cup, recognizing the blood of Jesus. He died for us. Matthew 26:19, 26-29 Knowing Jesus gives us life. John 6:53-58

4. The Lord's Supper is a continual reminder that Jesus died for our sins and that through faith in Him, we have new life. 2 Corinthians 5:7

When?
There's no direct command.
The Bible teaches that the Lord's Supper:
1. Was a part of the life of the very first church, Acts 2:42
2. Was celebrated weekly by an early church, Acts 20:7

Why?
1. We remember Jesus' sacrifice for us. 1 Corinthians 11:23-25
2. We proclaim Jesus' sacrifice to the world until He comes again. 1 Corinthians 11:26

What?
1. The bread we use is like the unleavened Passover bread, Exodus 12:39
2. The cup is filled with grape juice, the same as Jesus used. Mark 14:23-25

New Life Study #8
Knowing God's Will

God's Definite Will

1. God wills that all men be saved and come to Him.
   2 Peter 3:9
   1 Timothy 2:3-4
2. God wills for us to live a life committed to Him.
   Ephesians 5:17-21
   1 Thessalonians 4:3-8; 5:12-18ff

God's Will & Man's Free Will

1. Man is created in God's image.
   Genesis 1:27-28
2. Man is re-created by the Lord Jesus.
   2 Corinthians 5:17
3. The Christian has a renewed mind.
   Romans 12:1-2
   Hence, we are able to make decisions as God's responsible people.

Five Steps in Discerning God's Will in Your Life

Fill Your Mind with God's Word
Psalm 119:105

Obey God's Direct Will
James 4:17

Counsel with Mature Christians
Proverbs 1:5; 19:20

Ask the Lord's Guidance in Prayer
Matthew 7:7-8
James 1:5

Make Your Decision as a Christian and Walk with God
Matthew 28:20

New Life Study #9
Trained by Discipline

God Promises to Discipline His Children
Key Passage: Hebrews 12:5-15

Three Things to Realize

1. The purpose of discipline is so that we share in God's holiness. Hebrews 12:10

2. Not every hardship in life is sent by God. James 1:13 Many times, God allows difficulties to come our way and then promises us that He is powerful enough to work through even the hardest situation to bring about 'good' in our lives. Romans 8:28

3. Therefore, God can use every difficult situation in our lives to train us to be His people . . . if we allow Him to.

Three Ways to Handle God's Discipline

Stoicism

"I will get through this and tough it out." And yet through this they learn nothing. Some people say they have had 10 years' experience, but a stoic response means they have had 1 year of experience repeated 10 times.

Bitterness

. . . toward God and everyone else.
Heb. 12:15
The bitter person:
1. Has an unforgiving spirit, Heb. 12:4; Eph. 4:31-32.
2. Verbalizes to others ill treatment, Matt. 12:34.
3. Refuses to admit the bitterness and learn from the experience, Ps. 139:23-24.

Acceptance

Hebrews 12:11
1. When difficulties come, accept their reality and ask, "How can this situation lead me closer to the Lord?"; "What can I learn from this to make me a better person?"
2. The result will be the peaceful fruit of righteousness.

New Life Study #10
Obedient Christian Living

OBEDIENCE
1 John 2:3

What?

1. Obedience is doing God's will from the heart, Hebrews 10:15-17

2. Obedience is not:
   – Serving God on your own terms
   – Asceticism
   – Legalism

Why?

1. Because of God's love and worthiness, 1 John 4:19.

2. Because it proves your love, 1 John 5:3.

3. Because God demands it, Matthew 7:21.

How?

Step #4
Learn to Deal with Temptations
1 Cor. 10:13

Step #3
Have the Right Attitude: To Delight to Do God's Will
Ps. 40:8

Step #2
Draw on God's Power to Obey
Phil. 4:12-14
Rom. 8:11

Step #1
Know God's Commands
2 Tim. 3:14-17

Four Steps to Obedient Christian Living

This lesson has been adapted from *Dynamics of Personal Follow-Up* by Gary W. Kuhne.
Copyright © 1976 by the Zondervan Corporation. Used by permission of Zondervan Publishing House (www.zondervan.com).
Available at your local bookstore or by calling 800-727-3480.

Chapter 13
THE NEED FOR SMALL GROUPS IN MAKING DISCIPLES

Spiritual growth, like emotional growth, does not occur in a vacuum. It comes as we relate to others in the body of Christ, his church. Why then have so many Christians failed to find spiritual stimulation in their local church? One key reason is that churches today, in general, lack the essential community that characterized churches for centuries. The people you sat next to in church last Sunday very likely do not live in your neighborhood. And even if they do, chances are that they will move away in three years. These are the facts of life. We just don't get to know, really know, the people who are our brothers and sisters in Christ if we meet only in a large group that draws from a twenty-mile radius and that changes constantly. By meeting in smaller units we make intimacy at least possible.[1]

Ron Nicoles

Our goal, once we bring people into a saving relationship with Jesus Christ, is to lead them into maturity through the "Discipling Process." In the last chapter we saw how that process is carried out in four basic forms.

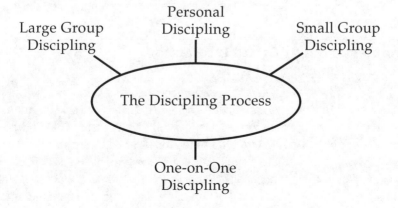

Large Group
Discipling

Personal
Discipling

Small Group
Discipling

The Discipling Process

One-on-One
Discipling

We have already looked briefly at each of these basic forms. One last area of the discipling process needs to be examined in greater detail because in the long run it holds the most promise for producing the image of Christ in the life of the new believer. This is called "small group discipling."

Five different categories of people are in attendance at any particular congregation on any given Sunday. They are:

1. Those assimilated into a small group which gives a meaningful experience before they formally join the congregation
2. Those entering a meaningful group after joining the church family
3. Those who assume a role after joining the church (teacher, usher, etc.)
4. Those who find a task in the church
5. Individuals who do none of the above. These are already in the process of dropping into inactivity within one year

This makes it obviously clear that every church family must work at developing meaningful small groups for the spiritual and social needs of its people.

Small groups are called by varying names in our local congregations. These groups include anything from Bible school classes, committee groups, women's circles, youth groups, cell groups, encounter groups, home Bible studies, supper-eights, fellowship-fours, ministry teams, care groups, to just "the gang" that gets together after services. At best these small groups are seen as dynamic, life-changing units which add not only to personal growth but also to the corporate body-life of the church. At worst, these small groups are seen as cliques that separate and alienate. One thing is for certain, every church that has grown larger than 30-35 in attendance will have "small groups" within its structure.

Christians need to consider the New Testament concept of small group discipling. I believe that it is impossible to carry out the mandates of disciplemaking without utilizing this important segment of the discipling process.

Examples of Small Group Interaction in the First-century Church

In the New Testament, the fact is undeniable that Christians met in private homes. However, it is difficult to base justification for small group ministry upon these scattered examples from the New Testament. The house churches (Acts 20:7-12; Rom. 16:5) mentioned in Scripture were just that, local congregations small enough to meet in a private home. This is considerably different from what many churches today wish to implement, which is the division of a single congregation into smaller groups centering on personal ministry. The fact that first-century Christians met in private homes could be explained simply by utilitarian reasons. They had neither the means nor the social standing to erect buildings suitable for public worship.

The house churches mentioned in Scripture were local congregations small enough to meet in a private home.

In order to find a more firm foundation for small group ministry, we must turn our attention to the Scripture's teaching on the nature and purpose of the church, seeing how these can best be implemented in our local church bodies by the use of small group ministry.

The Necessity of Small Group Interaction in New Testament Theology

God's call for His church to exhibit biblical fellowship cannot be realized without some sort of personal interaction on the part of the individual members of the local church family. A wide range of Christian scholars have spoken on this issue. There are numerous scriptural underpinnings for such a belief. Hadaway, Wright, and DuBoise make a keen observation concerning the nature and function of the church in relationship to its structure. They write:

> There is a direct line between nature, function, and structure. We can expect the church to assume certain functions growing out of its nature, and we can expect these functions to be translated into structures as the church takes root and grows in its cultural, social, economic, and political context. A theology of church structure, therefore, is the way in which we perceive structural forms as the reflection of the nature of the church and the essential functions which attest to that nature.[2]

In effect these authors are stating that a certain structure within the church may be better equipped and even necessary to allow the church to become what God has revealed in the Scriptures.

Christian scholar, Millard J. Erickson has written:

> The body is to be characterized by genuine fellowship. This does not mean merely a social interrelatedness, but an intimate feeling for and understanding of one another. There is to be empathy and encouragement. What is experienced by one is to be experienced by all.[3]

Much of the nature of the church as it is expressed in daily living is to be found worked out in the personal relationship between Christians.

Perhaps no one in the twentieth century has said this better than Dietrich Bonhoeffer. In his inspiring book *Life Together* Bonhoeffer forcefully declares that "Christianity means community through Jesus Christ."[4] These were not mere words for Bonhoeffer. They were lived out on a daily basis in the underground seminary which Bonhoeffer started in Nazi Germany. His words ring with intensity.

> Christian brotherhood is not an ideal which we must realize, it is rather created by God in Christ in which we may participate. The more clearly we learn to recognize that the ground and strength and promise of all our fellowship is in Jesus Christ alone, the more serenely shall we think of our fellowship and pray and hope for it.[5]

And for Bonhoeffer, Christian community was not simply a doctrine. Rather the doctrine had been transformed into the vehicle of experiencing the reality of Christian living. It was through Christian community that this martyred theologian found the daily grace of Christ in a nation ravaged by Nazi tyranny.

New Testament Images of the Church in Community

In studying the New Testament we find very few *definitions* of the church. What we do find are numerous word pictures showing us *descriptions* of what God has created His church to be and to do. Let's examine several of the major images used in the New Testament relating to the church as God's community in the world.

Family

One of the most prevalent images of the church presented to us in the New Testament describes the church as a "family." In his excellent study, Robert Banks goes so far as to declare that the family image is the most important image of the church contained within the New Testament. He writes:

> So numerous are these and so frequently do they appear, that the comparison of the Christian community with a "family" must be regarded as the most significant metaphorical usage of all. . . . More than any other images utilized by Paul, it reveals the essence of his thinking about community.[6]

While the actual phrase "the family of God" is not used in the New Testament, family terminology abounds. The most common address for God is the term "Father," occurring 259 times in the New Testament alone. G.E. Ladd relates that the most important phrase in the study of the self-disclosure of Jesus is the "Son of God."[7] Sonship was the best concept available to the Holy Spirit to inspire the authors of Scripture to describe the role relationship which Jesus shared with God the Father.

Christians are addressed as "brethren."[8] All of this points out that in God's mind the church is implicitly viewed as a family. Christians call God "Abba Father" (Gal. 4:6), are fellow heirs of the family holdings with Christ (Rom. 8:14-17), and call one another brother (1 Cor. 8:11, 13). This family concept even shows up in Paul's relationships with his colleagues. Paul refers to Onesimus as "my child, whose father I have become" (Phil. 10), and to Timothy as a son (Phil. 2:23; Col. 1:1) and a brother (1 Thess. 3:22). He even refers to Rufus's mother as his own (Rom. 16:13).

This "family image" of the church, presented so strongly in the New Testament text, has obvious ramifications for the type of relationships Christians are to develop. A family knows one another intimately. A family cares for one another and shares with one another. A family meets one another's needs. A family grows together. This is what God intends for His church to become.

A family cares for one another, shares with one another, meets one another's needs, and grows together. This is what God intends for His church to become.

Ralph Martin notes:

> The church at its best reflects all that is noblest and most worthwhile in human family life: attitudes of caring and mutual regard; understanding of needs, whether physical or of the spirit; and above all the sense of "belonging" to a social unit in which we find acceptance without pretense or make-believe. Home life is for many people a sphere where they can be "natural" as themselves. God's house shares this character when its worship and fellowship create an atmosphere in which there is free expression of our true selves, always in the hope that we can learn from one another and mature as we grow into our Elder Brother's likeness (Rom. 8:29; Eph. 4:13-15).[9]

With this understanding of the church, we have to ask ourselves the question: Can the spiritual needs of God's people be met without some sort of small group interaction? The fact is that God, through His Word, is calling His church to experience interaction; not simply in the context of community, but in the context of the closest community known in this life: the community of the family. In order to accomplish this, the local congregation, no matter how large, will have to provide the opportunity for Christians to grow in a family type of setting. This implies small group interaction. While family reunions may run into the hundreds, families grow normally in smaller cell groups.

Can the spiritual needs of God's people be met without some sort of small group interaction?

People of God

Another important image used in the New Testament is that of the church as "the people of God." A key text is found in 1 Peter:

> But you are a chosen race, a royal priesthood, a holy nation, a people for God's own possession, that you may proclaim the excellencies of Him who has called you out of the darkness into His marvelous light; for you once were not a people, but now you are the people of God; you had not received mercy, but now you have received mercy (1 Pet 2:9-10, NASB).

In this passage there are many different images (race, priesthood, nation) all centering around the concept of being "the people of God."

In our normal English usage of the term "people," we usually think of an aggregate mass of people being present at a certain place. Many view the church in this way; as a group of relatively unrelated individuals coming together loosely for an hour or two a week.

Paul Minear has been quick to point out that nothing can be farther from the truth.[10] He relates that *people in general* do not exist in a New Testament context; there are *only particular people*.[11]

> Each people has a separate and cohesive actuality of its own. Every person belongs to a particular people, just as he belongs to a particular tongue or nation or tribe; and this people is not reducible to the mathematical aggregate of its members. The people defines the person . . . . Hence when an individual shifts from one people to another, a drastic change in his status and selfhood is involved.[12]

Minear continues to relate a second misconception that our culture has forced upon the New Testament usage of the concept of a people. We often use the term "people" to denote a plural number of persons. When New Testament writers wish to refer to "all men," they speak of Adam as the representative of all men (Rom. 5:12-21; 1 Cor. 15:22; 15:45-49) or they speak of "all the peoples" (Rev. 10:11; 17:15). In the New Testament, humanity is not visualized as a worldwide census of individuals, but as the separate peoples that, taken together, comprise mankind as a whole. Each people retains its own discrete unity. Therefore, to identify a particular society as the people of God is immediately to set it over against all other peoples.[13]

In the New Testament there are a number of images that undergird the concept of the church as *the people of God*.[14] We have already examined the images laid out for us by the apostle Peter. Paul likens the church to the twelve tribes of Israel (1 Cor. 10:1-10; Rom. 15:8-10), the circumcision (Rom. 15:8-10), Abraham's sons (Gal. 3:29; Rom. 4:16), the remnant (Rom. 9:27; 11:5-7), the elect (Eph. 1:4; Rom. 11:28). All of these images are a comparison between the community life of the church and the community life of the literal nation of Israel. The intention of the biblical authors is to reflect that our belonging to the church of our Lord Jesus Christ is to be viewed with the same and perhaps even greater intensity of the faithful Jew to His people. The people of Israel centered their national life around the tabernacle and later the temple. As Christians, we are called to recognize that the temple worship central to the nation of Israel is now to be a reality within the life of every individual Christian (1 Cor. 6:19; Eph. 2:21). And as the spiritual needs of the Israelites were met by God through the levitical priesthood, now among the church as the people of God, every member of "God's new nation" is a priest (1 Pet 2:9).[15]

How can we, as priests, best minister to one another's spiritual needs?

In coming to grips with this image of the church as the people of God with every member as a priest, we immediately must ask the question: How can we, as priests, best minister to one another's spiritual needs? It is true that certain "priests" may have gifts to minister to large groups of people all at one time. However, "the people of God" have all been entrusted with gifts of ministry.[16] Can we expect the ministry of the "people of God" to one another to be carried on without some sort of small group interaction? The concept of the church as the people of God demands that the members of this special group of people minister to one another on a very personal level. One obvious way that this can be carried out is in a small group setting.

The Body of Christ

A third major image of the church in the New Testament is perhaps the most widely used image in popular Christian literature today. It is the image of the church as "the body of Christ" (1 Cor. 12:12-27; Rom. 12:4-5; Eph. 1:23; 4:4,12,16; 5:23,30). The "body" imagery was well known to the Greek culture. However it seems that in his writings, the apostle Paul did not regard the "body" concept in the same way the Greeks did. To the Greek mind, the body was only formed matter, but to Paul the body was an organism of acting members. No other image in the New Testament speaks of the necessity of small group interaction as does the "body" image. Christians are bound to one another through their relationship to Christ.

In the New Testament the sharpest picture of the church as the "body of Christ" can probably be found in 1 Corinthians 12:12-27. The apostle Paul concludes that section of Scripture by making an affirmation of God's view of His church.

> . . . so that there should be no division in the body, but that its parts should have equal concern for each other. If one part suffers, every part suffers with it; if one part is honored, every part rejoices with it. Now you are the body of Christ, and each one of you is a part of it (1 Cor. 12:25-27).

The bond between members of Christ's church is so strong that when something happens to any particular member, the life of the whole group is affected (12:26). In order for this to be realized in daily life, the local congregation would seem to have to be organized into groups small enough to allow such close interaction to take place. In a church of 300 worshiping members or above, it is not normally possible for any single believer to know everybody else, let alone be personally affected by the joys and sorrows of every member. However, if the larger congregation is organized into smaller cell groups (each group in itself constituting the "body of Christ" in its completeness), then this becomes more than a point of doctrine, it becomes a point of fact lived out in the real lives of brothers and sisters in Christ.

In a large church, it is not normally possible for any single believer to know everybody else.

This passage in 1 Corinthians 12 also relates another important aspect of the life of the church. Every member of the body is important and necessary to the life of the body as a whole (12:14-24a). While this can be realized in a somewhat practical sense in a large gathering, this concept is immediately appreciated in a small group setting. Just as a family cannot be a complete family unless all members are present, so a body cannot be a completed unity with some member missing. While in a gathering of several hundred this is true in theory, in a smaller group it is evident without having to be spoken. If a group of eight is meeting and one individual is missing, the discussion leader doesn't have to study 1 Corinthians 12 for the group to realize what has happened. The members simply look around and ask, "Where's Charlie?"

This oneness of the "body," the church, is idealized in the celebration of the Lord's Supper. The readers of the Corinthian letter would have immediately understood this imagery as the apostle Paul spoke of the body and blood symbolized in the bread and the cup and the unity and intimate interrelatedness to which they attest (1 Cor. 10:16-17).

The "body" has one head, according to Scripture, the Lord Jesus Christ. He is the "head of the body, the church" (Col. 1:18). Under His headship, both Jew and Gentile become one in Christ who "is all and in all" (Col. 3:11). In Him, the body is to "grow up in all aspects" (Eph. 4:15). And when the Lord has finished with His church, it will have grown "to the measure and stature which belongs to the fullness of Christ" (Eph. 4:13).

Millard Erickson writes:

> There is no such thing as an isolated, solitary Christian life . . . . Each member needs the other and each member is needed by the other. The body is to be characterized by genuine fellowship. This does not mean merely a social interrelatedness, but an intimate feeling for and understanding of one another. There is to be empathy and encouragement.[17]

This sort of interaction among Christians has to have an outlet. The local congregation must develop a form for the expression of these lofty ideals of Scripture. If the organizational structure of the local congregation is a hindrance to the attainment of the purpose of the church in the New Testament, then one of two things must take place. Either the local church will fail to become what Christ has willed in His Word, or the local church will find a way to reflect in its structure the best way to allow the church to become the "body of Christ." Small group ministry is an essential structural form in the life of a local congregation to enable the church to actualize its theology in day to day living. There are many other images of the church found in the New Testament which also relate to our topic, but these three, the family of God, the people of God and the body of Christ are sufficient to illustrate the need for the church to consider the viability of small group ministry.[18]

The Fourfold Aspect of Small Group Ministry

In his book *Good Things Come in Small Groups*, Ron Nicoles outlines a fourfold purpose for small group ministry.[19] These are aspects that need to be present in any group which hopes to function according to the principles of the New Testament and produce the type of atmosphere which will be conducive to the growth of a new Christian in the discipling process.

The first aspect is that of *nurture*. This involves growth in both mind and spirit (Rom. 12:2). God uses many ways to bring us to maturity in our Christian lives. For most small groups, nurture comes directly from studying the Bible. Every Christian needs the empowering words of God flowing into them if they are to maintain spiritual vitality and growth.

Second, discipling groups need to display the aspect of *worship*. Worship flows out of our knowledge of God into praising and honoring Him (Acts 2:43). Worship takes many forms such as singing and prayer. Every small group within the church should work at developing this aspect of group life.

Third, comes the aspect of *fellowship*. Every discipling group within the local congregation needs to display some aspect of the fellowship we have described earlier in this chapter. Christian fellowship is not merely a subjective feeling of belonging. It is related to the commitment of love and obligation we have toward members of our own family. It is devotion to one another based upon the experience we share as God's children in Christ.

Finally, every group in the local congregation which is serious about discipling needs to display the aspect of *mission*. Small discipling groups need to have goals and activities that are not centered upon themselves. Each group needs to develop the vision to reach out beyond the group to take the love of Christ to others in some special way. This may involve such activities as evangelism and social action. Small groups in the local church need to learn how to develop this aspect of mission.

Different Types of Groups within the Local Congregation

The typical congregation in America consisting of over 30 to 40 people naturally divides itself into small groups. The goal of those interested in discipleship is to make certain that these groups do in fact reflect the four aspects of spiritually healthy group life. This will ensure that the "theology" of the New Testament church can be lived out in the body life of a local congregation. When this occurs, discipleship will take place.

Each different group in a local church will probably emphasize one of the four group functions over the other three, but all must be present within any small group in order for that body of people to "grow" into what Christ desires. For instance, some groups within the church naturally emphasize *nurture*. These would include Bible school classes, Bible study groups, new member classes, etc. In these small groups, the study of the Word is the primary concern. However, time must also be found to display aspects of worship or the study will produce spiritually sterile intellects, filled with head knowledge, but no heart knowledge. A Bible study group must also seek for ways to enjoy fellowship activities, to allow members of the group to actually live out the doctrines they have been learning. Each study group should also involve itself in some aspect of mission, seeking ways to serve those outside its immediate boundaries.

Other small groups within the church center on *worship*. These might include choirs, other music groups, prayer groups, renewal groups, etc. Those involved in such groups make the aspect of worship the primary activity of their time together. However, if the aspects of nurture are ignored, the heart of the worshiper may wander into unbiblical expressions because it has been severed from the head. Worship groups must also plan times of fellowship and outreach if true disciplemaking is to take place.

A wide range of groups within a typical congregation may center on *fellowship*. These would include men's groups, women's groups, youth groups, home care groups, or others. Every church needs groups whose primary function is to provide the family atmosphere of caring and interactive joy that is one of the characteristic aspects of God's people in the church. However, a fellowship group which has no sense of mission and outreach can quickly degenerate into a social clique which accomplishes nothing to help lead people into becoming true disciples of Jesus Christ. Also, fellowship groups which lack aspects of nurture and worship can become introspective, unspiritual and unbiblical. It is amazing how many such groups exist within congregations across America. These groups have great interpersonal dynamics, but they become an actual hindrance to the cause of Christ. The reason is that these groups have neglected one or more of the spiritual aspects necessary for every small group to possess.

A fellowship group which has no sense of mission and outreach can quickly degenerate into a social clique.

Finally, some small groups in the church center the chief amount of their attention on *mission*. These groups might include evangelistic teams, almost all church committees, church boards, and elder boards. These groups have a certain function or mission to carry out in service of the church or the community. But even these groups need the other three aspects of small group life in order to function in a spiritually productive manner. How many church boards would benefit from incorporating aspects of worship, nurture, and fellowship into their meetings? The group that oversees the local community food distribution center needs to be studying the Bible of the God who loves the poor, so that they will not grow cynical toward those who are less fortunate. Aspects of worship could help the task to be seen as a joy instead of a duty, and aspects of fellowship are necessary so that the team can bear one another's burdens and so fulfill the law of Christ.

Our goal is simple and clear. Whenever a Christian becomes a part of a small group interaction within a local church family, he must find a spiritual atmosphere which will allow for his ultimate growth as a member of the body of Christ. While each group's main emphasis may differ, the goal is always the same. The group must aid in "making disciples" or it will find itself working against rather than for the purposes of God.

New Testament Thinking about Small Groups

In order for the church to function according to the principles laid out in the New Testament, the members of each local congregation must exhibit close personal relationships. It is not possible to develop close relationships in our postmodern society in the setting of a large group alone. Therefore, every church that is serious about functioning according to the principles laid down in the New Testament, must develop ways of plugging its members into some form of small group ministry.

The small group allows God's purpose for the church to be carried out in a very natural way. No church should have a goal to remain small because of what we have discussed. Rather, every church, whether it has fifty or five thousand members, should ask itself if it is realizing in a daily expression what God has called the church to be and to do. When large churches break their membership down into small groups, those groups will begin to translate the theology of the New Testament church into the daily lives of God's people. When this occurs, we will be well on our way to seeing the ultimate goal of the Great Commission carried out within the life of the church. We will be "making disciples."

1. Ron Nicoles et al., *Good Things Happen in Small Groups* (Downers Grove, IL: InterVarsity, 1985), p. 14.

2. C. Kirk Hadaway, Stuart A. Wright, and Francis M. DuBoise, *Home Cell Groups and House Churches* (Nashville: Broadman, 1987), p. 56.

3. Millard J. Erickson, *Christian Theology* (Grand Rapids: Baker, 1987), p. 1038.

4. Bonhoeffer expands on this concept in a bold three-part assertion. First he declares that a Christian needs others only because of Jesus Christ. Secondly, a Christian comes to others only through Jesus Christ. Finally, he contends that in Jesus Christ, we have been chosen from eternity, accepted in time, and united for eternity (both to Christ and each other). Dietrich Bonhoeffer, *Life Together* (New York: Harper and Row, 1976), pp. 21-26.

5. Ibid., p. 30.

6. Robert Banks, *Paul's Idea of Community: The Early House Churches in Their Historical Setting* (Grand Rapids: Eerdmans, 1980), pp. 53-54.

7. Ladd follows Gerhard Vos in pointing out that there are at least four ways the term "Son of God" is used in the New Testament: (1) a nativistic sense, in that humanity owes its existence to the creative activity of God; (2) a messianic sense, in that the Davidic king is designated the son of God (2 Sam. 7:14); (3) a theological sense, in that Jesus was Son of God in that He partook of the divine nature; and (4) a moral-religious sense which can be applied to men and to the nation of Israel. "In the New Testament, this concept is filled with deeper significance as Christians are described in terms of sonship to God by birth (John 3:3; 1:12) or by adoption (Rom. 8:14, 19; Gal. 3:26; 4:5)." G.E. Ladd, *A Theology of the New Testament* (Grand Rapids: Eerdmans, 1974), pp. 159-160.

8. There are 30 instances of this in Acts and 130 in the Pauline corpus. Han Freiherr von Soden, "ἀδελφός," *Theological Dictionary of the New Testament*.

9. Ralph P. Martin, *The Family and the Fellowship* (Grand Rapids: Eerdmans, 1979), p. 124.

10. Paul Minear, *Images of the Church in the New Testament* (Philadelphia: Westminster, 1975), p. 68.

11. There are only a few exceptions to this rule, the majority being in the Lucan writings. The only other exceptions are in Matt. 11:32; 14:2 and Mark 4:23; 26:5; 27:25,64. H. Strathmann, "λαός," *Theological Dictionary of the New Testament*.

12. Paul Minear, *Images*, p. 68.

13. Ibid.

14. The following Scriptures show that the concept of the church as "the people of God" had a major significance in the life of the early church: Acts 3:23; 7:34; 13:17-31; 15:14; 18:10; Rom. 9:25-26; 11:1-32; 15:10; 2 Cor. 6:16; Heb. 2:17; 4:9; 8:10; 10:30; 13:12; Rev. 18:4; 21:3.

15. For a good overview of this see Donald G. Bloesch, *The Essentials of Evangelical Theology*, vol. 2: *Life, Ministry, and Hope* (New York: Harper and Row, 1978), pp. 104-130.

16. First Corinthians 12:27-31 lists a variety of spiritual gifts, some of which seem to have the best application in the context of a larger group while others are seen to be carried out on a more personal level. The greatest gift of all, which 1 Cor. 13 outlines, cannot be fully realized outside of a small group setting where personal interaction takes place.

17. Millard J. Erickson, *Christian Theology*, pp. 1037-1038.

18 There are many other images that speak of the nature of the Christian community. Donald Guthrie has written concerning the vine allegory in John 15: "The vine allegory is . . . suggestive regarding the corporate character of the coming community . . . . The idea of many branches being knit together by being joined by one stem or stock is a valid illustration of corporateness. Not only can no branch exist without being in living contact with the vine but the

branches could have no relation to each other except through the vine. The illustration presents the concept of a community viewed not as an organization, but as an organism." Donald Guthrie, *New Testament Theology* (Downers Grove, IL: InterVarsity, 1981), p. 723.

Elton Trueblood spends much time talking of the military metaphor of the church found in the pages of the New Testament. Trueblood sees the commitment fostered in a military setting at the heart of the power of the early church. This means involvement and personal interaction. Trueblood has written: "The churches which are succeeding best are those in which the involvement of the rank and file of the members is most nearly complete." Elton Trueblood, *The Company of the Committed* (New York: Harper and Row, 1969), p. 39.

Perhaps the most complete listing of church images is given by Paul Minear. Minear lists thirty-two minor images of the church and four major images. Two of the major images listed by Minear, "the new creation" and "the fellowship in Faith," we did not discuss. Minear, *Images*, pp. 105-172.

19. Nicoles, *Good Things Happen in Small Groups*, pp. 22-37.

Chapter 14
SOME CONCLUDING THOUGHTS

And now you have an extraordinary opportunity, a day wherein Christ has thrown the door of mercy wide open, and stands in calling and crying with a loud voice to poor sinners; a day wherein many are flocking to him, and pressing into the kingdom of God. Many are daily coming from the east, west, north and south . . . are now in a happy state, with their hearts filled with love to him who has loved them, and washed them from their sins in his own blood, and rejoicing in hope of the glory of God. (The conclusion of the sermon: "Sinners in the Hands of an Angry God").

Jonathan Edwards

(The) men of Issachar, who understood the times and knew what Israel should do.

1 Chronicles 12:32a

The greatest opportunity in the world is to be able to take part in God's great work of bringing people back to Himself by sharing the message of what He has done through His Son and our Savior, the Lord Jesus Christ. In every age, the enemy has done his best to discourage God's faithful witnesses or to cloud the minds of those who need Christ. Our own present Postmodern Generation is no exception to that. Yet in every age God has poured out His blessings on those who make it their business to internalize the great drama of salvation as God has revealed it to us in history as recorded in the Christian Scriptures. God can use any of His faithful people to carry out His purposes. However, God will especially bless those who make it a point not only to understand the Scriptures, but also to understand the times. These servants will be able to know just the right methods to take the unchanging gospel message to the ever changing world around them. They will be like the "men of Issachar, who understood the times and knew what Israel should do" (1 Chr 12:32).

The task is simple in its concept, but complex in its execution. "Therefore go and make disciples of all nations, baptizing them in the name of the Father and of the Son and of the Holy Spirit, and teaching them to obey everything I have commanded you. And surely I am with you always, to the very end of the age" (Matt 28:19-20). In "going," we prepare ourselves with the gospel and with an understanding of the culture with which we plan to share that gospel. In "baptizing," we make contact with those who need Christ and help them to come in faith to the Lord Jesus. In "teaching them to obey everything" Jesus has commanded us, we begin a lifelong journey with our brothers and sisters in Christ "until we all reach unity in the faith and in the knowledge of the Son of God and become mature, attaining to the whole measure of the fullness of Christ" (Eph 4:13). This involves intensive discipling in the early months following conversion as well as utilizing the structures of the Discipling Process which will allow us to carry out the Lord's ultimate command. We are to "make disciples!"

The task is simple in its concept, but complex in its execution.

We began this study by sharing the conversion stories of some well known people who had been surprised by joy. I'd like to conclude by sharing one final story which will display the joyous work of evangelism as well as challenge each one of us for action. The story involves Edith Schaeffer, the wife of the late Christian philosopher, Francis Schaeffer. It occurred early in their ministry while they were living in the St. Louis area. Mrs. Schaeffer was preparing a message for a study group in her local church on the "Day of Atonement." After she had done her biblical analysis, she thought it might be a good idea to ask a contemporary Jew what the Day of Atonement meant to them. She inquired as to the location of one of the Jewish families living in her community and, although they were strangers, Edith walked up to their door and knocked.

When she was met by the lady of the house, she diffidently explained her mission. The lady offered to have her father explain their practices, as he knew more about the subject than she did. The elderly gentleman, stooped and gray-haired, was happy to reminisce about his boyhood memories of the Day of Atonement as practiced by the Austrian Jewish community. As a boy he would eagerly anticipate the coming of the day, and try hard to remember his sins of the previous year and be sorry for them one by one. Their fasting also included going without water and not even cleaning their teeth that day. When he finished his account by bringing his thoughts up to date, the daughter suddenly asked, "Please, would you tell me what makes your attitude so different from most Gentiles I have met?

You are so warm and I feel a love for us in your attitude. What is it that makes you love us? I can feel it . . . and I want to know why."

Mrs. Schaeffer told them that it would take longer than a simple answer to adequately explain this, and that she did not want to presume on their hospitality when she had already basically invited herself into their home with her own question. Yet if they wanted her to go ahead, she would gladly explain to them why she thought it only natural for anyone with a proper understanding of the Bible to love the Jews.

Receiving their permission, she began with a bird's eye overview of the Old Testament, giving her understanding of the central teaching of the Bible. When she got to the end of the Old Testament, she stopped and asked again for permission to proceed, not wanting to offend. When they admonished her not to stop, but go ahead, she continued right through the New Testament to the end of Revelation.

> When I finished, and the heavenly city had been described, and the whole story had come to its climax, the old Austrian Jew sighed a deep sigh, and turning his head to look up at his daughter said, "Daughter, have you ever heard anything so beautiful?"
> "No, Father, I never have."
> Then the father turned his head to look down at me. "For thirty years I have been a dentist in this city. For thirty years I have had Gentile patients. *Why* has no one ever told me all this before?"[1]

No Christian should be surprised by guilt on the day of judgment for lack of carrying out the Great Commission. How much better to be continually surprised by joy as we take part in our Master's greatest labor. Lord help us to Make Disciples!

---

1. Edith Schaeffer, *Christianity Is Jewish* (Wheaton, IL.: Tyndale, 1975), pp. 9-11.

APPENDIXES

Appendix A
BAPTISM IN ITS HISTORICAL PERSPECTIVE

Our goal is to give a brief (and admittedly somewhat superficial) overview of how the theological pendulum of thought has shifted through the centuries in regard to understanding the biblical teaching on the significance of baptism. There is such a wide view of baptism that those who write articles on baptism will most certainly offend someone. In fact, the *International Standard Bible Encyclopedia*'s article on baptism is written by the editor, Geoffrey Bromiley, with three other authors giving the Baptist, Reformed and Lutheran views of baptism, and each vehemently critiquing one another.

The swing of the theological pendulum has made a broad arch in the flow of Christian thought. Early on, the doctrine of baptism departed from the simple biblical teaching in the sacramental theology of Roman Catholicism and later continuing in Eastern Orthodoxy and most paedo-baptism traditions. Here, baptism becomes the entire conversion-transformational event without regard to the inner assent of the heart of the individual. In the time of the Reformation, the pendulum cut a sweeping arch in the opposite direction (specifically in the thought of Zwingli). Here, baptism is stripped of any significance in relationship to saving faith and becomes merely an optional appendage of postsalvation obedience. The bulk of the evangelical world still lives in the outer arch of the pendulum swing of the Reformation. Baptism merely signifies identification with a local congregation; or even worse, baptism is exegeted as merely a metaphor wherever it seems to relate to saving faith.

Let's briefly look at this swinging pendulum of thought and understand that the truth is to be found when the pendulum is at rest and can be used as a plumb line to reflect the mind of God reflected in the message of Scripture.

I. Early Christianity: The Pendulum Swings to the Right — The Action Becomes Everything

In the 2nd century, the church stood with a united understanding of Christian baptism. Baptism was an outward appeal of the inner conviction of the heart. The two were united. Hence baptism was seen as the act of faith through which God would grant the blessings of the finished work of Christ on the cross to the life of the individual. In the *Epistle of Barnabas* (believed to have been written by an Alexandrian Jewish Christian near 100 A.D.) we see that forgiveness of sins was understood as being received at the time of baptism.[1]

In the *Shepherd of Hermas* (traditionally believed to have been written near 160 A.D.) we see that these believers understood that at the time of their baptism they received God's forgiveness and the new life He has to offer.[2]

Justin Martyr (110-165), one of the first great apologists and martyrs for the faith, declared that an individual was "regenerated" at the time of his baptism, and he equated baptism with being "born again" (The first extra-New Testament reference to the term "born again" refers it to the time of baptism!!). He called baptism the "illumination" (a term that became popular in the Ante-Nicene period).[3]

Irenaeus (120-202) was a student of Polycarp who had been a student of the Apostle John. He taught that in baptism we receive forgiveness of sins, and that baptism was the seal of eternal life and the regeneration by which we become God's children.[4]

However, near the end of the 2nd century and continuing into the 3rd century, we begin to see a departure from the New Testament teaching. Tertullian (145-220) makes mention of a threefold immersion and admits that it is an "ampler pledge than the Lord has appointed in the Gospels."[5]

A much more troubling doctrine arises with Tertullian when he begins to teach that God grants a miraculous power to the water of baptism. While Tertullian saw that repentance was necessary and a prerequisite to baptism, yet he also taught that the water itself gained the power of sanctification through the work of the Holy Spirit.[6]

Here we have a direct departure from biblical teaching. The New Testament is clear that the Holy Spirit works His sanctifying power on the heart of man, not upon the waters of baptism! "And that is what some of you were. But you were washed, you were sanctified, you were justified in the name of the Lord Jesus Christ and by the Spirit of our God" (1 Cor. 6:11).

Biblically, the apostles understood that baptism was the time of the cleansing of conscience, but the Holy Spirit is the agent of that cleansing.

The apostles saw the outward act and the inward reality, though occurring simultaneously. And yet, they are not identical but rather quite separate in their nature. "Let us draw near to God with a sincere heart in full assurance of faith, having our hearts sprinkled to cleanse us from a guilty conscience and having our bodies washed with pure water." (Heb. 10:22) "And this water symbolizes baptism that now saves you also — not the removal of dirt from the body but the pledge of a good conscience toward God. It saves you by the resurrection of Jesus Christ" (1 Pet. 3:21).

Space will not allow us to examine the digression of the doctrine of baptism completely throughout the early Middle Ages. Eventually the concept of baptism evolved into what theologians called *ex opere operato* which means "done by the deed." The act of baptism itself, apart from the inner consenting faith of the heart, became the sacramental means of receiving the benefits of the finished work of Christ on the cross. The rise of the concept of original sin and the necessity of infant baptism fit very well into this line of thinking.[7]

Also the delay of baptism from the initial conversion of the heart was initiated to allow for proper penance.[8] This led to an unbiblical separation of what the New Testament saw as a unity. In Scripture the inner repentance and the outward baptism are always seen together (Acts 2; 8; 16 etc.)

Hence, in baptism the inner consent of the heart and the outward display of the action were separated. The inner aspect of faith was relegated to virtual insignificance (in infant baptism) and the outward action of baptism was given magical proportions. The theological pendulum had indeed swung to the right.

II. Reformation Christianity: The Pendulum Swings to the Left — The Action Becomes Nothing

With the coming of the Protestant Reformation of the 16th century, much study of a corrective nature was given to a great many Medieval doctrines and baptism was included. Of course, the great affirmation of the Reformers was the **doctrine of justification by faith.** This emphasis by Luther, Calvin and others came like a breath of fresh air to the suffocating sacramentalism of the increasingly pagan Medieval Catholic Church.

The Reformers sought to reestablish the absolute necessity of the inner aspects of faith. The trust of the mind in the message of the gospel and the turning of the will toward God through repentance were of great importance. So strong was their reaction to the "magical concept of the sacraments" that the "theological baby of baptism" was thrown out with the "muddy bath waters of sacramentalism." Whereas, once baptism had been the totality of coming to Christ, now it was removed from the picture altogether. Nowhere is this found more dramatically stated than in the writings of John Calvin's theological predecessor, Huldreich Zwingli.[9]

Zwingli (1484-1531) began as a faithful member of the Roman Catholic Church. He had always believed that baptism was for the remission of sins. However by 1523, he had not only repudiated the sacramental view of baptism, but he had also removed from baptism any concept of it relating to saving faith. He wrote: "In this matter of baptism all the doctors have been in error from the time of the apostles . . . . For all the doctors have ascribed to the water a power which it does not have and the holy apostles did not teach."[10] He went on to say that, "The Fathers were in error . . . because they thought that the water itself effects cleansing and salvation."[11]

Zwingli accepted the doctrine of the total sovereignty of God expressed in the concept of unconditional election. For Zwingli (and all Calvinists to follow) God has elected to salvation those He intends to save. This election occurred before the foundation of the world and was based upon His capricious will. Since election is the source and guarantee of salvation, baptism can obviously have nothing to do with saving faith. Zwingli believed that it was possible for people to be saved even without consenting faith (as in infancy). He wrote, "For the elect are ever elect, even before they believe!"[12]

This led Zwingli to reinterpret many of the key biblical passages on baptism. For instance, when Scripture plainly states in 1 Peter 3:21 "baptism now saves you," Zwingli wrote, "Baptism is sometimes used for the blood or passion of Christ . . . we are not to understand . . . the washing of baptism, but Christ Himself or His blood and death, for by these we have been redeemed . . . . How foolish, therefore, would anyone seem, who because of these words should maintain that we are washed clean of our sins by the baptismal waters."[13] Zwingli applied such a figurative understanding to passages like Eph. 5:26, Rom. 6:3-4, Gal. 3:27, Titus 3:5, in fact anywhere in Scripture where baptism seemed to be associated with salvation — even though such an interpretation goes against the united voice of all scholarship throughout church history and the sound principles of exegesis.

Zwingli taught a distinction between outward water baptism and what he called "the inner enlightenment and calling when we know God and cleave to Him."[14] This inner baptism of the Spirit is the only one necessary for salvation, for this is the time when the Spirit bestows the gift of faith. Zwingli was adamant about not confusing inner and outer baptism. For "though outer baptism is good and proper, only inner baptism is sure salvation to the one who has it."[15]

What developed in Zwingli's thought as to the actual reason for water baptism is quite involved (and exegetically bizarre!). He concluded that baptism had nothing whatsoever to do with the individual being baptized. The only reason to be baptized was for the sake of the audience witnessing the event. Zwingli wrote, "For baptism is given and received for the sake of fellow-believers, not for a supposed effect in those who receive it." [16]

Zwingli acted on the correct premise that a man is justified by "faith in Christ" and not by any magical sacramentalism involving baptism (or anything else). However, his theology developed an overreaction to the outward display of faith (in baptism) and, in one generation, swung the theological pendulum in the completely opposite direction. Now the inner aspect of faith (based upon the to-be-Calvinist doctrine of election) was elevated to being the sum total of biblical saving faith, while the outer aspect of faith displayed in water baptism was seen to have nothing whatsoever to do with salvation.

Unfortunately, much of current evangelical theology remains under the influence of Zwingli's overreaction to the excesses of pagan medieval Catholicism. One example of this is James Boice Montgomery. In his popular rewrite of Calvin's *Institutes,* he declares that while baptism is not necessarily metaphorical in all New Testament instances, he goes on to give examples that wherever baptism seems to relate to salvation, it must be viewed metaphorically. He then refers to such texts as Gal. 3:27 and Mark 16:16 as examples of his thesis, even though his interpretation goes contrary to the majority interpretation of the church for over 2000 years! [17]

Another example is found in popular Bible teacher John MacArthur in his New Testament commentary on Acts 1–12. MacArthur admits that literal baptism is spoken of in Acts 2:38, but following typical Zwinglian evangelical tradition goes on to point out that, contrary to the grammar and linguistic construction of the passage, baptism simply cannot be "for the forgiveness of sins." He goes on to give four reasons why his understanding of baptism can contradict the Apostle Peter's. All of these center on the necessity of faith in salvation and the separation of any outward activity from such saving faith (à la Zwingli). MacArthur concludes: "The order is clear, repentance is for forgiveness. Baptism follows that forgiveness, it does not cause it." [18]

Biblically, repentance is the inward action of faith upon the heart in which sin is rejected and Christ is desired. But baptism is the outer request for such forgiveness. The modern evangelical declares that the inner desire and the outer request cannot coexist. Scripture seems to state otherwise.

Conclusion

All this pendulum swinging of theological thought may cause some dizziness. What can we say in summary? The medieval theologians were correct — baptism is associated with the forgiveness of sin and the gift of the Holy Spirit. But the medieval theologians were also extremely wrong — baptism is nothing apart from the inner faith of an individual. It is not a magical sacramental act. How about the reformers? They were also correct — salvation comes through faith. But the reformers were also in error — biblically, faith is an act of the will inwardly which leads to an outward act of faith in Christian baptism. Biblically, true baptism is impossible without inward faith, and inward faith is less than what God has desired without outward baptism.

What is baptism? I believe biblically it is nothing other than an outward aspect of — faith! It is how Jesus instructed his apostles to make disciples (Matt. 28:18-20). It is the display of our death to sin, our burial with Christ, and our resurrection to new life through the power of Christ's resurrection (Rom. 6:1-11). Perhaps we need to read again that old Restoration sermon by Benjamin Franklin,[19] "Baptism for the Remission of Sins Is Justification by Faith." At first his title seems too inflammatory even for many in our movement. But look at what it says: There is nothing about baptism that is not a part of faith (while all would be quick to admit that there is quite a bit more to faith than water baptism).

If we would simply follow the examples of those who placed their faith in Christ as recorded in Holy Scripture, we would not even have to know the details of the theology recorded concerning baptism. However, God has given us in Scripture both example and theology (πράξεις and διδαχή) to declare what saving faith truly is.

At this point many in the evangelical world would probably raise an eyebrow and ask, "Are you saying, then, that baptism is necessary for salvation?"[20] I must admit a certain uneasiness every time I am asked that question. The answer to such a question has to be an emphatic NO!! Infants are saved in God's eternal plan whether baptized or not.

But aside from infants and small children, other serious questions arise. What of those who have not come to the conclusions we have stated in our study? What of those who have truly turned to Christ in their hearts but have not had the opportunity to display such faith in Christian baptism? I have opinions about their salvation based upon my understanding of the vast grace of God as outlined in the New Testament. Yet they remain only my opinions.

"Must I be baptized to be saved?" This is a question that I simply cannot answer. To do so, I would be placing myself in the place of God, and this I will not do. When asked this question, I usually point out to the questioner that, "I am in sales, not management!" It is not my place to sit on God's throne and make divine executive decisions.

When anyone asks me this question: "Do I have to be baptized to be saved?" I respond by saying, "You have asked me a question that I cannot answer. And I suspect it is not the real question you expect me to answer. Let me rephrase your question. I suspect your real question is, 'Must I be baptized to *display faith in Christ* as outlined in the preaching of Jesus' apostles as recorded in Holy Scripture inspired by the Holy Spirit?'" If this is what the individual wants to know then I do have an answer to that question. The answer is an emphatic YES! To require less than Christ and His apostles is to be untrue to Scripture and to the Christ of Scripture.

What of those who cannot agree with this position? We must be gracious and honor the inner assent of their hearts to the Jesus who has changed our hearts as well. At the same time we must teach what we see the Bible to teach. We must let God sort out the conclusion of these matters. We must speak the truth in love.

The pendulum is still swinging in the church today. Some want to see baptism as everything. Others seem to believe that church growth is "Mission Impossible" with the biblical doctrine as we have outlined it and want to disavow any knowledge of baptism's action. And while we must be gracious to all those who love Christ, we are responsible to attempt to turn attention away from the swinging pendulum to the plumb line of God's truth and measure all our theological musings against the written Word of God, which is the voice of the Holy Spirit.

Can we not say of baptism what Peter said so long ago:

> [It is] an appeal to God for a good conscience — through the resurrection of Jesus Christ (1 Pet. 3:21, NASB).

If that's not faith, I don't know what is.

---

1. Further, what says He? "And there was a river flowing on the right, and from it arose beautiful trees; and whosoever shall eat of them shall live for ever."(Ez 47:12) This meaneth, that we indeed descend into the water full of sins and defilement, but come up, bearing fruit in our heart, having the fear [of God] and trust in Jesus in our spirit. (*Epistle of Barnabas*, Ch. 11)

All quotes from the Fathers are taken from *The Ante-Nicene Fathers*, (1885 edition) A. Roberts and J. Donaldson, eds. Albany, OR: Sage Software, 1996. All future quotes from the Fathers are from this source unless otherwise noted.

2. And I said to him, "I should like to continue my questions." "Speak on," said he. And I said, "I heard, sir, some teachers maintain that there is no other repentance than that which takes place, when we descended into the water and received remission of our former sins." He said to me, "That was sound doctrine which you heard; for that is really the case. (Shepherd of Hermas, *Commands*, 4:3)

"They were obliged," he answered, "to ascend through water in order that they might be made alive; for, unless they laid aside the deadness of their life, they could not in any other way enter into the kingdom of God. Accordingly, those also who fell asleep received the seal of the Son of God. For," he continued, "before a man bears the name of the Son of God he is dead; but when he receives the seal he lays aside his deadness, and obtains life. The seal, then, is the water: they descend into the water dead, and they arise alive. And to them, accordingly, was this seal preached, and they made use of it that they might enter into the kingdom of God." (Hermas, *Similitudes*, 9:16)

3. I will also relate the manner in which we dedicated ourselves to God when we had been made new through Christ; lest, if we omit this, we seem to be unfair in the explanation we are making. As many as are persuaded and believe that what we teach and say is true, and undertake to be able to live accordingly, are instructed to pray and to entreat God with fasting, for the remission of their sins that are past, we praying and fasting with them. Then they are brought by us where there is water, and are regenerated in the same manner in which we were ourselves regenerated. For, in the name of God, the Father and Lord of the universe, and of our Savior Jesus Christ, and of the Holy Spirit, they then receive the washing with water. For Christ also said, "Except ye be born again, ye shall not enter into the kingdom of heaven." Now, that it is impossible for those who have once been born to enter into their mothers' wombs, is manifest to all. And how those who have sinned and repent shall escape their sins, is declared by Esaias the prophet, as I wrote above; he thus speaks: "Wash you, make you clean; put away the evil of your doings from your souls; learn to do well; judge the fatherless, and plead for the widow: and come and let us reason together, saith the Lord. And though your sins be as scarlet, I will make them white like wool; and though they be as crimson, I will make them white as snow. But if ye refuse and rebel, the sword shall devour you: for the mouth of the Lord hath spoken it." And for this [rite] we have learned from the apostles this reason. Since at our birth we were born without our own knowledge or choice, by our parents coming together, and were brought up in bad habits and wicked training; in order that we may not remain the children of necessity and of ignorance, but may become the children of choice and knowledge, and may obtain in the water the remission of sins formerly committed, there is pronounced over him who chooses to be born again, and has repented of his sins, the name of God the Father and Lord of the universe; he who leads to the layer the person that is to be washed calling him by this name alone. For no one can utter the name of the ineffable God; and if any one dare to say that there is a name, he raves with a hopeless madness. And this washing is called illumination, because they who learn these things are illuminated in their understandings. And in the name of Jesus Christ, who was crucified under Pontius Pilate, and in the name of the Holy Ghost, who through the prophets foretold all things about Jesus, he who is illuminated is washed (Justin Martyr, *First Apology*, ch. 61).

4. The Faith . . . as the Presbyters, the disciples of the Apostles have delivered it to us . . . above all teaches us that we have received baptism for the forgiveness of sins in the name of God the Father, and in the name of Jesus Christ, the Son of God, who was incarnate, died and rose again and in the Holy Spirit of God; and that this baptism is the seal of eternal life, and the regeneration to God by which we become the children, not of mortal man, but of the eternal and everlasting God (Irenaeus, *Demonstration of the Apostolic Preaching*, ch 3; as quoted in Kirsopp Lake, "Baptism (New Testament)" in *Encyclopaedia of Religion and Ethics*, James Hastings, ed., 1955).

5. Tertullian in speaking of the place of tradition as authoritative in Christian practice states:

To deal with this matter briefly, I shall begin with baptism. When we are going to enter the water, but a little before, in the presence of the congregation and under the hand of the president, we solemnly profess that we disown the devil, and his pomp, and his angels. Hereupon we are thrice immersed, making a somewhat ampler pledge than the Lord has appointed in the Gospel. Then when we are taken up (as new-born children), we taste first of all a mixture of milk and honey, and from that day we refrain from the daily bath for a whole week. We take also, in congregations before daybreak, and from the hand of none but the presidents, the sacrament of the Eucharist, which the Lord both commanded to be eaten at meal-times, and enjoined to be taken by all alike (Tertullian *De Corona*, ch. 3).

6. Moreover, a presumptuous confidence in baptism introduces all kind of vicious delay and tergiversation with regard to repentance; for, feeling sure of undoubted pardon of their sins, men meanwhile steal the intervening time, and make it for themselves into a holiday-time for sinning, rather than a time for learning not to sin. Further, how inconsistent is it to expect pardon of sins (to be granted) to a repentance which they have not fulfilled! This is to hold out your hand for merchandise, but not produce the price. For repentance is the price at which the Lord has determined to award pardon: He proposes the redemption of release from penalty at this compensating exchange of repentance. . . . That baptismal washing is a sealing of faith, which faith is begun and is commended by the faith of repentance. We are not washed in order that we may cease sinning, but because we have ceased, since in heart we have been bathed already. For the first baptism of a learner is this, a perfect fear; thence forward, in so far as you have understanding of the Lord, faith is sound, the conscience having once for all embraced repentance. Otherwise, if it is (only) after the baptismal waters that we cease sinning, *it is of necessity*, not of free-will, that we put on innocence (Tertullian, *On Repentance*, ch. 6).

Thus the nature of the waters, sanctified by the Holy One, itself conceived withal the power of sanctifying. . . . All waters, therefore, in virtue of the pristine privilege of their origin, do, after invocation of God, attain the sacramental power of sanctification; for the Spirit immediately supervenes from the heavens, and rests over the waters, sanctifying them from Himself; and being thus sanctified, they imbibe at the same time the power of sanctifying (Tertullian, *On Baptism*, ch. 4).

Notice that Tertullian's emphasis on repentance preceding baptism seems to be based on a belief that forgiveness of sins is automatic in the action of baptism itself! Hence repentance, leading to innocence must precede baptism to be of free-will, because after baptism innocence is "of necessity"!!

7. For a fine overview of how all of this took place see Boyd Lammiman, *Caught in the Crossfire: The Baptism that Demonstrates the Faith that Justifies* (Fort Worth: Star Bible Publications, n.d.), pp. 13-18.

8. See Henry F. Brown, *Baptism through the Centuries* (Mountain View, CA: Pacific Press Publishing Association, 1965), pp. 11-15. Be aware that Brown writes in the Reformed tradition.

9. In the following section on Zwingli I am indebted to the scholarship of Jack Cottrell, who did his doctoral dissertation of Zwingli's view of baptism. For a brief summary of this excellent study see Cottrell's "Baptism According to the Reformed Tradition" in David Fletcher, ed. *Baptism and the Remission of Sins* (Joplin, MO: College Press, 1990).

10. Ibid., p. 40.

11. Ibid. This understanding of Zwingli's seems only to be aware of the writings of the Fathers from Tertullian onward. The earliest Church Fathers (as we have shown earlier in this appendix) did not attribute magical properties to the waters. Zwingli was mistaken in his assessment of the teaching of 2nd-century Christians, which we would maintain, mirrored

New Testament teaching — seeing the connection between the inner and outer aspects of faith.

12. Ibid., p. 45.

13. Ibid., p. 46. Note again that Zwingli seems to ignore the nonsacramental views of the earliest Church Fathers.

14. Ibid., p. 47.

15. Ibid.

16. Ibid., p. 42.

17. He attempts to prove baptism as metaphorical by an appeal to Rev. 3:20 "Here I am! I stand at the door and knock. If anyone hears my voice and opens the door, I will come in and eat with him, and he with me." even though that Scripture is most definitely not talking about sinners coming to initial faith in Christ but rather to backslidden Christians. "He who has an ear, let him hear what the Spirit says to the churches" (Rev. 3:22). James Boice Montgomery, *Foundations of the Christian Faith*, Vol. 4: *God and History*, (Downers Grove, IL: InterVarsity, 1981), pp. 104-105.

18. John MacArthur, *The MacArthur New Testament Commentary: Acts 1–12*, (Chicago: Moody Press, 1994), pp. 72-75.

19. This Benjamin Franklin (1812–1878) was one of the early leaders in the Restoration Movement, and is not to be confused with his earlier and better-known namesake.

20. Some of this final argument also appears on pages 240-242 in chapter 11.

Appendix B
CONVERSIONS IN THE ACTS OF THE APOSTLES

A worksheet to display what Jesus' apostles taught concerning the meaning of accepting the gospel of Christ by faith.

Scripture	Preaching	Belief	Repentance	Baptism	Other
Acts 2:14-41: The setting is the Day of Pentecost. The miracle of tongues attracted a large crowd. Peter preached to this Jewish crowd in the temple area.					
Acts 3:11–4:4 The setting is the Beautiful Gate in the temple area. Peter and John have just healed a lame man and a crowd has gathered. They are arrested before Peter can finish his sermon.					
Acts 5:12-16 This is a very general description of many conversions taking place in the Jerusalem area.					
Acts 6:7 Another very general description of the rapid growth in Jerusalem.					
Acts 8:4-13 The church in Jerusalem is scattered under the persecution led by Saul. Philip traveled to Samaria and evangelized the people there.					

Scripture	Preaching	Belief	Repentance	Baptism	Other
Acts 8:26-40 Philip left Samaria and met an Ethiopian. He took the opportunity to lead him to Christ.					
Acts 9:1-19 This is the initial account of the conversion of Saul of Tarsus. Because of its great importance, this conversion is repeated two other times in the Book of Acts. Those are found in:					
Acts 22:1-16 Paul addresses an angry mob in the temple area in Jerusalem and retells his conversion.					
Acts 26:1-32 Paul once again retells his conversion as he addresses Herod Agrippa II about the charges that would lead him to trial in Rome.					
Acts 10:24-28 Peter preaches to the first Gentile convert, Cornelius, the Roman Centurion.					
Acts 11:4-18 Peter retells the events surrounding the conversion of Cornelius.					
Acts 11:19-21 The text relates that certain unnamed believers travel to Syrian Antioch where many Gentiles come to Christ.					
Acts 11:22-24 Barnabas is sent to Syrian Antioch and under his leadership a great number of people are brought to the Lord.					
Acts 13:4-12 Paul and Barnabas are sent to Cyprus where they convert the Roman proconsul.					

Scripture	Preaching	Belief	Repentance	Baptism	Other
Acts 13:44-49 Paul and Barnabas preach to the Gentiles at Pisidian Antioch.					
Acts 14:1-7 Paul and Barnabas preach the good news in the city of Iconium.					
Acts 14:20-21 After a near-death experience at Lystra, Paul and Barnabas have a successful ministry in the city of Derbe.					
Acts 16:1-5 A general account of the beginning of the 2nd missionary tour where Paul visits the churches he had planted on his 1st journey.					
Acts 16:11-15 Paul and his associates make the first convert on the European continent at Philippi in the household of a wealthy business woman named Lydia.					
Acts 16:22-34 Paul is arrested in Philippi and leads his jailer to the Lord in a dramatic manner.					
Acts 17:1-4 A general description of Paul's ministry in the Greek city of Thessalonica.					
Acts 17:10-12 Another general description of the work of Paul in the Greek city of Berea.					
Acts 17:16-34 A recount of Paul's sermon to the philosophers on Mars Hill and the response.					
Acts 18:7-8 Paul leads Crispus, head Rabbi of the synagogue in Corinth, to faith in Christ.					

Scripture	Preaching	Belief	Repentance	Baptism	Other
Acts 18:24-26 While Paul was beginning his 3rd mission tour, Priscilla & Aquila lead a powerful preacher named Apollos to a fuller understanding of the gospel.					
Acts 19:1-7 At Ephesus, Paul met men who only knew the baptism taught by John the Baptist. Paul baptized them all in the name of Jesus.					
Acts 18:17-20 A general description of Paul's 2-year ministry in Ephesus and the dramatic effect of the gospel on the people there.					
Acts 28:17-31 Paul arrived in Rome and was under house arrest. He preached to the Jewish leaders and then turned to the Gentiles. His prison ministry here lasted for 2 years while he waited for his trial before Nero.					

As you study the conversion accounts recorded in the Acts of the Apostles, what conclusions do you make concerning what the Bible teaches about how to accept Christ by faith?

BIBLIOGRAPHY OF WORKS CITED

Aldrich, Joe. *Life-Style Evangelism*. Portland: Multnomah, 1981.

Allen, Diogenes. *Christian Belief in a Postmodern World*. Louisville: Westminster/John Knox Press, 1989.

Aquinas, Thomas. *Summa Theologica*. Westminster, MD: Christian Classics, 1948.

Arn, Win and Charles. *The Master's Plan for Making Disciples*. Monrovia, CA: Church Growth Press, 1991.

Banks, Robert. *Paul's Idea of Community: The Early House Churches in Their Historical Setting*. Grand Rapids: Eerdmans, 1980.

Barna, George. *User Friendly Churches*. Ventura, CA: Regal, 1991.

_____. *What Americans Believe*. Ventura, CA: Regal, 1991.

Barnes, Albert. *Notes on the New Testament: Acts of the Apostles*. Grand Rapids: Baker, 1953.

Barth, Karl. *The Teaching of the Church Regarding Baptism*. London: SCM Press, 1948.

Baxter, Richard. *The Reformed Pastor*. Portland: Multnomah, 1982.

Beasley-Murray, G.R. *Jesus and the Kingdom of God*. Grand Rapids: Eerdmans, 1986.

_____. *Baptism in the New Testament*. Grand Rapids: Eerdmans, 1981.

Bloesch, Donald G. *The Essentials of Evangelical Theology*. 2 volumes. New York: Harper & Row, 1978.

Blomberg, Craig L. *The New American Commentary: Matthew*. Nashville: Broadman, 1992.

Bloom, Allan. *The Closing of the American Mind*. New York: Simon & Schuster, 1987.

Bonar, Horatius. *Words to Winners of Souls*. Phillipsburg, NJ : Puritan and Reformed, 1995.

Bonhoeffer, Dietrich. *The Cost of Discipleship*. Translated by R.H. Fuller. New York: Macmillan, 1961.

_____ . *Life Together*. New York: Harper & Row, 1976.

_____ . *The Cost of Discipleship*. Translated by R.H. Fuller. New York: Macmillan, 1961.

Bork, Robert. *Slouching toward Gomorrah*. New York: Harper Collins, 1996.

Brown, Colin, ed. *Dictionary of New Testament Theology*. Grand Rapids: Zondervan, 1981.

Brown, Harold O.J. *The Sensate Culture*. Dallas: Word, 1996.

Brown, Henry F. *Baptism through the Centuries*. Mountain View, CA: Pacific Press, 1965.

Bruce, A.B. *The Training of the Twelve*. Grand Rapids: Kregel, 1971.

Bruce, F.F. *The Acts of the Apostles: The Greek Text with Introduction and Commentary*. Grand Rapids: Eerdmans, 1990.

Bunyan, John. *The Pilgrim's Progress*. Westwood, NJ: The Christian Library, n.d.

Calvin, John. *Institutes of the Christian Religion*. Translated by Henry Beveridge. Grand Rapids: Eerdmans, 1979.

Campbell, Alexander and N.L. Rice. *A Debate between Rev. A. Campbell and Rev. N.L. Rice on the Action, Subject, Design and Administrator of Christian Baptism*. Cincinnati: Standard, 1917.

Chandler, Russell. *Racing toward 2001*. Grand Rapids: Zondervan, 1992.

Coleman, Robert. *The Master Plan of Evangelism*. Old Tappan: Fleming H. Revell, 1980.

Colson, Charles. *Against the Night*. Ann Arbor: Servant Publications, 1989.

Cosgrove, Francis M., Jr. *Essentials of Discipleship*. Colorado Springs: NavPress, 1980.

Cullmann, Oscar. *Baptism in the New Testament*. Philadelphia: Westminster, 1950.

Douglas, J.D., ed. *Proclaim Christ until He Comes: Calling the Whole Church to Take the Whole Gospel to the Whole World*. Minneapolis: World Wide Publications, 1990.

_____ . *Let the Earth Hear His Voice*. Minneapolis: World Wide Publications, 1975.

Erickson, Millard J. *Christian Theology*. Grand Rapids: Baker, 1987.

_____ . *Modernizing the Faith: Evangelical Responses to the Challenge of Postmodernism*. Grand Rapids: Baker, 1998.

Fant, Clyde, Jr. and William Pinson. *Twenty Centuries of Great Preaching*. 16 volumes. Waco: Word, 1974.

Fletcher, David W., ed. *Baptism and the Remission of Sins*. Joplin, MO: College Press, 1990.

Frend, W.H.C. *The Rise of Christianity*. Philadelphia: Fortress, 1984.

Gibbs, Eddie. *In Name Only: Tackling the Problem of Nominal Christianity*. Wheaton, IL: Victor Books (BridgePoint), 1994.

Gorman, Julie A. *Community That Is Christian*. Wheaton, IL: Victor Books, 1993.

Green, Michael. *Baptism: Its Purpose, Practice and Power*. Downers Grove, IL: InterVarsity, 1987.

Guthrie, Donald. *New Testament Theology*. Downers Grove, IL: InterVarsity, 1981.

Hadaway, C. Kirk, et al. *Home Cell Groups and House Churches*. Nashville: Broadman, 1987.

Haenchen, Ernst. *The Acts of the Apostles*. Translated by Basil Blackwell. Philadelphia: Westminster, 1971.

Harnack, Adolf. *The Expansion of Christianity in the First Three Centuries*. Translated by James Moffett. New York: Books for Libraries Press, 1904.

Hawking, Stephen. *A Brief History of Time*. New York: Bantam Books, 1990.

Hawkins, Don. *Master Discipleship*. Grand Rapids: Kregel, 1996.

Hemphill, Ken. *The Antioch Effect*. Nashville: Broadman & Holman, 1994.

Hendee, John. *Ambassadors for Christ: Training for Evangelism*. Cincinnati: Standard, 1984.

Henderson, David W. *Culture Shift: Communicating God's Truth to our Changing World*. Grand Rapids: Baker, 1998.

Hendriksen, William. *New Testament Commentary: John*. Grand Rapids: Baker, 1953.

Hestenes, Roberta. *Using the Bible in Groups*. Philadelphia: Westminster, 1983.

Hinckley, K.C. *Living Proof: A Small Group Discussion Guide*. Colorado Springs: NavPress, 1993.

Hodges, Zane C. *Absolutely Free: A Biblical Reply to Lordship Salvation*. Grand Rapids: Zondervan, 1989.

Hunter, George G., III. *How to Reach Secular People*. Nashville: Abingdon, 1992.

Hybels, Bill. *Becoming a Contagious Christian*. Grand Rapids: Zondervan, 1994.

Jacks, Bob and Betty. *Your Home a Lighthouse*. Colorado Springs: NavPress, 1986.

Jenni, Ernst and Claus Westermann, eds. *Theological Lexicon of the Old Testament*. Peabody, MA: Hendrickson, 1997.

Jervis, L. Ann. "Becoming like God through Christ: Discipling in Romans," in *Patterns of Discipleship in the New Testament*. Edited by Richard Longenecker. Grand Rapids: Eerdmans, 1996.

Jewett, Paul K. *Infant Baptism and the Covenant of Grace*. Grand Rapids: Eerdmans, 1978.

Kennedy, James D. *Evangelism Explosion*. Wheaton, IL: Tyndale, 1970.

Kittel, Gerhard and G. Friedrich, eds. *Theological Dictionary of the New Testament*. 10 volumes. Grand Rapids: Eerdmans, 1977.

Kroft, Peter and Ronald K. Tacelli. *Handbook of Christian Apologetics*. Downers Grove, IL: InterVarsity, 1994.

Kuhne, Gary W. *The Dynamics of Personal Follow-up*. Grand Rapids: Zondervan, 1981.

Ladd, G.E. *A Theology of the New Testament*. Grand Rapids: Eerdmans, 1974.

_____ . *Crucial Questions about the Kingdom of God*. Grand Rapids: Eerdmans, 1952.

Lammiman, Boyd. *Caught in the Crossfire: The Baptism that Demonstrates the Faith that Justifies*. Fort Worth: Star Bible Publications, n.d.

_____ . *Response to Grace: Putting Baptism in Its Place*. Self-published, 1998.

Lasch, Christopher. *The Culture of Narcissism*. New York: W.W. Norton, 1978.

Lawrence, John W. *The Seven Laws of the Harvest*. Grand Rapids: Kregel, 1975.

Little, Paul. *How to Give Away Your Faith*. Downers Grove, IL: InterVarsity, 1966.

Long, Jimmy. *Generating Hope: A Strategy for Reaching the Postmodern Generation*. Downers Grove, IL: InterVarsity, 1997.

Louw, Johannes and Eugene Nida, eds. *Greek-English Lexicon of the New Testament Based on Semantic Domains*. New York: United Bible Societies, 1988.

Luther, Martin. *The Babylonian Captivity of the Church* (1520), contained in *Luther's Works*. Edited by Helmut T. Lehmann; vol. 36: Word and Sacrament II. Philadelphia: Fortress, 1959.

MacArthur, John. *The MacArthur New Testament Commentary: Acts 1–12*. Chicago: Moody, 1994.

_____ . *The Gospel According to Jesus: What Does Jesus Mean When He Says, "Follow Me?"* Grand Rapids: Zondervan, 1988.

Marshall, I. Howard. *The Acts of the Apostles*. Grand Rapids: Eerdmans, 1980.

Martin, Ralph P. *The Family and the Fellowship*. Grand Rapids: Eerdmans, 1979.

——————. *Worship in the Early Church*. Westwood: Fleming H. Revell, 1964.

McDowell, Josh. *A Ready Defense*. San Bernadino, CA: Here's Life, 1991.

—————— *Evidence That Demands a Verdict*. San Bernadino, CA: Here's Life, 1979.

——————. *More Evidence That Demands a Verdict*. San Bernadino, CA: Here's Life, 1981.

——————. *Tolerating the Intolerable: A Mandate to Love*. Campus Crusade for Christ Staff Conference Handout, n.d.

McIntosh, Gary. *Three Generations*. Grand Rapids: Revell, 1995.

Middleton, J. Richard and Brian J. Walsh. *Truth Is Stranger than It Used to Be: Biblical Faith in a Postmodern Age*. Downers Grove, IL: Inter-Varsity, 1995.

Miles, Delos. *Introduction to Evangelism*. Nashville: Broadman & Holman, 1983.

Minear, Paul. *Images of the Church in the New Testament*. Philadelphia: Westminster, 1975.

Montgomery, James Boice. *Foundations of the Christian Faith*. 4 volumes. Downers Grove, IL: InterVarsity, 1981.

Morison, Frank. *Who Moved the Stone?* Grand Rapids: Zondervan, 1958.

Morris, Leon. *The Atonement: Its Meaning and Significance*. Downers Grove, IL: InterVarsity, 1983.

——————. *The Gospel According to John*. Grand Rapids: Eerdmans, 1971.

Naisbitt, John and Patricia Aburdene. *Mega Trends 2000*. New York: William Morrow and Company, 1990.

Nicoles, Ron, et al. *Good Things Happen in Small Groups*. Downers Grove, IL: InterVarsity, 1985.

Niles, D.T. *That They May Have Life*. New York: Harper & Brothers, 1951.

Ogden, Greg. *Discipleship Essentials: A Guide to Building Your Life in Christ*. Downers Grove, IL: InterVarsity, 1998.

Packer, J.I. *Evangelism and the Sovereignty of God*. Downers Grove, IL: InterVarsity, 1961.

Petersen, Jim. *Living Proof: Sharing the Gospel Naturally*. Colorado Springs: NavPress, 1992.

Peterson, James and Peter Kim. *The Day America Told the Truth*. New York: Prentice Hall, 1991.

Pinnock, Clark. *Reason Enough: A Case for the Christian Faith*. Downers Grove, IL: InterVarsity, 1980.

Ratz, Calvin, Frank Tillapaugh, and Myron Augsburger. *Mastering Outreach and Evangelism*. Portland: Multnomah, 1990.

Ridderbos, Herman. *The Coming of the Kingdom*. St. Catherines, ON: Paideia Press, 1962.

Roberts, Alexander and James Donaldson, eds. *The Ante-Nicene Fathers*. 11 Volumes. Grand Rapids: Eerdmans, 1978.

Ryrie, Charles C. *So Great a Salvation: What It Means to Believe in Christ*. Wheaton: Victor Books, 1989.

Sagan, Carl. *Cosmos*. New York: Random House, 1980.

Schaeffer, Edith. *Christianity Is Jewish*. Wheaton, IL: Tyndale, 1975.

Schaeffer, Francis A. *The Complete Works of Francis A. Schaeffer*. 5 volumes. Westchester, IL: Crossway Books, 1982.

Schaff, Philip. *History of the Christian Church*. 10 volumes. Grand Rapids: Eerdmans, 1910.

Schuller, Robert H. *Self Esteem: The New Reformation*. Waco: Word, 1982.

Seeburg, Reinhold. *History of Doctrines*. Grand Rapids: Baker, 1977.

Sider, Ron. *Rich Christians in an Age of Hunger*. Downers Grove, IL: InterVarsity, 1977.

Sire, James W. *The Universe Next Door*. Downers Grove, IL: InterVarsity, 1988.

Snaith, Norman H. *Distinctive Ideas of the Old Testament*. New York: Schocken Books, 1964.

Soards, Marion L. *The Speeches in Acts*. Louisville: Westminster/John Knox Press, 1994.

Spurgeon, Charles H. *The Soul Winner*. Eerdmans, 1963.

Stark, Rodney. *The Rise of Christianity: A Sociologist Reconsiders History*. Princeton, NJ: Princeton University Press, 1996.

Stein, Robert. "Baptism and Becoming a Christian in the New Testament." *The Southern Baptist Journal of Theology*, Vol. 1, No. 1 (Spring 1998): 6-17.

Stewart, James S. *The Wind of the Spirit*. Grand Rapids: Baker, 1984.

Stott, John R.W. *The Cross of Christ*. Downers Grove, IL: InterVarsity, 1986.

_____. "The Great Commission." In *One Race, One Gospel, One Task*, Vol. 1. Edited by Carl F.H. Henry and W. Stanley Mooneyham. Minneapolis: World Wide Publications, 1967.

——————. *The Message of Acts*. Downers Grove, IL: InterVarsity, 1990.

Strobel, Lee. *Inside the Mind of Unchurched Harry and Mary*. Grand Rapids: Zondervan, 1993.

Trueblood, Elton. *The Company of the Committed*. New York: Harper & Row, 1969.

VanGemeren, William A., ed. *New International Dictionary of Old Testament Theology and Exegesis*. Grand Rapids: Zondervan, 1996.

Warren, Rick. *The Purpose-Driven Church*. Grand Rapids: Zondervan, 1995.

Watson, Alan. *I Believe in Evangelism*. Grand Rapids: Eerdmans, 1976.

Wenham, John W. *Christ and the Bible*. Grand Rapids: Baker, 1984.

White, R.E.O. *The Biblical Doctrine of Initiation*. Grand Rapids: Eerdmans, 1960.

Wilson, Carl. *With Christ in the School of Disciple Building*. Grand Rapids: Zondervan, 1979.

Witherington, Ben, III. *The Acts of the Apostles: A Socio-Rhetorical Commentary*. Grand Rapids: Eerdmans, 1998.

Zustiak, Gary. *The Next Generation: Understanding and Meeting the Needs of Generation X*. Joplin, MO: College Press, 1996.

About the Author

Terry A. Bowland since 1993 has been Professor of New Testament and Christian Ministries at Ozark Christian College in Joplin, MO. Prior to his teaching career, Brother Bowland was involved in the preaching ministry for 17 years in churches in Nebraska and Illinois.

He received his D.Min. from Trinity Evangelical Divinity School, M.A. and M.Div. from Lincoln Christian Seminary and his B.A. and B.Th. from Nebraska Christian College.

Dr. Bowland was selected as an Outstanding Young Man of America in 1987 and appears in *Who's Who in American Education* in 1994 and *Who's Who in the World in 1997*. Since coming to Ozark, Dr. Bowland has traveled extensively throughout the United States and abroad preaching revivals and leading in seminars. He has published works in numerous religious journals.

Terry has been happily married to his wife, Carol, since 1975. They have two daughters, Crystal (Mrs. Andy Melton) and Tiffany, and one granddaughter.